THE RECIPE
for **STUDENT
WELL-BEING**

5 key ingredients
for **social**, **behavioral**, and **academic** success

BRIAN H. SMITH
CLAYTON R. COOK
ARIA E. FIAT

Solution Tree | Press

Copyright © 2024 by Solution Tree Press

Materials appearing here are copyrighted. With one exception, all rights are reserved. Readers may reproduce only those pages marked "Reproducible." Otherwise, no part of this book may be reproduced or transmitted in any form or by any means (electronic, photocopying, recording, or otherwise) without prior written permission of the publisher.

555 North Morton Street
Bloomington, IN 47404
800.733.6786 (toll free) / 812.336.7700
FAX: 812.336.7790

email: info@SolutionTree.com
SolutionTree.com

Visit **go.SolutionTree.com/SEL** to download the free reproducibles in this book.

Printed in the United States of America

Library of Congress Cataloging-in-Publication Data

Names: Smith, Brian H., 1959- author. | Cook, Clayton R., author. | Fiat, Aria E., author.

Title: The recipe for student well-being : five key ingredients for social, behavioral, and academic success / Brian H. Smith, Clayton R. Cook, Aria E. Fiat.

Other titles: 5 key ingredients for social, behavioral, and academic success

Description: Bloomington, IN : Solution Tree Press, [2024] | Includes bibliographical references and index.

Identifiers: LCCN 2023043520 (print) | LCCN 2023043521 (ebook) | ISBN 9781951075613 (paperback) | ISBN 9781951075620 (ebook)

Subjects: LCSH: Affective education. | Social learning. | Emotional intelligence. | Academic achievement. | Teacher-student relationships--Psychological aspects. | School environment--Social aspects.

Classification: LCC LB1072 .S544 2024 (print) | LCC LB1072 (ebook) | DDC 370.15/34--dc23/eng/20231012

LC record available at https://lccn.loc.gov/2023043520

LC ebook record available at https://lccn.loc.gov/2023043521

Solution Tree
Jeffrey C. Jones, CEO
Edmund M. Ackerman, President

Solution Tree Press
President and Publisher: Douglas M. Rife
Associate Publishers: Todd Brakke and Kendra Slayton
Editorial Director: Laurel Hecker
Art Director: Rian Anderson
Copy Chief: Jessi Finn
Production Editor: Paige Duke
Copy Editor: Madonna Evans
Proofreader: Charlotte Jones
Text and Cover Designer: Kelsey Hoover
Acquisitions Editor: Hilary Goff
Assistant Acquisitions Editor: Elijah Oates
Content Development Specialist: Amy Rubenstein
Associate Editor: Sarah Ludwig
Editorial Assistant: Anne Marie Watkins

ACKNOWLEDGMENTS

Solution Tree Press would like to thank the following reviewers:

Erin Adams
Associate Principal
Pulaski Community Middle School
Pulaski, Wisconsin

David Chilson
Principal
Theodore Roosevelt Elementary
 School
Binghamton, New York

Doug Crowley
Assistant Principal
DeForest Area High School
DeForest, Wisconsin

John D. Ewald
Educational Consultant
Frederick, Maryland

Louis Lim
Vice Principal
Richmond Green Secondary School
Richmond Hill, Ontario, Canada

Debra Lane
Director of Talent Development
Alexandria City Public Schools
Alexandria, Virginia

Agnes Miller
Test Coordinator / Instructional
 Coach
Charlotte, North Carolina

Bruce Preston
Assistant Superintendent of
 Curriculum and Personnel
Howell Township Public Schools
Howell, New Jersey

Christie Shealy
Director of Testing and Accountability
Anderson School District One
Williamston, South Carolina

Kory Taylor
Reading Interventionist
Arkansas Virtual Academy
Little Rock, Arkansas

Visit **SolutionTree.com/SEL** to download the free reproducibles in this book.

TABLE OF CONTENTS

Reproducible pages are in italics.

About the Authors xi

INTRODUCTION 1

A Comprehensive Approach to Student Well-Being 1
The Role of Social-Emotional Learning 2
Book Overview 4

CHAPTER 1

THE SEL RECIPE 7

What Is Comprehensive SEL? 8
    SEL for Adults 10
    Safe, Predictable, and Positive Environments 10
    Positive Relationships 11
    SEL Curriculum and Instruction 11
    Assessment 12
Why Is SEL Important? 12
    Academic Achievement 12
    Social, Emotional, and Behavioral Well-Being 14
    Trauma-Informed Practice 15
    Equity-Focused Practice 18
    Twenty-First Century Skills 19
How Can Schools Effectively Deliver Comprehensive SEL? 20

    Putting Together a Distributed Leadership Team 21
    Securing Buy-In 22
    Engaging in Continuous Improvement 25
    Allocating Protected Time and Resources 26
    Gathering Fidelity Data and Providing Feedback 26
    Training and Coaching 27
Conclusion 28
Next Steps 29
Reflecting on the SEL Recipe 30
Planning for SEL Practices 32

CHAPTER 2

SEL FOR ADULTS 33

What Is SEL for Adults? 34
    Educator Well-Being 34
    SEL Understanding 36
Why Is SEL for Adults Important? 36
How Can Leaders Support SEL for Adults in Schools? 38
    Environment Matters 39
    Strategies to Improve Adult Stress Coping and Well-Being . . . 42
Conclusion 47
Next Steps 48
Reflecting on SEL for Adults 49
Planning for SEL for Adults 50
Reviewing Research-Based Strategies for Educators to
   Improve Stress Coping and Resilience 51

CHAPTER 3

SAFE, PREDICTABLE, AND POSITIVE ENVIRONMENTS 53

What Kinds of Environments Support SEL? 54
    Safe 54

    Predictable 56
    Positive... 58
Why Do Safe, Predictable, and Positive Environments Matter? ... 59
    Motivation and Engagement 60
    Social-Emotional Competence 60
    Social-Emotional Well-Being............................... 61
    Academic Achievement 62
    Equity 63
    Stress Coping 63
    Person and Environment 64
How Can Educators Create Safe, Predictable, and
    Positive Environments? 64
    Positive Behavioral Interventions and Supports 65
    Proactive Classroom Management.......................... 68
    PROMPT Method... 75
    Multitiered System of Supports............................. 77
Conclusion 79
Next Steps 79
Reflecting on Safe, Predictable, and Positive Environments 80
Planning for Safe, Predictable, and Positive Environments 82

CHAPTER 4

POSITIVE RELATIONSHIPS 83

What Are Positive Relationships? 83
Why Are Positive Relationships Important? 84
How Can Educators Intentionally Cultivate and Support
    Positive Peer-to-Peer Relationships? 87
    Positive Peer Reporting 87
    Classroom Meetings 91
How Can Educators Intentionally Cultivate and Support
    Positive Student–Teacher Relationships? 93
    Use the Establish, Maintain, Restore Model 94
    Get Out of Relationship Ruts............................... 111

Student–Teacher Relationships and Equity 113
Conclusion 114
Next Steps 114
Reflecting on Positive Relationships 115
Planning for Positive Relationships 117
Restoring Positive Relationships 120

CHAPTER 5
SEL CURRICULUM AND INSTRUCTION 123

What Is SEL Curriculum and Instruction? 124
    Based on Curriculum, Not Infusion. 125
    Comprehensive, Not Single Topic. 126
    Developmentally Differentiated. 126
    Engaging for Students 127
    Culturally Responsive 127
    User Friendly and Easy to Deliver 128
    Pedagogically Sound 129
    Supportive of Generalization 130
    Backed by Research 131
Why Should Schools Implement a Research-Based
    Curriculum or Program? 132
    Schoolwide Delivery 132
    Effective Implementation 133
How Can Schools Choose an SEL Program? 134
    School Resources 134
    Evidence of Effectiveness. 137
    Developmental Appropriateness. 139
    Support for Generalization. 140
How Can Schools Effectively Implement SEL Curriculum
    and Instruction? 142
    Secure Educator Buy-In 142
    Protect Time for Delivery 142

Avoid Initiative Overload................................... 143
Offer Training and Professional Development.............. 143
Make It a Priority.. 144
Employ a Team Approach 145
Ensure Implementation Fidelity............................ 146
Support Content Beyond Lessons 147
Conclusion 149
Next Steps 150
Reflecting on SEL Curriculum and Instruction 151
Planning for SEL Curriculum and Instruction 153

CHAPTER 6
ASSESSMENT 155

What Is SEL Assessment? 155
    What to Assess... 157
    Screening.. 159
Why Is SEL Assessment Important? 160
How Can Schools Conduct SEL Assessment? 161
    SEL Team... 162
    Approaches to SEL Assessment: Pay or Do It Yourself...... 162
How Can Schools Gather SEL Assessment Data? 163
    Establish a Comparison 164
    Consult Administrative Records 165
    Disseminate Surveys.................................... 165
How Can Schools Assess SEL Ingredients? 167
    SEL for Adults.. 168
    Safe, Predictable, and Positive Classroom and
       School Environments................................ 168
    Positive Relationships With Teachers and Peers............ 168
    SEL Instruction... 169
    Student Engagement.................................... 171
Conclusion 172
Next Steps 172

Reflecting on Assessment 173
Planning for SEL Assessment 175
Reviewing Resources for SEL Assessment 176

Epilogue 179

References and Resources 181

Index 203

ABOUT THE AUTHORS

Brian H. Smith, PhD, has been a leader in translating research into effective social-emotional learning (SEL) programs for nearly twenty years. He headed the design and development of multiple revisions of the preK–8 Second Step curriculum as senior research scientist at the Committee for Children as well as the revision of the K–12 SEL curricula as director of research at CharacterStrong. Dr. Smith has presented to educators in several states on SEL-related topics and worked directly with schools to improve their SEL planning and implementation.

Prior to attaining his doctorate, Dr. Smith worked in schools in a variety of roles, including as elementary counselor, early intervention and prevention specialist, mental health specialist, school social worker, and substance abuse counselor.

Dr. Smith received both his master's degree and doctorate from the School of Social Work at the University of Washington. He has published book chapters and articles for both research and educator audiences.

Clayton R. Cook, PhD, is the chief development officer at CharacterStrong, an organization that aims to create a more loving world through education by designing low-burden, high-impact multitiered solutions. Dr. Cook has been a professor and researcher at three universities—Louisiana State University, the University of Washington, and the University of Minnesota—studying topics such as youth mental health, educator well-being and resilience, SEL, and implementation of evidence-based practices. He has obtained over $20 million in grant funding for his research and published more than a hundred peer-reviewed scientific articles, producing scholarship that has influenced everyday policy and practice in schools. He has delivered more than forty keynote presentations and numerous invited breakout sessions to educational leaders, teachers, and support staff.

Dr. Cook formerly held the John W. and Nancy E. Peyton Faculty Fellowship in Child and Adolescent Wellbeing at the University of Minnesota and also cofounded the School Mental Health Assessment, Research, and Training Center at the University of Washington. His work has been featured in *The New York Times*, *Time* magazine, NPR, Edutopia, and other outlets.

Aria E. Fiat, PhD, is an assistant professor and pediatric psychologist at Cincinnati Children's Hospital Medical Center. She is committed to making mental health care more equitable and accessible through integrated systems of service delivery that emphasize prevention. As a clinician, researcher, educator, and consultant, Dr. Fiat works to enhance the capacity of systems to promote behavioral health and wellness, with an emphasis on supporting the educators and caregivers who help students thrive. She is particularly focused on initiatives that enhance organizational well-being as a key facilitator of systems change.

Dr. Fiat has coauthored more than three dozen peer-reviewed articles, book chapters, and conference proceedings on topics related to school mental health. Dr. Fiat is the creator of the Seven Cs: A Tool Kit for Caregivers Coping in a Crisis and a codeveloper of the Adult Resilience Curriculum, a wellness-promotion program that has been implemented in school districts across the country to counteract educator stress and burnout. Dr. Fiat belongs to the National Association of School Psychologists, the American Psychological Association, and the Society of Pediatric Psychology. She is also a certified instructor of Yoga Calm for Children. Outside of her role as a psychologist, Dr. Fiat is the cofounder of and vice president on the board for Supplies for Dreams, a Chicago-based nonprofit dedicated to mitigating educational inequities.

Dr. Fiat received a bachelor's degree in education and social policy from Northwestern University and a master's degree and doctorate in educational psychology from the University of Minnesota–Twin Cities.

To book Brian H. Smith, Clayton R. Cook, or Aria E. Fiat for professional development, contact pd@SolutionTree.com.

INTRODUCTION

For any person to perform to the best of their capabilities, they need to *be well*. Well-being is a critical enabler to both school and life success. Well-being can be broken down into social, emotional, and mental aspects. To be socially well means feeling like you belong and have the skills to build and maintain healthy relationships, collaborate with others to achieve a common goal, and resolve conflicts productively. To be emotionally well means you experience positive emotions and can regulate your emotions in response to challenging situations. To be mentally well means you have positive thoughts and beliefs about yourself, others, and the future—as well as the skills to identify unhelpful thoughts and reframe them to be more helpful. Together, these dimensions of well-being combine to promote school engagement and enable students to fulfill their potential. The good news is that well-being is malleable and can change in response to enriching experiences that educators can intentionally create through the practices they consistently implement day to day. This book is about those practices: what they are, why they matter, and how to put them into practice.

A Comprehensive Approach to Student Well-Being

As anyone who works in education knows, many children and youth are struggling with mental health challenges. The Surgeon General of the United States recently stated that youth mental health needs have become "the defining public health crisis of our time" (Peetz, 2023). What does a book about universal approaches to supporting student well-being have to do with mental health?

Science has increasingly shown that having mental health is more than simply not having mental illness. The World Health Organization defines mental health as, "a state of mental well-being that enables people to cope with the stresses of life, realize their abilities, learn well and work well, and contribute to their community" (World Health Organization, n.d.). In recent years, therapeutic practice has shifted its focus: from fixing deficits to developing well-being by targeting factors shown to promote young people's abilities to *thrive* (Kobau, 2011; Shek, 2019). World expert on resilience, Anne Masten, argues that, in addition to addressing psychiatric emergencies, "we also need an infusion of knowledge and ordinary strategies to support mental health on the positive side" (Abrams, 2023).

Schools are underequipped to shoulder the burden of meeting the mental health treatment needs of children and youth (Schaeffer, 2022). Consequently, this book showcases and explains how to implement five effective, scientifically supported strategies to improve student well-being. The beauty of this book's approach is that the strategies support healthy student development for those who are struggling as well as for those who seem to be doing OK. Research shows that a focus on increasing student well-being can promote positive mental health, enhance the effectiveness of mental health treatment, and protect students from developing mental health challenges in the future (Suldo, 2020).

The Role of Social-Emotional Learning

Social-emotional learning (SEL) initiatives are increasingly used in education to support comprehensive student well-being, especially in developing and supporting mental health. SEL is a rapidly evolving field, and educators have realized the critical role it plays in achieving the varied missions of the K–12 school system: increasing academic achievement; improving school climate and student safety and well-being; creating productive learning environments in classrooms; and preparing students for the challenges, opportunities, and responsibilities of adulthood.

Here at the start of this book, we'd like to clearly articulate an objective understanding of SEL. SEL aims to ensure that all students receive what they need socially, emotionally, and behaviorally to develop and maintain their well-being, engagement, and academic growth in school and to support their eventual success in work, civic, and private aspects of adult life. To this end, we offer a unique resource in the SEL field.

A solid foundation of research supports all the approaches covered in this book. And the great news is that evidence clearly states that a full range of effective strategies is available for educators to use to nurture the development of students. Humans are complex, and human development is influenced by what individuals learn and how they are taught as well as by their environments and relationships. A number of vital component parts, then, form the basis of a comprehensive approach to supporting student well-being: the social-emotional competence of educators, the culture and climate educators create in schools, the relationships they build with and among students, and their effective delivery of culturally responsive SEL instruction. Much like ingredients in a recipe, these discrete items work synergistically to yield something remarkable—in this case, the conditions under which students can be successful in school and grow into the adults that a strong, healthy society needs.

Because this kind of SEL doesn't happen without the guidance and support of leaders, this book is aimed at educators with leadership capacity—whether formal (for example, school and district administrators) or informal (for example, teacher leaders, school psychologists, counselors, social workers, and paraprofessionals)—to drive meaningful changes in practice within schools to promote equitable social, emotional, and behavioral outcomes for students. Employing a straightforward format, we will help you understand why a comprehensive approach to SEL is important and outline *what* a recipe for SEL success entails, including what each ingredient is, *why* it matters for student success, and, perhaps most important, *how* those practices can be effectively woven into the fabric of schools' day-to-day operations. By showing how each of the SEL ingredients contributes to *all* the goals of education, and by laying out practical, concrete strategies for providing students with what they need to thrive in school and in life, we'll bust the myth that comprehensive support for students' social-emotional development piles far too much onto educators' already full plates.

By that same token, school-based SEL is intended to add to, not take the place of, the learning experiences and growth opportunities students experience in their families and communities. Educators can appreciate the extent to which factors outside school affect students' social and emotional development, such as students' home and neighborhood environments, what they learn there, and the quality of the relationships they have with the adults in their lives—all of which highlight the applicability of the SEL recipe beyond school settings. While these factors are largely beyond teachers' control, the good news is that decades of research show the interconnectedness of students' social, emotional, and academic growth as well as the power of teacher practices to foster student growth.

As educators ourselves, we have spent years working in and with schools. But we also have research backgrounds and know that there is solid science that can help us be more effective in our work with students. The information and strategies in this book come from our synthesizing the strongest research across education, psychology, neuroscience, and many other fields. But we didn't write this book for researchers—we wrote it for educators in the field. Our goal was to translate the science on how to support the social-emotional well-being and development of students into practical guidelines educators can use to improve their practice.

Book Overview

Each chapter in this book is organized into three main sections that capture the what, why, and how of the topic discussed. Following chapter 1, in which we present our comprehensive SEL approach as a simple five-ingredient recipe, each subsequent chapter covers *what* exactly a given SEL ingredient is, the evidence for *why* that ingredient matters, and *how* schools can effectively mix it into their operations. To illustrate, we'll begin a tour through the chapters with a little more detail on the what, why, and how for chapter 1.

In chapter 1, we explain *what* we mean by comprehensive SEL by laying out each of the components of our research-based model of universal SEL. We then focus on *why* this approach to SEL matters for student outcomes, synthesizing the research on student social-emotional development and academic learning to show that SEL is critically important to student success in all areas of life—including academics. Finally, we detail *how* district and school leaders can successfully support the implementation of the SEL ingredients laid out in the rest of the book.

Chapter 2 focuses on one of the major shortfalls in the field of SEL—SEL for the adults in schools. Teaching is a highly stressful profession, and teacher social and emotional well-being have powerful effects on students. In this chapter, we discuss what it means to support the social-emotional competence and resilience of the adults in schools and what SEL for educators might include. We also review the research on the power of supporting teacher well-being and on why SEL for educators can positively impact both teachers' and students' social and emotional growth. Finally, we cover how schools can effectively support adult SEL. Given the shortage of available resources that support SEL for educators, we also cover some strategies educators can use to manage stress and enhance their well-being.

Chapter 3 covers the SEL ingredient of creating safe, predictable, and positive school and classroom environments. First, we discuss what characterizes environments that help all students thrive and provide powerful support to students with additional social and emotional needs. We then explain the reasons our approach to SEL includes attention to the environment by synthesizing the extensive research on the impact of school and classroom environments on student academic achievement a nd social-emotional growth. Finally, the chapter goes into detail on concrete, practical strategies educators can use to create the environments that help students thrive.

Chapter 4 focuses on the promotion of positive relationships both between teachers and students and among students themselves. The chapter explains the key components of positive relationships and summarizes why these relationships are critically important for promoting academic achievement, positive student behavior, and social-emotional development. The chapter then lays out the concrete steps educators can take to support and build the positive relationships that enhance everyone's experience, including teachers'.

Chapter 5 explores the most common approach to SEL—direct instruction of social and emotional competencies through implementation of standardized SEL curricula or programs. The *what* section gives a brief history of SEL curricula and lays out the key characteristics of effective SEL programs. Next, the chapter offers substantial evidence for why direct instruction is a critical part of comprehensive SEL, summarizing research on the positive impacts of well-implemented SEL programs. Finally, the *how* section explains what it takes to get those results—through how to choose and then effectively implement your curricula, from the school level down to how lessons are delivered and supported.

Chapter 6 discusses the role of SEL assessment and the use of data in a comprehensive SEL initiative. First, we provide some perspective on what to assess in order to gather data that you can use to effectively improve your SEL support for students. Next, the chapter explains why assessment is an important part of a data-based decision-making process to increase both overall effectiveness and equity in your SEL efforts. Finally, we dive into the details of how to gather data on all the SEL ingredients and use them to power up your SEL initiatives through practical, time-efficient, data-based decision making.

This book lays out a comprehensive suite of practices that educators can use to truly educate the whole student while making schools and classrooms healthier and happier places for everyone. Throughout the book, we strongly make the case that SEL is much more than a lesson students get once a week. Both the work of education and the work of SEL need to be focused on how we can most effectively create environments and experiences that fully support the healthy development of students intellectually, socially, and emotionally. This work is crucial to the mission of schools, and a comprehensive approach to SEL provides a road map to the specific practices shown to be the most important ways schools can help students succeed academically and become resilient people who can help create healthy families and communities.

CHAPTER 1
THE SEL RECIPE

Wouldn't it be great if there was one simple thing we as educators could do that effectively met students' developmental needs? Of course it would! But that's like saying wouldn't it be great if it was easy for anyone to step into a classroom and automatically be a fantastic teacher. Meeting students' needs, like teaching, is a complex endeavor. All three of the authors have made careers out of studying and figuring out how to apply the best science in education, child development, neuroscience, psychology, and other fields.

Our laser focus has been on one question: What works? This begs a few other questions: What approaches and strategies are both doable in real-world schools and shown to benefit students? Which ones have the most bang for their buck? And what are the key ingredients that *work together* best to support student well-being and social, behavioral, and academic development?

Every strategy in this book can make a difference. But the reason we use the recipe metaphor is that, when all strategies are combined, the whole is absolutely greater than the sum of the parts: all the ingredients work to strengthen and increase the effectiveness of the others.

In this chapter, we provide an overview of the key ingredients that make up the SEL recipe; discuss why comprehensive SEL matters and is important for student well-being, growth, and success; and look at some powerful ways to ensure successful SEL implementation.

What Is Comprehensive SEL?

Delivering SEL is analogous to following a baking recipe—you need to include all the right ingredients to get the best results. In combining distinct practices to produce the desired outcomes for students, too often, schools fall into the trap of using only some of the ingredients in a recipe for success, which is like trying to bake chocolate chip cookies without sugar or butter. The reality is that single-ingredient approaches are not enough to provide the full range of supports needed to promote students' social-emotional success, prevent problems from emerging, and lay the foundation for more intensive interventions to work for the subset of students who need them. To be effective, schools must use a recipe that combines the key SEL ingredients in order to produce desired social, emotional, and academic outcomes.

High-quality SEL that effectively supports the full range of positive student outcomes includes five key ingredients.

1. SEL for adults
2. Safe, predictable, and positive environments
3. Positive relationships
4. SEL curriculum and instruction
5. Assessment

Figure 1.1 (page 9) shows the five key ingredients of SEL.

To take the recipe analogy a little further, you don't simply bake each ingredient of your chocolate chip cookies separately. To get the right outcome, you need all the ingredients mixed together. The same is true with SEL. Each ingredient is powerful on its own. But the real impact is achieved through the synergy that comes when each increases the power of the others. Direct SEL instruction has more power when delivered in a classroom with a positive climate, by socially and emotionally skilled teachers to whom students feel connected, in the context of a school environment that spells out clear expectations and encourages the use of social-emotional skills. It's easier for students to meet school and classroom expectations when they've learned skills for self-management. Likewise, students are in a better position to master those self-management skills when positive norms for behavior motivate them to put the skills to use. Clear norms, expectations, and routines also provide the framework for staff to create predictability and

FIGURE 1.1: The five SEL ingredients.

consistency that support students to employ and fine-tune SEL skills they learn through lessons. When students feel connected to their teachers and other students, they are not only more motivated to follow positive class norms but also more open to engage in learning experiences, which makes SEL lessons and other academic instruction more impactful. And everyone benefits from a more proactive and positive learning environment in which educators are able to both detect and assist early on those students who have extra needs for support. Let's take a look at the key SEL practices that together set all students up for success.

SEL FOR ADULTS

Students are not the only ones who can benefit from the skills taught in SEL. Teaching is one of the most difficult and stressful professions, and educator well-being impacts students' experience in school and helps support teachers' ability to meet the many challenges of the profession (Doan, Steiner, Pandey, & Woo, 2023; Jennings & Greenberg, 2009; Oberle & Schonert-Reichl, 2016). In addition, having some understanding and even competence in many of the topics covered in SEL lessons boosts teachers' abilities to effectively support student development and mastery of SEL competencies. The more resilient teachers are, the better they can handle the stress and workload involved in teaching, which supports their ability to create positive classroom environments and form positive relationships with students.

SAFE, PREDICTABLE, AND POSITIVE ENVIRONMENTS

This practice or ingredient of the SEL recipe highlights the fact that schools and classrooms are powerful developmental contexts. And it's not that they *can be* but that they *are*—for better or for worse. It may be tempting to think of students as self-contained, that their development is an internal process or perhaps something that is primarily affected by what goes on outside school. But the reality is that students spend a huge amount of their time at school, and the experiences that they have there impact their development not just intellectually but socially, emotionally, and behaviorally. This means that students' environments during the school day have the potential to influence their development in either positive or negative ways that really matter (Eccles & Roeser, 2011).

POSITIVE RELATIONSHIPS

Humans are fundamentally social beings. We are wired to connect with others, and positive relationships are one of the most powerful factors in healthy development, learning, and happiness. We know from experience and extensive research what kinds of relationships lead to beneficial outcomes for all students. According to researchers Kelly Allen, Margaret L. Kern, Dianne Vella-Brodrick, John Hattie, and Lea Waters (2018), all students benefit from feeling like they belong; from being able to trust and respect others; and from feeling like they are wanted, valued, and welcomed members of a place. Educators have the ability to intentionally cultivate positive relationships with students and promote relationships among students, both of which are essential to students' sense of belonging and connection to school.

It might not be immediately obvious why positive relationships comprise one of the ingredients of a high-quality comprehensive approach to SEL. But the fact is that SEL is largely a *socially driven* process based on a core human need: a sense of belonging. The connections students have with their teachers and other students, as well as the relationship between school and home, powerfully affect students' ability to benefit from both academic and SEL instruction.

In their work on human development and education, professors Terri J. Sabol and Robert C. Pianta (2012) confirm that positive student–teacher relationships help drive student engagement in both SEL and academic lessons, increase student motivation to practice and employ social and emotional skills, and help provide the safety and support students need to develop the competencies to regulate themselves while striving to achieve meaningful short- and long-term goals they set for themselves. Positive peer relationships help students feel accepted and valued for who they are. Positive relationships between school and home, especially when they include sharing information with families about the SEL work happening at school, can help families and schools work together to promote the social-emotional well-being of students.

SEL CURRICULUM AND INSTRUCTION

This ingredient captures what comes to mind for most people when they think of SEL: directly teaching students social and emotional skills and knowledge. The most common way schools do this is by implementing an SEL program or curriculum. Too often, people think that *is* doing SEL—that SEL is a one-ingredient recipe.

SEL curricula have many strengths. The best ones are easy to deliver, carefully developed, based on science, and shown to work (CASEL, n.d.a). But the strengths of the curricula approach to SEL can also be its weakness. It's easy to think that simply purchasing a program and delivering lessons once a week means you've taken care of SEL. The reality is that not only are the other ingredients necessary, but important aspects of implementing SEL curricula are too often missed. It's critical that educators understand what it takes to maximize the effectiveness of this key ingredient.

ASSESSMENT

SEL-related assessment can provide important information schools and districts can use to strengthen and improve their SEL efforts across each of the other SEL ingredients laid out in this book. Gathering information related to the different SEL ingredients can inform a data-based decision-making approach to SEL that helps schools focus their limited resources on where they're likely to be most effective at improving student outcomes (McKown & Herman, 2020). Once schools use assessment data to ensure they are properly supporting and implementing key SEL practices, they can also use assessment to gauge the various impacts of their providing students and staff with support for their social-emotional competence and well-being.

Why Is SEL Important?

Developing social-emotional competence is fundamental to student academic and life success for a wide variety of reasons. In this section, we summarize evidence for the diverse benefits of SEL, homing in on academic achievement; social, emotional, and behavioral well-being; trauma-informed practice, equity-focused practice; and 21st century skills.

ACADEMIC ACHIEVEMENT

There never seems to be enough time in education. But what if spending time on SEL actually *increases* rather than takes away from academic learning? The great news is that decades of research show that is exactly what happens. In large-scale studies of the impacts of SEL, researchers Joseph A. Durlak, Roger P. Weissberg, Allison B. Dymnicki, Rebecca D. Taylor, and Kriston B. Schellinger (2011) have found increased social and emotional skills, better behavior, and less emotional distress—but they also show that SEL programs increased student academic achievement by 11 percent. And the effects of SEL have staying power. The work of Rebecca D. Taylor, Eva Oberle, Joseph A. Durlak, and Roger P. Weissberg (2017) reveals that over three years *after* students participated in an SEL program, their academic performance was 13.5 percent higher than students who had not received SEL. There is no question: SEL can increase academic achievement. But *why* does time spent on supporting students' social and emotional development help increase learning?

We have come a long way since the days when we thought of a teacher's job as simply to pour knowledge into students like coffee into a cup. Research in human development, educational psychology, neuroscience, and educational practice and policy have come together to establish that learning is not just an intellectual act. Learning is impacted by and depends on social, emotional, cognitive, linguistic, and academic development. Neuroscientists C. Daniel Salzman and Stefano Fusi (2010) show that the brain circuits involved in cognition and emotional and physiological regulation are all interconnected. Any experienced teacher knows that motivation, engagement, and academic performance are highly dependent on students' interest level, mindsets, self-confidence, and persistence. Students don't just use their IQs to learn; their emotions help drive engagement and effort. Learning also has powerful social dimensions. Success in the classroom requires the social awareness and skill to read social cues, avoid or handle conflicts, collaborate with peers, and contribute to a positive learning climate.

One of the biggest factors that drives student achievement is engagement. What and how you teach simply doesn't matter that much if students are not engaged. We know, and research shows, that student engagement has important emotional, behavioral, and cognitive components that are all affected by SEL. Researchers Hanke Korpershoek, Esther T. Canrinus, Marjon Fokkens-Bruinsma, and Hester de Boer (2020) find that students who feel connected and like they belong in their school have greater self-efficacy and higher levels of both behavioral and cognitive engagement. Similarly, authors Camille Farrington, Shanette Porter, and Joshua Klugman (2019) show that student engagement is impacted by the quality of classroom environments.

SEL can also help level the educational playing field by ensuring all students develop the social, emotional, and behavioral strengths they need to be fully engaged. Research indicates that students who possess social and emotional competencies like social skills, empathy, and self-control do better in school and are more likely to be academically successful from elementary through high school (Mahoney, Durlak, & Weissberg, 2018). But the simple fact is that students don't show up at school with equal levels of those competencies, nor do they all learn them as quickly or easily as others. If we want to promote equity and support the academic success of all students, we need to ensure that they all receive the support needed to develop critical social and emotional competencies.

Academic achievement is not a solitary endeavor. Even highly motivated and skilled students can fail to realize their potential in dysregulated classrooms. Students who lack social-emotional competence can create disruptive classroom environments, and researchers Carmel Blank and Yossi Shavit (2016) show that disruptive behavior lowers the achievement of all students, not only those exhibiting the behavior. According to educators Scott E. Carrell, Mark Hoekstra, and Elira Kuka (2018), high levels of emotional dysregulation within classrooms decreases the long-term educational outcomes even for students with strong emotion regulation skills. So when students in a classroom are able to self-regulate, all students in the class learn and achieve more, benefiting both directly and indirectly from SEL.

SOCIAL, EMOTIONAL, AND BEHAVIORAL WELL-BEING

In their work for the Centers for Disease Control and Prevention, Ruth Perou and colleagues (2013) note that as many as one out of every five students aged three to seventeen have a mental, emotional, developmental, or behavioral disorder, and many more exhibit milder social, emotional, and behavioral problems that impair their functioning. These latter problems hinder academic success and are linked to interpersonal challenges at school, truancy, and eventual dropout. SEL gives students the support they need to increase their social, emotional, and behavioral well-being. As discussed in the introduction, enhancing student well-being is a powerful tool for supporting the effectiveness of mental health treatment, preventing the onset of mental health challenges, and improving the experience and capabilities of all students.

Research clearly shows that SEL improves student behavior (Durlak, Weissberg, & Pachan, 2011), including in the classroom, lunchroom, hallways, and on the playground. The great thing about improving social-emotional competence is that the effects are not just short term; changing skills, attitudes, mindsets, and norms can ripple out into long-term gains for students, schools, and society as a whole. In their longitudinal research that follows the same individuals over decades, authors Mona Alzahrani, Manal Alharbi, and Amani Alodwani (2019) have shown that students' social-emotional competence has powerful positive effects years down the road. For example, research from clinical psychologist Terrie E. Moffitt and colleagues (2011) indicates that students' social-emotional skills in kindergarten lead to real improvements in their young adult educational and career attainment and reduce their involvement in criminal activity, substance abuse, and mental health disorders.

Students who receive a high-quality SEL program are more prosocial, get in less trouble, have fewer conduct problems, and experience less emotional distress (Durlak et al., 2011). This increased social, emotional, and behavioral well-being creates a real difference in their ability to make friends, benefit from instruction, and stay in school and achieve. But supporting the social, emotional, and behavioral competence of students who struggle is a powerful support to all students—as well as to teachers. Struggling students need support from teachers. But sadly, the challenges of difficult student behavior can make that support harder to deliver by dramatically increasing teacher stress and frustration. Improving students' social, emotional, and behavioral well-being can support teacher effectiveness and well-being, which makes a real difference for both students and educators.

TRAUMA-INFORMED PRACTICE

Behavioral scientist Phyllis Holditch Niolon (n.d.) writes that many students come to school impacted by a variety of traumas and chronic stressors, many of which are categorized as adverse childhood experiences (ACEs), such as physical, sexual, and emotional abuse; physical and emotional neglect; domestic violence; parental substance abuse; parental mental illness; the incarceration of a parent; and divorce. ACEs also encompass *adverse community environments*, such as poverty, discrimination, poor housing, lack of opportunity, community disruption, and community violence (Niolon, n.d.). Professor of public health Karen Hughes and colleagues (2017), along with researchers Patricia Logan-Greene, Sara Green, Paula S. Nurius, and Dario Longhi (2014), show that without proper support, ACEs can result in worse life outcomes into adulthood, including higher rates of addiction, criminal behavior, incarceration, and medical problems severe enough to compromise health and even lead to early death.

The Center on the Developing Child at Harvard University (n.d.) reports the following findings about stress in children. When children experience relatively short-lived mild-to-moderate stressors in the context of supportive relationships with adults, it helps them develop a healthy stress response system and build resilience.

During a healthy, manageable stress experience, heart rate and stress hormone levels briefly rise to meet the challenge and then fall again soon after. But when a child experiences intense, frequent, or prolonged adversity, especially without nurturing adult support, it creates toxic stress in the form of chronically elevated stress hormones. This lasting elevated stress response impacts brain development in ways that can make it more difficult for students to learn and harder for them to manage their emotions and behavior. Over time, ACEs, other trauma, and chronic toxic levels of stress result in greater activation of the parts of the brain, like the amygdala, that are designed to detect and respond rapidly to threats. At the same time, toxic stress can impair the development of the parts of the brain, like the prefrontal cortex, involved in learning, thinking, impulse control, long-term planning, and the ability to manage difficult thoughts and feelings—with obvious impacts on learning and behavior.

Emotion regulation is one of the competencies most impacted by trauma (Short, Boffa, Clancy, & Schmidt, 2018). Students affected by ACEs and toxic stress are more likely to show up at school with their brains attuned to signs of danger. The National Scientific Council on the Developing Child (2020) offers the following explanation: From an evolutionary survival standpoint, if you experience your environment as unsafe, it's better to see danger when it may not be there than to miss out on spotting a real threat. Some students burdened by toxic stress have very specific triggers they respond to, but it's common for trauma-affected students to have a threat response system that can be set off by a wide range of things that other students might tolerate without a problem. Once the brain of a student impacted by toxic stress detects a threat, whether it's real or not, the student is more likely to respond impulsively before the thinking function of the brain can engage. This heightened reactivity and rapid, emotionally driven impulsive responsiveness, combined with a lowered capacity to reason through problems and think before acting, causes problems for these students and their teachers and can negatively impact the classroom and school environment for all students.

Although some students impacted by trauma may be prone to conflicts and disruptive behavior, others often fly under the behavioral radar. Neuroscience research like that of Michael A. P. Bloomfield, Robert A. McCutcheon, Matthew Kempton, Tom P. Freeman, and Oliver Howes (2019) shows that toxic stress and trauma impact the dopamine system in the brain in ways that can increase depression. The students in your class with their heads on their desks or buried in their hoods may just be behind on sleep from too much late-night gaming or social media, but they may also be overloaded by stress and psychologically and emotionally shut down.

Whether acting out or trying to go unnoticed, students with traumatic histories are suffering, less able to learn, and in need of support.

It can be hard for us as educators to think about how many of our students are suffering in these ways. And it can also be difficult to have our best-planned lessons blown up when students act in disruptive ways or disengage because of toxic stress. But the good news is that not only do we have a lot of knowledge about how serious adversity impacts students; we have also learned a lot about the kinds of support they need.

So what does SEL have to do with ACEs and the impacts of toxic stress? It's tempting—and frankly pretty scary—to think that teachers need to become therapists, or maybe "abuse detectives," trying to figure out which of their students have been through exactly what kinds of horrific experiences. Fortunately, perhaps the most effective way educators can help students with traumatic histories grow, develop, and succeed is by creating positive relationships in the context of safe, predictable environments and by supporting the development of students' social-emotional competence. In other words, the appropriate educational response to ACEs, trauma, and toxic stress is not primarily targeted at identifying and "treating" individual students. Although some students suffering from the effects of trauma do need more targeted or intensive support, schools can make a powerful contribution to the well-being of students impacted by toxic stress through a dedicated implementation of the core ingredients of SEL laid out in this book.

Essentially, what implementing comprehensive SEL practices does is supply students with the critical supports they need to grow their brains in healthy ways, gain skills to help counteract the impacts of toxic stress, and improve their ability to learn in school and grow into thriving adults. Supporting the development of social-emotional competence, especially emotion regulation, works to help students overcome the emotional dysregulation and lack of impulse control caused by long-term stress. Much of what drives trauma and toxic stress are the intertwined problems of fractured relationships with caregivers and unsafe environments. Relationships are foundational to human development, and when we create positive connections with students, we are providing them with critical developmental support. The same goes for creating safe, secure, predictable classroom and school environments. Traumatized students' brains cannot calm down and develop in a nonstressed state while they feel unsafe. We can give students a powerful developmental gift by helping them feel like they are safe enough to let their guard down, know what's going to happen when, and don't have to be on alert for danger or sudden changes. Students spend a large part of their lives in school. If we can help make that a period of time when their brains can develop normally—free from constant worry, fear, and stress—it will go a long way toward righting the wrongs they have experienced.

EQUITY-FOCUSED PRACTICE

Educational equity means ensuring that all students receive the supports they need to develop into healthy and successful adults. Of course, that involves rigorous academic instruction as well as high expectations for *all* students. It also entails working to make sure our discipline policies and practices are constructive, rather than simply punitive, and implemented fairly so they do not feed lower-income students and students of color into the school-to-prison pipeline. But equity is also about providing all students with SEL supports that fit their needs, delivered in culturally responsive ways.

It is easy and perhaps traditional for educators to assume that students' social-emotional development will be taken care of by parents and the out-of-school experiences families make available to their children. But this does not take into account the inequitable distribution of opportunities for young people to develop social-emotional competence outside school. Across all ages, students from families with fewer financial resources and more challenges have less access to the myriad of enrichment experiences that support the social-emotional development of more privileged students, like sports, music, gymnastics, performing arts, summer camps, high-quality preschool and before- and after-school programs, martial arts, internships, mentorships, and more. According to the Office of Juvenile Justice and Delinquency Prevention (2023), children living in poverty in the United States are three times more likely to have a single-parent caregiver. The challenges of single parenting along with the many difficulties of parenting with fewer financial resources mean students often receive lower-quality day care and preschool and parents have less time and energy to support student growth and development at home.

A greater understanding of the challenges many of our students face should inspire us to focus on the importance of how we as educators can support the development of the whole student. In their research on schools serving economically disadvantaged neighborhoods, Matthew J. Irvin, Judith L. Meece, Soo-yong Byun, Thomas W. Farmer, and Bryan C. Hutchins (2011) of the National Research Center on Rural Education Support clearly tell us that students can benefit from the right experiences at school despite poverty and disadvantage. The daily actions of educators matter for all students.

Engagement is critical to student learning, yet students of color and economically disadvantaged students on average show lower levels of engagement (Bingham & Ogaki, 2012; Yazzie-Mintz, 2007). Educators can advance student development and help buffer the effects of poverty and racism when they intentionally work to create culturally responsive and developmentally appropriate relationships with students, ensure all students have the opportunity to learn in safe and welcoming environments, and actively provide students with the supports they need to develop social and emotional competencies. Schoolwide efforts to implement comprehensive SEL can make important contributions to increasing equity in our schools.

TWENTY-FIRST CENTURY SKILLS

Educators and parents aren't the only people interested in and pushing for SEL. There is a growing realization that social-emotional competence is critical for success in the workplace. One person who has done a lot to make a strong evidence-based case for the importance of supporting students' social and emotional development is Nobel Prize-winning economist James Heckman. His research shows that social-emotional competence is critical to long-term success, including in the workplace, and he has been a powerful advocate for interventions like SEL as a way to strengthen the U.S. workforce and economy (Heckman, 2000).

When key research and policy institutes on both the right and left ends of the political spectrum worked together to produce a joint report on reducing poverty and restoring the American dream, one of their key recommendations was an increased focus on educating the whole student to "promote social-emotional and character development as well as academic skills" (AEI/Brookings Working Group on Poverty and Opportunity, 2015, p. 5). Their report highlights the widely supported fact that students' social-emotional competence impacts their educational attainment, employment, and earnings as much as or more than their standardized achievement test scores.

Employers themselves make it clear that ensuring students have academic or even technical knowledge is not enough. In one survey of 900 executives, 92 percent said social-emotional skills such as problem solving and communication are as important as—if not more important than—technical skills for worker success (Davidson, 2016). In another workforce study, computing and information systems experts Evan Schirf and Anthony Serapiglia (2017) found that even in the information technology field, the lack of social-emotional skills such as communication, problem solving, interpersonal skills, motivation, and positive attitude is often a bigger problem than a shortage of technical skills.

Even young people themselves say they need more support for social-emotional development to help them succeed. In a study conducted by researchers Jennifer L. DePaoli, Matthew N. Atwell, John M. Bridgeland, and Timothy P. Shriver (2018), less than half of recent high school graduates in the United States said they were prepared for success after high school or ready for a job or career. But that was not true across the board. Fully 80 percent of recent graduates from "strong SEL" schools felt they were prepared for a job or career, but that was true of only 8 percent of students from "weak SEL" schools. The students also highlighted the need for more SEL, with less than half of recently graduated high school students saying that their school did at least a pretty good job of helping them develop their SEL skills (DePaoli, Atwell, Bridgeland, & Shriver, 2018).

No educator went into the profession with the sole goal of producing good workers. But if our students cannot ultimately get jobs, thrive in the workplace, and contribute to a strong economy, we all lose.

How Can Schools Effectively Deliver Comprehensive SEL?

This chapter has introduced you to the key practices that make up an effective, comprehensive approach to SEL, and each will in turn be covered in detail in the following chapters. But we must keep in mind that students cannot benefit from practices they do not receive. *Implementation* refers to whether and how practices are delivered in your classroom, school, or district. As important as it is to embrace good SEL practices, ultimately implementation is what will make or break positive outcomes for your students.

Too often, schools get caught up in the "flavor of the month" trap, rapidly adopting a new program or initiative and then just as quickly moving on to something else. One side effect of this tendency is that nothing truly gets a fair chance to work, because high-quality implementation takes time and focused effort. Educators may be left simply waiting for one fad to be replaced by the next and are not surprised when the latest big idea fails to make a difference.

Educators should be working at both the district and school levels to ensure that students receive well-implemented SEL supports. School districts make SEL happen through aligning policies, resources, procedures, and practices. At a building level, implementation is most effectively supported by a distributed leadership team in the building that oversees implementation and embeds it in a continuous improvement process. Ultimately, you can be sure your school is effectively implementing SEL when you have data that indicate your educators deliver the practices with fidelity—all the active ingredients delivered as intended—and that demonstrate your students are increasingly able to meet the social and academic demands of school and more fully engage in and therefore benefit from their learning experiences.

Throughout this chapter, you've encountered the ingredients for SEL. What does successful implementation look like? Successful implementation of SEL ingredients includes six key elements: (1) putting together a distributed leadership team, (2) securing buy-in, (3) engaging in continuous improvement, (4) allocating protected time and resources, (5) gathering fidelity data and providing feedback, and (6) training and coaching. The following text briefly describes each of these implementation ingredients, and subsequent chapters discuss how to support specific SEL practices by leveraging each of these ingredients.

PUTTING TOGETHER A DISTRIBUTED LEADERSHIP TEAM

The first and most important ingredient in the recipe for successful SEL implementation is a dedicated distributed leadership team. When putting together this team, choose a diverse team of both formal and informal leaders who can work collaboratively. The team should be charged with the following.

- Strategic decision making and action planning around the implementation of the specific SEL practices you're seeking to put in place
- Managing potential competing priorities and demands to maintain focus on a given implementation effort and avoid initiative overload and staff burnout
- Supporting the collection and use of fidelity data to monitor implementation, problem-solve barriers to implementation, and

develop and put in place action plans that include strategies that target improving implementation

Considering all of this, the distributed leadership team owns responsibility for implementation in the building and oversees the other ingredients in the recipe for implementation success.

SECURING BUY-IN

Gaining teacher buy-in is a prerequisite to successful implementation. Half-hearted delivery of SEL practices isn't likely to be very effective. Buy-in means people understand why the practices are important and are committed to doing the work to make sure students get the high-quality SEL supports they need. Jumping into implementing a new program without bringing staff on board and ensuring buy-in is a recipe for weak delivery that doesn't last.

We can think of buy-in as readiness. When we use the term *ready* in everyday life (for example, "Are you ready for dinner?" or "Is the team ready for the game?"), what we are referring to is whether individuals are prepared. In an article for *Implementation Science,* researchers Christopher M. Shea, Sara R. Jacobs, Denise A. Esserman, Kerry Bruce, and Bryan J. Weiner (2014) describe *readiness* as "the extent to which organizational members are psychologically and behaviorally prepared to implement organizational change." From an educational perspective, the question is whether staff demonstrate the commitment and willingness needed to motivate them to invest time and energy into implementing and continuously improving SEL practices over time.

Psychological preparation means staff have the beliefs, attitudes, and motivation needed to put the SEL practices into action. These come about through intentional exposure to content and experiences that enable staff to learn about the benefits of the SEL practices, how educators like them are able to successfully integrate the SEL practices into their workflow, and why the SEL practices align with their values as educators. The following are ways to increase psychological preparedness among staff.

- Providing initial training on the SEL practices
- Disseminating research briefs highlighting the evidence supporting certain SEL practices
- Exposing staff to testimonials from other educators who emphasize the benefits of the SEL practices

- Arranging site visits to other schools already undertaking the implementation of certain SEL practices
- Sharing stories from students and families about the reasons why the SEL practices are needed

Behavioral preparation is about developing a keen understanding of the actions that one will be expected to perform to implement an SEL practice with fidelity. This behavioral preparation comes through didactic training, rehearsal or practice opportunities, modeling, video simulations, and other ways in which people can internalize the actions they will be expected and supported to perform to implement chosen SEL practices.

Educator buy-in will make or break an SEL initiative. A more detailed understanding of buy-in comes from Bryan J. Weiner, Cara C. Lewis, and Kenneth Sherr (2023), whose research indicates there are four components that drive motivational readiness to implement: (1) why the practices are needed, (2) positive expectations, (3) social proofs, and (4) self-efficacy.

Why SEL Is Needed

Buy-in is strengthened by a deep understanding of the reasons *why* integrating SEL practices into the fabric of educational programming will meet important student developmental needs and improve academic performance and school climate. If educators don't believe that SEL practices will make a critical contribution, then they are likely to have low motivational readiness to implement. The effective approach to building a strong sense of why SEL is essential is to appeal to educators' hearts and minds through a combination of data and stories. Leaders can use data to highlight how SEL practices can effectively meet student needs in ways proven to contribute to positive educational and developmental outcomes. For example, leaders could use data to show that 35 percent of students report that they don't feel a sense of belonging and connection to their school. Educators want all students (100 percent) to experience a sense of belonging in school because they know it is a powerful driver of student well-being and achievement. Recognition that three out of every ten students, or nine students out of a class of thirty, do not feel like they belong heightens educator awareness of a need that intentional implementation of student-facing relationship practices can meet.

Positive Expectations

Educators are more likely to implement practices they believe will lead to positive outcomes for students and themselves. Positive expectations motivate behavior change. One way to boost positive expectations for SEL practices is to share scientific research on the effects of SEL. For example, the Collaborative for Academic, Social, and Emotional Learning (CASEL; https://casel.org/fundamentals-of-sel/what-does-the-research-say) offers resources that highlight the consistently positive outcomes educators observe when schools implement SEL. By definition, evidence-based SEL practices should be supported by rigorous research studies demonstrating their positive effects. Sharing this evidence with educators delineates the outcomes they can expect if they commit to integrating and implementing evidence-based practices. Throughout this book, we've included evidence to support the ingredients of our SEL recipe. Stories or narratives from others are also a powerful way to cultivate positive expectations. This means bringing in the voices of students, other educators, and families about the benefits of SEL to help educators recognize the value of investing in SEL practices. Ultimately, positive expectations help educators believe that the benefits of SEL significantly outweigh the costs of the energy, effort, and time needed to bring SEL to life.

Social Proofs

Social proofs are a compelling way to increase motivational readiness to implement, as they rely on the idea that people are heavily influenced by the behaviors and actions of others like them. *Social proof* refers to the tendency of individuals to conform to the actions and behaviors of others particularly when they are uncertain about what to do in a given situation. In an educational context, if you want to encourage educators to adopt a new teaching method, you can provide evidence or testimonials from other educators who have successfully implemented it. This demonstrates that behavior change is not only possible but also widely accepted and practiced by their peers, increasing the likelihood of adoption. Social proofs are also used to establish unwritten social norms and expectations that a given practice is what trusted and respected colleagues are investing in to achieve important outcomes for students. Knowing how many schools are implementing SEL can also help educators understand that engaging in SEL practices is the norm in education, not the exception. For example, in one large study, advisory firm authors Gates Bryant, Sean Crowley, and Caroline Davidsen (2020) find that more than 90 percent of K–12 schools and districts report they are working to support student SEL.

Self-Efficacy

Self-efficacy has a direct impact on a person's intentions and commitment to engage in specific behaviors. It reflects individuals' confidence in their ability to engage in specific behaviors in the face of challenging or competing demands for their time and energy. This is why boosting educators' self-efficacy is an important way to increase motivational readiness to implement. A number of strategies can help increase self-efficacy. For example, "Seeing is believing" means allowing educators to see particular practices in action to give them the confidence that they can replicate those practices. Protecting time on the front end to allow educators to think more deeply about how they can integrate SEL practices into their daily workflow can also boost confidence, especially when lack of time threatens self-efficacy. Also, knowing that coaching, mentoring, and modeling will be available to them throughout implementation helps increase self-efficacy by assuring educators that if they get stuck, they can get unstuck by tapping into resources available to them. Ultimately, self-efficacy is needed for educators to have the internal motivation and confidence that they can pull off integrating and implementing SEL practices along with the other things that are on their metaphorical plates.

ENGAGING IN CONTINUOUS IMPROVEMENT

Continuous quality improvement consists of systematic and persistent actions by the distributed leadership team that lead to measurable improvements in the delivery of SEL practices and student social, emotional, and academic outcomes. A process of continuous quality improvement recognizes the direct link between improved implementation of SEL practices and desired student outcomes. To ensure continuous quality improvement, your distributed leadership team must meet regularly to look at data and reflect on implementation. Your team can empower staff to work together more effectively to support students and improve outcomes by focusing on the following questions.

- How well are the educators in the building adhering to delivering the SEL practices as planned?
- Are the educators delivering the right amount, or dosage, of each SEL practice?
- Are educators delivering the practices in an engaging and effective way?

During implementation, it is important to protect time for staff to come back together in groups to collaborate, reflect on implementation, and revisit plans around implementation. This collaboration could occur in established professional learning communities or grade-level, department, or whole-staff meetings. The aim is to dedicate collaborative time for staff to reflect on and incrementally improve the delivery of SEL practices to reach high fidelity. An example of a structured process leaders can use to facilitate collaboration among staff to drive continuous improvement is the plan-do-study-act cycle (Deming, n.d.). This cycle supports an implementation effort by helping staff to develop a plan to implement specific SEL practices, carry out the plan, observe and learn from the consequences of the plan, and determine what improvements should be made to the plan before putting them into action. Plan-do-study-act cycles are repeated over time to enable continuous improvement. Ensuring time is protected for staff to collaborate in such a structured way is an important ingredient to successful implementation.

ALLOCATING PROTECTED TIME AND RESOURCES

School leaders show what they value by how they allocate precious staff time and school resources. If educators lack the time and supportive resources they need to competently implement new practices, it can sink your SEL initiative. To be successful, leadership will need to make it clear that SEL work is a priority, particularly by ensuring staff have protected time and resources to devote to the work. Protected time provides opportunities for educators to learn about, reflect on, and plan how to integrate specific practices into their regular routines. It also enables them to collaborate with their peers to problem-solve barriers to implementation. Being intentional about providing the financial and informational resources necessary to support implementation ensures that educators have what they need to deliver specific practices.

GATHERING FIDELITY DATA AND PROVIDING FEEDBACK

Students can't benefit from an intervention or practice that they don't receive. However, it's not realistic to expect educators to be immediate experts at implementing SEL practices, especially given that much of SEL falls outside the training teachers typically receive. One critical way to support effective implementation is by providing performance-based feedback on the quality of SEL supports teachers are providing and students are receiving. As teachers progress in their implementation, it's important to gather and share data on how effectively they are delivering the SEL practices. This feedback will help teachers improve their practice over time and thereby increase the positive impact on students.

One of the most important aspects of performance-based feedback is to gather data on the delivery of critical components of the practice (discussed in greater detail in chapter 6, page 163, in the context of SEL assessment). Gathering fidelity data requires capturing the core components of the practices that drive student outcomes, including how much the practice should be implemented (that is, what dose of the practice students should receive). Once leaders gather data using the fidelity tool, they use it to determine the degree to which students are receiving the practice in a way that is likely to promote better outcomes. Once leaders have gathered fidelity data, it's important for them to figure out not only when they'll present the data to staff but also how they'll deliver the data as feedback. Performance-based feedback can be verbal (communication on which components teachers have implemented well and which components they are currently missing) or visual (graphs and images that depict how well and completely teachers have implemented various components). Performance-based feedback helps address a common barrier to successful implementation: thinking a practice is being implemented better than it actually is. Feedback based on objective data can clarify what is being done well and what needs improvement. Ultimately, finding nonjudgmental ways of providing feedback can help staff accurately understand how well they're doing and incrementally improve their delivery of the SEL practices in ways that are likely to achieve desired student outcomes.

TRAINING AND COACHING

Training and coaching are cornerstone implementation support strategies that help educators learn about and apply specific practices over time. One-and-done trainings are not enough to ensure high-quality implementation. Initial training provides an opportunity for staff to learn about and get motivated to apply SEL practices. It's equally important to follow up training by providing coaching. Harness the expertise and experience of school or district staff or bring in expert, trained coaches who are dedicated to helping your educators get incrementally better at delivering specific practices with fidelity.

Training and follow-up coaching address knowledge and self-efficacy gaps that otherwise undermine successful delivery of SEL practices. Quality training provides staff with knowledge of background information, theory, and philosophy, the rationale behind the practices, and opportunities to practice new skills and receive feedback in a safe environment. Educator Jana Hunzicker (2010) explains that to enhance teachers' ability to learn new skills, training must include "active" learning opportunities, or activities that engage teachers "physically, cognitively, and emotionally" (p. 6). Active learning includes problem-solving activities, sharing and discussion, simulations and role playing, observation of others modeling the practices, review of student or classroom scenarios, collaborative reflections, and physical movement. Quality training can be delivered in person, virtually, and synchronously or asynchronously. The aim is for the training to actively engage adult learners in a process of learning about the why, what, and how of SEL practices they ultimately are expected to implement.

Examining teacher training and coaching in an important early meta-analysis—a research study that combines the results of many individual studies—educators Bruce Joyce and Beverly Showers (2002) indicate that even when training consisted of theory, discussion, demonstration, practice, and opportunities for feedback, few teachers transferred the practices with fidelity to the classroom. It was only when follow-up coaching was added that large gains were seen in knowledge and ability to demonstrate practices with fidelity in the classroom. Coaching, according to researchers Allison G. Kretlow, Nancy L. Cooke, and Charles L. Wood (2012), is characterized by an expert or experienced colleague providing a less-experienced educator with advice about or demonstrations of the new practices, as well as feedback on the implementation of the newly learned practices. Quality coaching is fundamentally a relational process that occurs in the context of supportive, trusting relationships. It is important for leaders to identify individuals either outside or inside the school who can build trusting relationships with staff and provide coaching support to staff who may be struggling with implementation.

Conclusion

In this chapter, we addressed the what, why, and how of SEL. Our answer to the question "What is comprehensive SEL?" is a five-ingredient recipe: (1) SEL for adults; (2) safe, predictable, and positive environments; (3) positive relationships; (4) SEL curriculum and instruction; and (5) assessment.

We also addressed why comprehensive SEL is important to student success in school and in life. Our SEL recipe is a powerful universal approach to increasing academic achievement and student and staff social-emotional competence and overall well-being. It also provides effective support to the many students impacted by trauma and chronic stress, can be an important part of equity work, and helps develop students who can contribute to a high-skill workforce.

Finally, this chapter addressed how educators can effectively collaborate and how leaders can support them in delivering these powerful SEL ingredients to students. A distributed leadership team needs to take ownership and guide and support SEL efforts—but, to be sure, SEL cannot succeed by issuing edicts: educators need to understand why SEL practices are important as well as buy into the work required to implement and continuously improve those practices. And that requires leaders to show they consider SEL a priority by allocating protected time and ensuring availability of the resources educators need to effectively implement the full range of SEL ingredients laid out in this book.

Next Steps

Pause and consider: What are the next steps for leveraging the information in this book to advance implementation of a comprehensive approach to SEL in your building?

Reflecting on the SEL Recipe

Consider the following questions as they relate to your school or district and the SEL recipe.

- Where is your school or district in its readiness to implement SEL? Do you need to work on increasing educator buy-in to SEL in your school or district? If so, how will you do that?

- Do you have a multi-disciplinary team in place that can take a leadership role in your SEL initiative? Which school roles do team members represent?

- Which ingredients of the SEL recipe do you anticipate focusing on first?

- If you are planning on implementation of an SEL curriculum, how will you ensure planned and protected time for lesson delivery?

- Which aspects of the SEL recipe do you anticipate being most challenging for your school or district to implement?

- What challenges have you run into or do you foresee in your school or district SEL implementation?

- How would you explain the SEL recipe to others to help them understand the ingredients that combine to yield positive student outcomes?

Planning for SEL Practices

Use the following chart to consider practices to advance SEL implementation. In the space provided, note necessary steps involved in achieving each goal as well as key dates to remember aligned with implementation.

Implementation Goal	Necessary Steps	Key Dates
Establish a team responsible for leading implementation of SEL through putting in place supports that drive successful implementation.		
Support educators' recognition of the need or problem, understanding of the positive outcomes they can expect, perceptions that other trusted and respected educators are doing this work, and self-efficacy around their ability to implement SEL among other demands competing for their time.		
Support active implementation through training and coaching, allocating protected time for collaboration, and monitoring and providing feedback on fidelity.		

The Recipe for Student Well-Being © 2024 Solution Tree Press • SolutionTree.com
Visit **go.SolutionTree.com/SEL** to download this free reproducible.

CHAPTER 2
SEL FOR ADULTS

Imagine being tasked with teaching students a subject you yourself know very little about and have minimal experience with. Unfortunately, this is too commonly what happens with SEL instruction in schools. Yet how much training and practice do most educators have with teaching SEL lessons and supporting the other ingredients to student well-being laid out in this book? One answer comes from a 2020 Education Week survey. School administrators said 17 percent of their novice teachers were "completely unprepared" to address social-emotional learning, one-third were "somewhat unprepared," and only 5 percent were rated as "completely prepared" (Will, 2020).

Now consider another question: "How many of the common goals of SEL are competencies that educators frequently need to be successful in the classroom as well as their personal lives?" Think about competencies such as stress coping and resilience, managing strong emotions, good decision making under pressure, maintaining motivation, solving interpersonal problems effectively, empathy and perspective taking, and communication and relationship skills.

In this chapter, we begin our deep dive into the SEL recipe by discussing how addressing SEL for adults helps set up both students *and* educators for success in and beyond the classroom. We'll explain what SEL for adults entails, why it matters specifically for student outcomes, and how leaders can support SEL for adults in the school building.

What Is SEL for Adults?

SEL for adults should have two aims. One is to help educators *develop* social-emotional competencies to support their own well-being. The other is to *understand* the SEL skills, competencies, knowledge, and mindsets they will be supporting their students in acquiring.

EDUCATOR WELL-BEING

SEL doesn't always look the same for adults and students, but the competencies teachers need to stay motivated, cope with daily stressors, and thrive in their profession are largely the same ones they are trying to develop in their students. And like students, teachers deserve intentional support to help them develop these competencies and strengthen their resilience to better handle the daily challenges of teaching and their own lives. A fundamental goal of SEL for adults, then, should be improving the well-being of educators by both providing support for improving social and emotional competencies and ensuring the supportive environment needed to foster their development as well as support well-being directly.

Essential Competencies

Ensuring educators cultivate the competencies needed for their own well-being entails, among other things, helping them get better at recognizing, understanding, expressing, and regulating their own emotions—especially in difficult situations. Indeed, teaching often presents emotionally challenging experiences where it is crucial to have the ability to thoughtfully respond rather than let strong emotions drive reactions. So developing this kind of emotional intelligence can help teachers weather not only students' but also their own emotional storms.

Self-awareness is another fundamental SEL competency that can benefit educators. A key piece of this is a strong connection to a sense of purpose—to a clear and meaningful answer to the question of why they are teaching. Educators are in a unique position to influence the development and future lives of their students. Staying connected to their reasons for going into education in the first place can help educators maintain perspective and can provide a strong anchor that keeps them centered in a sense of purpose.

Positive relationships are also a powerful support for educator well-being. This includes meaningful connections with colleagues as well as students. Building and maintaining healthy, supportive relationships with colleagues requires educators to have the personal and social awareness, empathy, and communication skills that they strive to cultivate in their students. Empathy and perspective-taking skills are critical tools that help educators in their work to bridge the gap between themselves and their diverse students.

Teaching is one of the most stressful professions. Learning ways to effectively cope with stress and increase personal well-being should be central to SEL for adults. At the same time, if we want to value our educators and honor their dedication and hard work, we need to provide them with tools to manage stress and create well-being for themselves.

Environmental Support

While we believe SEL for adults can contribute to improving educators' well-being and ability to cope with stress, we want to be clear that we are not saying teachers can or should be expected to thrive regardless of the environmental challenges they face daily at work. Environments matter. Educators, like students, are most likely to experience well-being and develop resilience in a workplace that is safe, predictable, and positive. One way school climate for adults can be judged is by how educators answer the question, *Does it feel good to be here?*

Most teachers spend the majority of the day in their rooms working with students with little to no adult interaction, much less feedback and praise. People want to know they're doing a good job, and educators all benefit from recognition when they work hard and show a commitment to making a difference in the lives of their students. Teachers are constantly trying new ideas, implementing new curricula, and putting in the work to stick with something long enough to see whether it's effective. Getting better at anything requires learning from your mistakes, and like other professionals, teachers need to be appreciated for the risks they take and the many times they pick themselves up and keep going in the face of challenging new initiatives. School administrators have a responsibility to provide teachers with recognition for their efforts and successes. A higher ratio of positive to negative or neutral interactions is important for supporting students—the same is true for teachers (Losada & Heaphy, 2004).

Decades of research, including that of organizational scholars Amy C. Edmondson and Zhike Lei (2014), have identified psychological safety as the key characteristic of healthy and productive workplaces. *Psychological safety* is the belief that you will not be punished, negatively judged, or criticized if you speak up or admit to a shortcoming. It means people feel like they can be themselves at work, that they can be honest and open and trust their peers and supervisors to give them the benefit of the doubt rather than be quick to criticize. A psychologically safe school environment for staff means people are not afraid to take risks because they know that their peers and school leaders will support their growth rather than just look to find fault and assign blame. Psychological safety is a big part of what distinguishes workplaces focused on learning and getting better and those centered on criticizing performance and penalizing mistakes.

SEL UNDERSTANDING

Most high-quality SEL curricula provide lessons that are relatively easy to teach. Nevertheless, just like with academic subjects, teachers are much more likely to be able to effectively support student learning in SEL lessons if they themselves have a good understanding of, as well as competence in, the topics being covered. And the importance of adult SEL understanding to directly supporting student development of social-emotional competence goes beyond skillfully teaching lessons. The reality is that students are not terribly likely to learn and master new skills and competencies from one brief lesson per week. We know that's not how learning works, whether we are talking about academic subjects or SEL. For SEL curricula to be effective, students need opportunities to put new skills and understandings into practice. This means teachers must understand SEL content well enough to be able to anticipate or spot practice opportunities in order to cue students to try out or use what they've been learning. It's also important to help students see how the skills they're learning in SEL lessons can be used to meet classroom and school expectations as well as peer challenges. We also know that practicing new competencies is most effective when students receive feedback on both how well they are doing and how to improve their skills. All this requires educators to have a solid understanding of SEL content.

Why Is SEL for Adults Important?

Being a teacher can be incredibly rewarding—and also challenging and exhausting. Teachers are under pressure to simultaneously motivate and manage students, produce high test scores, learn and implement new curricula, and run a classroom all day, often with barely enough time to use the restroom or grab a bite to eat. Teachers daily face the stress of needing to constantly make decisions on the fly. And teaching isn't just an intellectual, organizational, and logistical challenge—it's also one of the professions that involves what is sometimes called *emotional labor*. Essentially, the term emotional labor recognizes that teaching requires educators to manage and control their own emotions in the service of meeting the needs of their students (Kariou, Kousimani, Montgomery, & Lainidi, 2021). Teachers must bring their own emotional resources to the challenge of creating and maintaining relationships with dozens of students as well as families and their own colleagues. Helping students navigate conflicts and cope with their own powerful emotions is itself emotionally taxing. Students constantly challenge teachers in ways that strain their emotional resilience. Finally, too often educators must manage the challenges of teaching largely on their own, with too little support from other adults and inadequate time and support for building and practicing their own coping skills.

According to professors of psychology Christina Maslach and Michael P. Leiter (2016), when stress piles up beyond a person's ability to cope, it triggers emotional exhaustion that can lead to feelings of inadequacy, depression, anger, and frustration, in addition to increased job dissatisfaction, absenteeism, and health consequences like high blood pressure, headaches, and illness. Additionally, the research of Eva Oberle and Kimberly A. Schonert-Reichl (2016), professors at the University of British Columbia, confirms that if teachers get overwhelmed by stress, the impacts ricochet out across their personal lives but also affect the stress levels of their students (Oberle & Schonert-Reichl, 2016).

When teachers have the social and emotional skills to help them handle the stress of teaching, it improves both their personal well-being and their ability to support students' academic and developmental growth. Reducing burnout keeps caring, talented people from leaving the profession. When teachers have the ability to stay resilient and manage stress, their students learn more and their classrooms have more positive climates. On the other hand, research measuring the levels of teacher and student cortisol—a primary stress hormone—shows that when teacher stress is high, the stress levels of their students go up as well (Oberle & Schonert-Reichl, 2016).

Resilient teachers contribute to a positive school and classroom climate by modeling healthy emotional coping for their students and colleagues. Teachers with strong social and emotional skills are good at building relationships with others, and that, combined with empathy and perspective-taking skills, can help them meet the growing need to connect with diverse students with whom the teachers may initially feel they have little in common. And, of course, positive relationships with students and colleagues are themselves a source of strength and resilience that can buffer the daily stress of teaching.

Teacher social-emotional competence also improves teachers' ability to deliver SEL instruction. Teaching and supporting student SEL is not unlike academic instruction in the sense that it's difficult to teach competencies that you don't possess yourself. Teacher social-emotional knowledge and competence support the three student-focused SEL ingredients: (1) safe, predictable, and positive environments; (2) positive relationships; (3) and SEL curriculum and instruction. Social-emotional competence helps teachers form positive relationships with their students, especially those who may be harder to reach. Teacher stress management and social-emotional skills also strongly impact their ability to create the safe, structured classroom environments that traumatized students need and all students benefit from. Finally, the quality of SEL curricula delivery and generalization support are strongly dependent on teachers' own knowledge and understanding of SEL content. Teachers' social-emotional competence can enhance their delivery of even highly scripted SEL lessons, but perhaps more importantly, teachers' own social-emotional competence impacts how well they are able to support students in using and mastering social-emotional skills throughout the school day beyond the lessons.

Training in stress coping and resilience increases teacher sense of well-being, reduces emotional exhaustion, and boosts resilience—all of which in turn improves student–teacher interactions, which of course lead to better academic performance and more positive classroom behavior.

Supporting educator resilience benefits students and improves the school environment. But it also supports teacher well-being, and that alone makes it important. Our dedicated teaching workforce deserves the support they need to be able to maintain their mental health and thrive despite the challenges that come with striving to educate and support students every day.

How Can Leaders Support SEL for Adults in Schools?

To support SEL for adults in earnest, leaders have a number of options for creating an environment in which educators can thrive, as well as strategies they can share with teachers to improve their well-being and ability to cope with stress.

ENVIRONMENT MATTERS

Although this chapter is mostly focused on helping teachers individually and collectively become more resilient, better at coping with stress, and able to teach both SEL and academics effectively with a higher sense of personal well-being, as we have said, the responsibility for promoting teacher well-being should not just fall to the teachers themselves. While increasing educators' abilities to be more resilient and enhance their individual and collective well-being is important and the focus of this key SEL practice, we must recognize that school leaders can do a lot to make schools a supportive environment for staff as well as students. Teachers, like students, thrive in supportive environments with positive relationships. Consider the following tips for fostering such an environment.

- **Foster genuine connection with teachers.** Administrators need to let teachers know they're valued for who they are, not just what they do. In the same way that it's essential for educators to foster positive relationships with and among students (a topic discussed in depth in chapter 4, page 83), it's important for school leaders to connect with and get to know teachers as individuals as well as professionals. That might mean taking the time to check in and see how teachers are doing, learning a little more about who they are and what's going on in their lives, and making the effort to create an interpersonally rich school environment from the top down by setting a good example.

- **Encourage mentorship.** One of the stressful aspects of teaching is isolation. Though they're surrounded by students all day, teachers often suffer from a shortage of social support from both school administrators and fellow teachers. Mentoring can be helpful for many teachers, particularly those new to the profession. Having to handle all the challenges of teaching on their own is especially stressful for new teachers, many of whom don't receive adequate training around student behavior in their teacher training programs. Effective mentoring involves practices such as both regularly scheduled and impromptu meetings, visiting and observing in each other's classrooms as well as some time spent co-teaching, maintaining confidentiality so that both mentor and mentee feel a sense of safety, and tailoring mentoring to the specific needs of new teachers (Weinberg, 2022).

- **Create opportunities for connections.** One of the most powerful ways people cope with stress and boost their personal happiness is through connecting with others. Research shows that supporting inclusion and belonging among people who work together is a powerful way to promote well-being (Office of the Surgeon General, 2022). School leaders as well as teachers all need to take responsibility for finding ways to create more opportunities for positive social connections. A simple but powerful approach we've seen in action is starting staff meetings with an opportunity for people to express appreciation for things their fellow educators have done. Carving out time for teachers to connect and build a sense of community is important and shouldn't be an afterthought. Planning social activities outside the school day can go a long way toward building a positive culture and helping people develop relationships they can draw on when times get tough.

- **Prioritize a manageable workload.** It's also important to pay attention to the demands of the job itself. Initiative overload is widespread in schools. Even if the new approaches or efforts are all good ones, there are still limits to how much teachers can take on at once without being overloaded. School leaders need to keep a sharp eye on the pace of their demands for change and adoption of new practices and initiatives, which often means making hard decisions about priorities. New initiatives, SEL or otherwise, are more manageable and less likely to pile too much stress on teachers if leaders ensure educators have protected time to devote to the new practices; get useful feedback on how they're doing; and receive the technical assistance, resources, and professional development support they need for effective implementation.

- **Identify and mitigate sources of stress.** School leaders should assess the work-related root causes of teacher stress and target those when possible. For example, managing challenging student behavior is a common stressor. If that challenge is a major source of teacher stress, leadership can work to help teachers build more tools to proactively address and prevent student problem behavior or provide nonjudgmental consultative support to help teachers devise plans to prevent and respond to specific challenging behaviors in the classroom. Supporting positive student behavior is more effective when norms and expectations are explicitly taught to students, are consistent across classrooms and other school spaces, and when students are noticed and reinforced for positive behavior.

- **Create avenues for self-care.** Self-care is part of what it takes to be an effective educator but is equally important for school leaders. It is valuable when leaders model prioritizing their own well-being such as by setting boundaries between work and home life. And, of course, when leaders focus on their own social and emotional competence and self-care, they benefit personally and are better able to handle the enormous stressors of the job as well as support teachers and staff (Mahfouz, King, & Yahya, 2022). At the building level, principal well-being should be made a serious priority, which may include providing professional development support aimed at principal wellness as well as embedding well-being as a goal in strategic plans and budgets. School leaders benefit from improving their own self-regulation as a tool to help cope with the massive demands of the role. Unlike teachers, principals typically have no direct peers in their building and are often too socially isolated. School leaders can benefit from intentional efforts to build positive relationships both within and outside their profession (King, Yahya, & Mahfouz, 2022).

Over stressed teachers are more likely to develop mental health problems over time, and high stress levels can impair the job performance of even highly skilled teachers (Bottiani, 2019; Skaalvik & Skaalvik, 2018). But it is important to say in this context that the primary causes of teacher stress are outside teacher control, including workload, accountability pressures, and challenging student behavior (Brasfield, Lancaster, & Yonghong, 2019). We are not saying that teachers are responsible for simply self-caring their way out of the stress and difficulties involved in teaching.

Leaders can take an active role in promoting the self-care of their staff by (1) creating a culture of open communication where educators feel psychologically safe to discuss their needs, perhaps through regular check-ins or one-on-ones; (2) organizing workshops, seminars, or training sessions on stress management, time management, mindfulness, and other SEL skills; and (3) regularly recognizing and acknowledging accomplishments (either publicly or privately) to boost morale and foster a sense of belonging.

While we do not want to suggest the solution to educator stress is self-care, it's also important to recognize that self-care can help teachers reduce and manage stress. Research shows that SEL for teachers results in increased personal well-being and greater development of social and emotional competence for students (Greenberg, Brown, & Abenavoli, 2016). Increased social support is essential for educators, as it's been shown to improve teacher well-being and ability to cope with stress (Li, Sheng, & Jing, 2022). Although principals have limited leeway, research shows that when school leaders make efforts to address challenges with workload, scheduling, and responsibilities, teachers experience that as an important form of social support (Maas, et al., 2022).

- **Adopt habits that foster psychological safety.** There are many ways leaders can work to create psychologically safe school environments for adults. A big one is modeling. Educators are more likely to experience psychological safety based on what school leaders do versus what they say. Effective school leaders support educator well-being by themselves being willing to admit mistakes, making it clear that they're open to feedback, and acknowledging and showing support when people offer new ideas. School teams also thrive when members get structured opportunities to get to know one another as individuals in addition to colleagues.

  School leaders seeking to promote psychological safety don't give everyone a pass regardless of behavior. But they do model approaching mistakes or errors as opportunities for learning and growth. We live in a rapidly changing world, and education is constantly challenged to rise to the occasion and find new and better ways to help students thrive, learn, and grow. For schools to be learning organizations, educators should ideally receive adult SEL training within a supportive and positive environment.

STRATEGIES TO IMPROVE ADULT STRESS COPING AND WELL-BEING

Figuring out how to provide effective SEL to adults is a challenge. The following section explores some promising practices that have been shown to contribute to teacher resilience and well-being: reining in one's emotions, tapping into one's sense of purpose, practicing gratitude, shifting one's stress mindset, getting adequate sleep, and embracing social support.

Reining In One's Emotions

Most teachers face plenty of situations throughout the day when it would be easy to lose their cool. When teachers mishandle these challenges, they behave in ways that can escalate difficulties and conflicts; they *react* instead of *respond* to difficulties. Despite the intense feelings that arise in those moments, as adults we know it's easier to rein in our emotions before they leap out of control. Putting out a campfire is easy; putting out a forest fire sometimes isn't even possible. Just like students, teachers need to get better at noticing their thoughts and feelings and learning skills that help with deciding how to respond thoughtfully instead of just going in the direction powerful emotions might be pushing them.

One of the simplest ways to rein in strong emotions, explains Daniel J. Siegel (2013), professor of clinical psychiatry, is to simply put a name on them. Neuroscience research shows that when we make the conscious effort to name the emotions we're feeling, it shifts brain activity away from the more impulsive parts of the brain to the regions that help us problem-solve and make good decisions. Siegel (2013) coined the phrase "Name it to tame it" to capture this emotion-management technique (p. 61). One key piece of this technique is to pay attention to the specifics of your self-talk around emotions. Telling yourself "I *feel* angry" helps more than reinforcing your immersion in the emotion by saying "I *am* angry." And, like so much in SEL for adults, this technique works great for students of all ages as well as adults.

Various forms of mindfulness and meditation are accessible tools many people find helpful for improving their ability to pay attention to the powerful winds of difficult thoughts and feelings before they get blown off course. The internet is loaded with sites and apps that support a variety of approaches to mindfulness and often provide guided meditations that can make the practice easier. As a starting point, visit Headspace (www.headspace.com), Healthy Minds (hminnovations.org/meditation-app), or Mindful (www.mindful.org/meditation/mindfulness-getting-started).

With consistent practice, meditation rewires the brain to achieve what neuroscientist Ethan Kross (2021) calls *self-distancing*. If we can step back from or outside our powerful thoughts and feelings, it makes it easier to decide how to handle a challenge and makes us less likely to be swept up and carried away. Simple ways to practice self-distancing include talking to yourself in the second person—"*You're* feeling really angry" instead of the usual "*I'm* feeling really angry!" (you can see how this approach combines self-distancing with "Name it to tame it.") You can also take that a step further by talking to yourself in the third person, using your own name—"Brian is feeling really angry." Next time you're upset or feeling a strong emotion you don't want to let take over the situation, try talking to yourself in the second or third person by identifying the emotion and then walking yourself through the situation, problem-solving as if you're talking about somebody else. See if that doesn't turn down the intensity by giving you a little distance from the thoughts and feelings.

Most of us have seen that it's often easier to give others perspective and advice on how to handle challenges than to do it for ourselves. Self-distancing offers you a trick in difficult situations to ask yourself what advice you'd give close friends if they were in the situation you find yourself in. You can also try using mental time travel to step back and gain perspective by asking yourself how you'd view the situation in a year or even five or ten years from now. Whether naming the emotion, practicing and applying mindfulness, or using a self-distancing technique, the goal is to help yourself be more consciously aware of what you're thinking and feeling so you can make better decisions and respond thoughtfully instead of impulsively reacting to difficult situations.

Tapping Into One's Sense of Purpose

SEL for adults should not only help us develop better awareness of our thoughts and feelings—it should also help us get better at consciously staying connected to our values and our sense of purpose. Having those anchors can help us ride out emotional and cognitive storms. Being in touch with our values and what we really care about works like a compass to help us make sure we're going in the right direction, especially when things get rough. Having a clear sense of purpose is a powerful tool for stress coping. Although it's tempting to fall for the myth that the ideal life is stress-free, the reality is that stress inevitably comes with doing and pursuing things we care about and value. If we can remind ourselves of how our stress is connected to what's important to us, it helps us to transform difficulties from experiences that are simply bad to those that are part of our fighting for what we care about and believe in. A simple analogy is being a parent. The stressors and hassles are endless, but when we stay connected to our love for our children and our hopes and dreams for their futures, it lightens the load and makes us stronger and more resilient. Connecting to our care and hopes for our students can work in the same way.

Practicing Gratitude

Another strategy that can pay big dividends when it comes to SEL for adults is routinely focusing on what's positive and going right in our lives and work. The survival pressures of evolution shaped us to prioritize safety, and that can translate into a tendency to focus on what's going wrong instead of right.

A simple practice for orienting us to the positives in life is increasing our sense of gratitude. Psychologists Robert A. Emmons, Jeffrey Froh, and Rachel Rose (2019) find that increasing gratitude makes people more energetic, emotionally intelligent, forgiving, and socially connected and optimistic, as well as happier and less depressed, anxious, and lonely. These benefits illustrate the link between gratitude and neuroplasticity: when we repeatedly focus on things we're grateful for, we're literally training our brains to scan for and focus on the positives in life. There are lots of ways we can increase our sense of gratitude for what we have. A simple one that has been shown to make a real difference is daily gratitude journaling—taking a moment to reflect on our day and write down three things we're grateful for, capturing not only the big, more obvious positives but the small everyday things we're happy to have in our lives (Fekete & Deichert, 2022). Another technique is to think about things we tend to take for granted and imagine what our lives would be like if we didn't have them.

Shifting One's Stress Mindset

Stress is an unavoidable part of life. In fact, it's completely impossible to pursue a rich and fulfilling life without encountering a lot of stress. Yes, stress can be harmful, especially if one lacks the skills and mindsets needed to handle it or encounters way too much stress. But it's also crucial to keep in mind that it's through coping with stress that people grow stronger and more resilient. Believing that stress is only a negative and harmful part of life that one should seek to avoid is itself harmful. This stressing over stress magnifies challenges, saps coping resources, and can push people to avoid things they care about in an effort to escape the stress that comes with them. On the other hand, seeing stress as an integral part of life that one can use to grow stronger, wiser, and more resilient helps people develop those very qualities and improves stress coping. One of the keys to successful stress coping is *actively* working to acknowledge and identify ways to deal with stressors, whether that means solving problems or working to stay strong and take care of ourselves in the face of stressors we cannot change. Efforts to deny, avoid, or escape stress too often backfire and make things worse.

Getting Adequate Sleep

If SEL is about supporting the ability to be more resilient, thrive, and build well-being, sleep must be an integral part of the discussion. As neuroscientist Matthew Walker (2018) explains, sleep is perhaps the single most important ingredient to physical and mental health and well-being, and lack of sleep is a major contributor to the full range of both physical and mental health problems. When adults get fewer than seven hours of sleep, their decision making, reasoning, impulsivity, and ability to learn get markedly worse. But the strongest negative effects of insufficient sleep are on mental health. Poor sleep causes significant increases in depression and anxiety. To be fully resilient and have social-emotional competence, adults should ideally get at least seven hours of good-quality sleep each night. Keep in mind that alcohol and sleeping pills actually disrupt sleep, as does caffeine later in the day (Thakkar, Sharma, & Sahota, 2015; Walker, 2018). Making a full night's sleep a non-negotiable wellness strategy is one of the best ways to greatly boost resilience and well-being. To learn more about sleep science and ways to improve your sleep, try an internet search on "sleep hygiene." Depending on your life circumstances, getting a full night of sleep may feel like a privilege you don't have. However, prioritizing actions to improve the quality and quantity of your sleep can greatly enhance health and well-being.

Embracing Social Support

A final, critical topic in SEL for adults is social support. Both globally and in the United States, adults have a serious problem with loneliness. Research shows that loneliness is becoming a significant public health issue around the world (Surkalim et al., 2022). Loneliness, isolation, and lack of connection is serious enough in the United States that an advisory on the problem was recently put out by the U.S. Surgeon General (Murthy, 2023). In one survey, 36 percent of people in the United States said they felt lonely "frequently" or "almost all the time" in the prior four weeks, and that number went up to 61 percent for young people aged eighteen to twenty-five (Weissbourd, Batanova, Lovison, & Torres, 2016). An individualistic culture like the one in the United States can fool educators into thinking that people ideally should just take care of themselves on their own, yet that flies in the face of everything we know about evolution and our brains. Humans are fundamentally social beings. And one of the most powerful ways we can cope adaptively when we're stressed is through accessing social support. This triggers what psychologist Shelley E. Taylor (2012) calls the *tend and befriend* stress response. Research shows that in fact, getting social support is often the quickest and most effective way to calm down when upset, and turning to others increases the hormone oxytocin—which increases bonding and even provides some of the extra courage needed to care for others in difficult circumstances (Taylor, 2012).

Although school leaders should be creating opportunities for staff to build relationships and bond, educators can also embrace this important connection-focused approach to enhancing well-being. Leaning on others can be a healthy way to cope with difficult and stressful times. When stress and emotions are high, it can be difficult to think clearly. Having a friend, family member, or colleague who can support you through this time, whether by helping you solve a problem or by providing comfort, can help ease some of the stress you're feeling. Plus, there is a reason why the saying "It takes a village" endures: you don't have to do it alone.

Often when we think about people who can help and support us, we think about family members. But friends can be a great source of support, as can neighbors, coworkers, and community members. Spending time with people who are trustworthy, encouraging, and caring is good for your mental health. And building relationships means more people who are willing to help you out—and who you can help out in return.

However, keep in mind that it's possible for social support to backfire. Turning to others is not always a guaranteed way to improve how we feel. In fact, it's possible for others to make us feel worse. When someone turns to a friend for support and instead comes away feeling worse, it's often due to what psychologists call *co-rumination*. It happens when the friend you turn to only doubles down on your misery, inflames your sense of injustice, magnifies your feeling of hurt, and keeps the conversation stuck on the problem without moving toward problem solving, getting perspective, or finding a way to help you feel better in the moment. So watch how you support coworkers and how they support you. If talking to someone only makes you feel worse, or if you find yourself just adding the fuel of your own anger or sadness to your friend's, without finding a way to move beyond the problem, you might be falling into the co-rumination trap.

Conclusion

Supporting SEL for adults boosts educator well-being and resilience and leads to improved outcomes for students. No one is getting rich through teaching. The job is demanding, and teachers deserve to get the supports they need to be able to thrive both at work and at home. Helping educators understand, and ideally develop their own, social-emotional competence is also a powerful part of delivering effective SEL to students.

Striving to meet the needs of students brings huge challenges, and we can't do our best work without taking care of ourselves. School leaders need to work to create safe and positive work environments that support educator well-being. They also need to find ways to ensure educators have opportunities to develop the social and emotional skills they need to cope with the challenges they face. Both administrators and teachers should work to create positive relationships and cultures among the adults in schools to make education the rewarding and sustainable calling it should be.

Next Steps

Pause and consider: What are the important next steps you want to take to maintain or improve SEL for adults? What plans need to be enacted (considering the what, when, how, and by whom) to implement what you've learned from this chapter?

Reflecting on SEL for Adults

Consider the following questions as they relate to your school or district and SEL for adults.

- What organizational strategies do leaders consistently employ to promote the well-being and engagement of educators in your building?

- How is your school or district supporting positive connections among educators?

- What are leaders in your school or district doing to avoid initiative overload?

- How much opportunity do your educators have for professional learning to support development of strong classroom management skills?

- What are leaders doing to ensure educators both understand the SEL content they're expected to deliver to students and have opportunities to build the same skills and knowledge for themselves?

Planning for SEL for Adults

Use the following chart to consider practices to advance SEL for adults. In the space provided, note necessary steps involved in completing each goal as well as key dates to remember aligned with implementation.

Implementation Goal	Necessary Steps	Key Dates
Boost collective efficacy through targeted professional development in areas of low efficacy.		
Free up time for staff members by removing something from their plates.		
Increase educators' experience of being valued and appreciated through recognition and acknowledgment.		
Promote psychological safety through modeling vulnerability and proactively building relationships among staff.		

The Recipe for Student Well-Being © 2024 Solution Tree Press • SolutionTree.com
Visit **go.SolutionTree.com/SEL** to download this free reproducible.

Reviewing Research-Based Strategies for Educators to Improve Stress Coping and Resilience

Consider the following research-based strategies for coping with stress and building resilience.

NAMING YOUR EMOTIONS

- Pay attention to what you're feeling.
- Put a label on the emotion. For example, say to yourself, "I'm feeling really frustrated."

PRACTICING MINDFULNESS AND MEDITATION

- Practice meditation to cultivate greater mindfulness and awareness of your thoughts and feelings.
- Try using an app (for example, Headspace) or internet resources to help with mindfulness and meditation.

SELF-DISTANCING

- Talk to yourself in the second person. For example, instead of saying, "I'm feeling really angry," say, "You're feeling really angry."
- Talk to yourself in the third person. For example, instead of saying, "I'm feeling really angry," say, "Brian is feeling really angry."
- When struggling with a difficult situation, ask yourself what advice you would give a good friend.
- Think of someone you know who is good at handling difficult or stressful situations, and ask yourself what that person would do; then do that.
- Ask yourself how you think you'll view a challenging situation one, two, or ten years from now.

STAYING CONNECTED TO YOUR SENSE OF PURPOSE

- Remember your why. Why did you become an educator? Why is that important and meaningful to you?
- Remind yourself of how the stressful situation connects to what's important to you.

The Recipe for Student Well-Being © 2024 Solution Tree Press • SolutionTree.com
Visit **go.SolutionTree.com/SEL** to download this free reproducible.

PRACTICING GRATITUDE

- Keep a daily gratitude journal: write down three things you're grateful for each day.
- Try paying attention to small things you're grateful for.
- Cultivate gratitude by challenging yourself to think about important things in your life you tend to take for granted and ponder how your life would be without them.

AVOIDING AVOIDANCE

- Try to embrace the mindset that stress is a natural part of life and that we can get stronger, wiser, and more resilient by learning to get better at solving stressful problems or by learning to cope with challenges that we cannot solve.
- Avoid avoidance! Watch out for the natural tendency to try not to experience difficult thoughts or feelings. Too often, the things we do to avoid challenges end up making things worse for us.

GETTING ADEQUATE SLEEP

- Do an internet search for "sleep hygiene" to learn ways to improve your sleep.
- Watch out for caffeine late in the day: you'll still experience a quarter of the effect twelve hours later.
- Avoid too much bright light or screen time before bed.

EMBRACING SOCIAL SUPPORT

- Social support works in both directions: you benefit from both giving and getting it. Make the effort to reach out to others.
- Look at the different areas of your life for ways to make more social connections: work, family, neighbors, friends, church, and other community experiences.

CHAPTER 3

SAFE, PREDICTABLE, AND POSITIVE ENVIRONMENTS

Dr. Smith's son unfortunately had an early elementary teacher who yelled at her students when she was angry, particularly targeting certain students. His son was clearly upset by it and felt uncomfortable in her classroom. When he tried to comfort his son by saying, "But she isn't yelling at you," the seven-year-old child replied, *"But it feels like she is!"*

The classroom and school environments educators create are crucially important for student growth and success. The good news is, there are key characteristics that make schools and classrooms places that effectively promote academic engagement and achievement as well as positive student behavior and well-being. And in this chapter we spell out the what, why, and how of practical approaches shown to create those kinds of environments.

This chapter is about shifting our view away from thinking of SEL solely as an *inside-out* process of helping all students to develop and apply their own self-regulatory skills and toward understanding that it's also an *outside-in* process that requires support from the school and classroom environments we create. This chapter will discuss the research behind this process and provide concrete strategies educators can collaborate on to co-create school environments that more effectively support students, especially those who need it the most.

What Kinds of Environments Support SEL?

The school and classroom environments that support students' social and emotional development and well-being have three specific qualities—they are (1) safe, (2) predictable, and (3) positive.

SAFE

Researchers Roger P. Weissberg and Mary Utne O'Brien (2004) explain that when students feel safe in school, it supports positive behavior and facilitates their academic learning and acquisition of social-emotional skills. A safe environment is not just one where students aren't afraid of getting *physically* injured. Our brains are wired so they respond to psychological, emotional, and social danger much the same way they do to physical danger. In fact, neuroscience studies like that of psychology professors Geoff MacDonald and Lauri A. Jensen-Campbell (2011) show that the emotional pain from bullying or other social injuries are experienced in the same brain regions as physical pain.

The harmful neural impacts of an unsafe environment don't kick in only when something bad actually *happens* to a student. Just anticipating or fearing possible harm is enough to trigger unhelpful mental states and a rise in stress hormones, according to researchers Jens Gaab, Nicolas Rohleder, Urs M. Nater, and Ulrike Ehlert (2005) and neuroscientist Luke R. Johnson (2016). Researcher Michela Lenzi and colleagues (2017) state that a safe school environment means staff and students aren't worried about potential threats to their physical, psychological, and emotional well-being. It means an environment free of bullying, discrimination, racism, aggression, and, of course, actual physical violence.

A great deal of research, including that of authors Carly Taylor, Maureen F. Dollard, Anna Clark, Christian Dormann, and Arnold B. Bakker (2019), has been conducted to figure out what kinds of environments make people most productive, promote teamwork, and allow people to bring their best selves to the challenges of working and learning together. Studies all point to one critical factor called *psychological safety*, which you may remember from the preceding chapter, discussed in the context of SEL for adults. In environments where people feel psychologically safe, they trust that they won't be criticized, made fun of, or in some way socially punished if they take a risk, express their opinion, or try using skills they're still learning. In a nutshell, psychological safety means people feel like it's safe to be and express their genuine selves. As this matters for educators, this matters for all students. But, as researchers Whitney W. Black, Alicia L. Fedewa, and Kirsten A. Gonzalez (2012) show, it can be especially valuable for students who don't necessarily fit the perceived school norm, who struggle in ways other students might not, or who don't share the backgrounds or home experiences of a lot of their peers or teachers (Voight, Hanson, O'Malley, & Adekanye, 2015). And increasing psychological safety is a critical part of how schools can help students struggling with trauma and toxic stress. In their research supported by Northwestern University, scholars Dorainne J. Levy, Jennifer A. Heissel, Jennifer A. Richeson, and Emma K. Adam (2016) find that a safe environment lowers such students' stress hormones and helps their brains to develop and function in healthy ways that support learning and growth.

Environments do not automatically affect all students equally. It is critical to think about whether schools are intentionally creating environments that support the needs of all students. For example, students need to be affirmed, seen, and known for who they are and supported with the tools and opportunities to engage with academic challenges and develop a sense of agency and determination. Equitable environments come about when students feel their cultural backgrounds and values are acknowledged, honored, and respected; they feel seen and respected by adults and peers; they know that others have high expectations for and positive beliefs about them; and they have access to the opportunities and supports they need to meet important goals they set for themselves. The policies, procedures, and practices in schools need to be scrutinized from this perspective to ensure that what students experience is not advantaging one group and systemically undermining the well-being and potential of another group. All of this requires intentional work, especially when the demographic makeup of the educators does not mirror that of the students.

Table 3.1 shows the percentage of male and female teachers in U.S. public schools.

TABLE 3.1: Percentage of Male Versus Female Teachers in U.S. Public Schools

Teacher Demographics in U.S. Public Schools, School Year 2020–2021	
Elementary schools	87% female
	12% male
Middle schools	72% female
	28% male
High schools	60% female
	40% male
Total	77% female
	23% male

Source: NTPS, "Public School Teacher Data File," 2017–2018

Table 3.2 shows the percentage distribution of teachers in U.S. public schools by race.

TABLE 3.2: Percentage Distribution of Teachers in U.S. Public Schools by Race

Teacher Demographics in U.S. Public Schools, School Year 2020–2021			
Teachers		Students	
White	80%	White	45%
Hispanic	9%	Hispanic	28%
Black	6%	Black	15%
Asian	2%	Asian	5.4%
American Indian/Alaska Native	Less than 1%	American Indian/Alaska Native	1%

Source: NCES, 2023

Before students are going to want to strive for competence, they need to feel like both the skills taught and the norms promoted in the environment are a reasonable fit for them. Realistically, educators are a relatively homogenous group—primarily White, college educated, and female. According to the Institute of Education Sciences (2020), even in schools whose student populations are predominantly Black or Hispanic, only about a third of the teachers come from racial and ethnic backgrounds similar to their students'. We need to take care that the environments we create are not just tailored to best fit students with the same backgrounds and experiences as their educators. Environments and school "culture" that are a mismatch for some students can result in what may look like students failing to try to acquire or use skills when in fact the expectations and supports from the environment don't fit with or align to their needs or preferences. Instead, educators should be seeking to create a strong fit for each student so students are able to consistently access the experiences and supports that enable them to be well, engage fully in their learning experiences, and develop and grow important competencies that set them up for life success.

PREDICTABLE

A predictable school environment produces consistency and means students can anticipate and trust what is going to happen. An example that illustrates both the value of predictability and the danger of overfocusing on individual characteristics comes from a famous research study called the marshmallow test, conducted by psychologists Walter Mischel and Ralph Metzner (1962). The original study involved giving children a marshmallow, telling them they could have another one if they waited and didn't eat the first one, and then seeing who waited and for how long. Researchers followed the children and found that the ones who waited for the second marshmallow had better outcomes across many areas of life well into adulthood. Researchers Tyler W. Watts, Greg J. Duncan, and Haonan Quan (2018) show that this has largely been interpreted as proving the value of differences in individual abilities around self-control and delay of gratification.

But researchers Celeste Kidd, Holly Palmeri, and Richard N. Aslin (2013) repeated the marshmallow test experiment, this time with a crucial new twist, which Lillie Moffett, Carol Flannagan, and Priti Shah (2020) elaborate on in their extension study. First, children were given paper and a crayon and asked to draw a picture. But they were told that if they waited, the adult would bring them a *big* box of crayons and markers to use. When the researcher returned, half the children got the big box, but the other half were told that they had run out of big boxes and they would have to draw their picture with the one crayon they had after all.

So, before any marshmallows were introduced, some students experienced the adults in their environment showing they could be trusted and counted on, while for others the adults were shown to be unreliable. After this, researchers conducted the standard marshmallow test, giving the children one marshmallow and telling them that if they waited before eating it they could have another one. And the results showed the power of environmental predictability. The children who got the big box of markers, as the adult promised, were much more likely to wait for the second marshmallow. On the other hand, the children who found out that the adult could not be relied on to follow through on what they told them were more likely to simply eat the first marshmallow and not wait. When the experiment was run this way, it showed that what really mattered was not how much individual self-control children had; it was how much they could trust adults. That is, it was the predictability of the environment that made the biggest difference in their behavior.

This simple experiment demonstrates that behaviors we might think are just reflections of students' individual skills and abilities are often strongly reflective of their environments, including the ones we create in schools and classrooms. What mattered in who waited for the second marshmallow was not just individuals' ability to delay gratification; it was also their experience of whether they could count on adults to deliver on what they said they'd do. In other words, *predictability* determined whether participants used skills they possessed. It's up to us educators to recognize that not all students come to school assuming they can trust and rely on adults. Many adults in schools tend to assume that because of their position as educators, they will naturally have the trust and respect of students. The reality, especially with minoritized students, is often that adults must show students they can be entrusted to guide their development. Creating a predictable environment is an important way we can work to support all students' social and emotional development.

Providing predictability can be as simple as posting a clear, visual schedule in the classroom of what is going to happen when, and ideally reviewing it periodically, especially with younger students. Educators can also establish predictability by having clear routines and expectations for each area in the school and each part of the day. This helps students avoid having to worry about unpleasant surprises, or constantly wonder what's coming next and how they should behave in different situations. Educators can create more predictable environments through their own actions when they respond to students in consistent ways and use common language throughout the school to model, prompt, and reinforce positive behaviors. The color wheel, which psychologist Emily R. Kirk and colleagues (2010) explore in their research, is one example of how educators can develop and teach behavioral expectations for different learning activities, clarifying for students what it looks like to be successful in class. The color wheel links different categories of learning activities to a color: green for free or other less-structured time; yellow for whole- or small-group instruction; blue for independent work; and red for transitions between activities. Students then learn specific behavioral expectations for each category, and colors are used to cue students about which behaviors are expected given the activity so they can switch quickly from one set of expectations to another. When educators spell out clear expectations to students, they help to reduce chaos and ensure students know not only what is expected of them but also what to expect from their peers.

POSITIVE

In addition to the importance of safety and predictability, students thrive best in positive environments. Simple acts such as offering greetings, farewells, and check-ins help both staff and students feel recognized and valued (Cook, Fiat et al., 2018). A positive environment also means students get opportunities to do things in school that they view as fun, exciting, and enjoyable. We can think of a positive environment as comprising two parts: (1) acknowledging and rewarding students for the energy and effort they put into helping create a positive learning environment and (2) maintaining a positive environment by preventing negative experiences for students at school. This includes educators setting clear limits and enforcing them in consistent, compassionate ways that teach students that behaviors have consequences while striving to avoid punitive approaches that harm students' feelings of belonging in the school and classroom community.

Why Do Safe, Predictable, and Positive Environments Matter?

According to the foundational work of developmental psychologist Urie Bronfenbrenner (1992), people are fundamentally social beings who are powerfully impacted by their social environments and their interactions and relationships with others. That is especially true of children and adolescents. Thinking about how school and classroom environments affect students' social and emotional development and well-being reminds us that SEL is a *developmental* process, as researchers Jessica Newman and Linda Dusenbury (2015) explain. School is where students spend the largest amount of their time outside the home, and some students have more time with the adults at school than at home, especially during the week.

According to researchers Roisin P. Corcoran, Alan C. K. Cheung, Elizabeth Kim, and Chen Xie (2018), safe, predictable, and positive school environments support academic achievement as well as social, emotional, and behavioral success—they help students gain and use both academic and social-emotional competencies. This kind of environment also naturally supports students' social and emotional well-being. So although educators have limited ability to influence the conditions in students' lives outside school, the classroom and school environments we create powerfully impact all aspects of student development (Wang & Degol, 2016). Note we did not say they *can*; the reality is that they *do*. The question is how intentional and skilled we are in creating safe, predictable, and positive environments—because when we provide these environments for all our students, we're supporting their motivation and engagement, freedom to practice and fine-tune social-emotional competencies, social-emotional well-being, and academic achievement, as well as achieving greater equity, improving student stress coping, and ultimately fostering a powerful symbiotic relationship between SEL and classroom climate.

MOTIVATION AND ENGAGEMENT

Research like that of educational psychologists Jennifer A. Fredricks, Amy L. Reschly, and Sandra L. Christenson (2019) clearly shows that student motivation and engagement are critically important drivers of positive behavior and academic achievement in school. It can be easy for educators to mistakenly think that all students should arrive at school fully motivated to engage in learning, and that when they don't, it reflects deficits in the students or in their lives outside school. But the reality, say researchers Tim Urdan and Erin Schoenfelder (2006), is that motivation and engagement in learning are powerfully influenced by educators through the classroom and school environments they create. Students who do not feel safe or like they belong at school are likely to withdraw and disengage, while students who feel like they are valued members of a school community and who feel physically and emotionally safe at school are likely to be more engaged and benefit more from their school experiences (Cook, Thayer, Fiat, & Sullivan, 2020).

Indeed, authors Carolyn Côté-Lussier and Caroline Fitzpatrick (2016) explain that unsafe classrooms with higher levels of conflict not only damage relationships between students and foster aggression but also harm students' academic focus. Accordingly, educators Linda Darling-Hammond and Channa M. Cook-Harvey (2018) advocate a whole-student approach, which understands that students live within webs of relationships and environments, and that those experiences—including at school—have considerable impacts on achievement, behavior, and well-being.

We know better than to buy into a model of schools as assembly-line factories. But it's still easy to forget how much the way students *feel* in school impacts their behavior and learning. Motivation is as much emotionally as intellectually driven. Emotional engagement in school is strongly influenced by how much students feel safe, able to anticipate what will happen, and valued and appreciated for their presence (Cook et al., 2020).

SOCIAL-EMOTIONAL COMPETENCE

Social-emotional competence is how we traditionally think about what SEL instruction is designed to teach—the acquisition and use of knowledge, skills, and attitudes. But we know that teaching SEL lessons alone is not enough to result in student social-emotional competence. Similar to mathematics and reading, it takes motivation and ongoing supported practice for students to go from learning something in lessons to working to make it part of what they naturally do.

As Stephanie M. Jones and Jennifer Kahn (2017) convey in their report for the National Commission on Social, Emotional, and Academic Development, if we want to see students applying what they learn in SEL lessons on a routine basis, we need to ensure that a healthy and supportive environment is in place that encourages students to consistently practice and use social and emotional skills. Acknowledging and recognizing student use of social-emotional competencies help create a reinforcing environment that motivates students to continue to put into practice what they're learning in SEL lessons.

Context matters. Consider, for example, Carol Dweck's (2016) enduring idea of growth mindset, a key goal of which, explain professor of developmental psychology David S. Yeager and colleagues (2019), is to help students embrace and learn from mistakes. Individual mindsets matter, but how safe students feel in the classroom informs how likely they are to take risks, try new approaches, and risk failure. And feeling safe is not a mindset—it's a student's response to a healthy and supportive environment. Mastering skills and building competence requires practice and risk taking, in both academics and social-emotional competence. To learn from mistakes, students need to feel confident they won't be criticized and made fun of by others if they try something and it doesn't go well, or admit when they're struggling and ask for help.

New skills and behaviors feel unfamiliar and can be a little clunky at first. In a safe classroom or school, students benefit from consistent performance feedback that helps them learn the behaviors that enable their own and others' success in school. The right environment can support students in building connections with each other, including across groups, by making it safe to use their social-emotional skills to get to know people different from them. Safe, predictable, positive environments can help students be open to learning about and accepting people with different perspectives or life experiences. A positive classroom setting works to support the development of SEL competencies like emotion management and executive functions. When students have a sense of safety from bullying and violence, it helps them try out and master nonviolent conflict resolution skills and promotes cooperation, inclusion, and productivity.

SOCIAL-EMOTIONAL WELL-BEING

Social-emotional well-being reflects how students think and feel about their experiences in a given context, such as a school or a classroom. Social well-being includes a sense of belonging and connection to others, which results in students feeling like valued, respected members of a community. Students experience emotional well-being when they feel satisfied with school and in a regulated and positive emotional state. There is a bidirectional relationship between social-emotional competencies and social-emotional well-being. For example, a strong sense of belonging and connection fosters engagement in learning and mastering social-emotional competencies, and students and staff who possess social-emotional competence are better able to co-create environments where they and others feel a sense of belonging and connection.

Social-emotional well-being is also strongly dependent on the environments we shape for students. Social-emotional well-being covers a lot of ground, including students' thoughts about themselves, peers, and adults; how much they feel a sense of belonging and connection; the emotions they experience; their behavior and how it affects themselves and others; and how they communicate with peers and adults throughout the school day. Students' individual social-emotional competence helps support their well-being. But well-being is also strongly impacted by the social-emotional competence of both their peers and the adults around them, including their educators. Fundamentally, SEL is about helping students develop the social-emotional competence to successfully tackle life's challenges while also ensuring that the environments we create for them are culturally appropriate, reinforce putting SEL into practice, and promote their social and emotional well-being (Greenberg, Domitrovich, Weissberg, & Durlak, 2017).

ACADEMIC ACHIEVEMENT

A positive school climate has been shown to improve attendance, test scores, and high school graduation rates (National Center on Safe Supportive Learning Environments, n.d.a.). The work of professors of clinical psychologists Linda D. Ruiz, Susan D. McMahon, and Leonard A. Jason (2018), as well as that of researchers Ming-Te Wang and Jessica L. Degol (2016), shows that strong, healthy school climates support academic achievement but can also help protect students' academic achievement from the negative effects of poverty. On the other hand, a negative school climate has been shown to decrease academic achievement and increase school violence and bullying (National Center on Safe Supportive Learning Environments, n.d.a.).

In a study by the University of Chicago Consortium on School Research, James Sebastian, Elaine Allensworth, and Haigen Huang (2016) find that the primary way school leaders influence academic achievement is through improving school climate–particularly how well they support the creation of a safe and orderly school environment. Just as a sense of safety is important for students it is valuable for teachers. One way principals can support a positive school climate is through a "no-fault" approach to improvement (Cohen, Espelage, Twemlow, Berkowitz, & Comer, 2015). In a nutshell, this involves working from a shared assumption that educators are doing their best, and that working to identify and target areas for improvement does not include looking for who to pin blame on but rather focusing on how to make the school a better place for students and staff.

Research into school climate effects across seventeen secondary schools found a mechanism for that effect: student achievement is higher in schools where students have a stronger psychological identification with the school, which was driven in the study by school climate (Maxwell et al., 2017). Ensuring that students experience school as a safe, predictable, and positive place is a powerful way to increase school identification and, through that, improve academic achievement.

EQUITY

There is no equity until *all* students feel like they belong. In fact, educators Mary C. Murphy and Sabrina Zirkel (2015) say that a sense of belonging can be an especially important asset for minoritized students. Unfortunately, many minoritized students do *not* feel it, due to systemic and interpersonal discrimination. Educators can increase equity in schools by working to reduce disproportionate punitive and exclusionary discipline toward these students, such as suspension, that diminishes emotional engagement and perpetuates the racist school-to-prison pipeline (Fredricks, Ye, Wang, & Brauer, 2019; Huang & Anyon, 2020; Skiba, Arredondo, & Williams, 2014). Moving away from harsh and inequitable discipline is critically important, but so is making sure we create positive emotional experiences for all students in our schools.

STRESS COPING

Creating a safe, predictable, and positive classroom and school environment is also an important part of trauma-informed practice. Educators are increasingly learning about the negative impacts from and sadly high prevalence of adverse childhood experiences (ACEs) and other childhood traumas. But knowing how trauma impacts students does not by itself tell us what to do. Fortunately, research from Robert D. Sege and Charlyn Harper Browne (2017), senior fellows at the Center for the Study of Social Policy, shows that creating safe, predictable, and positive environments can go a long way toward mitigating the harms of toxic stress.

Many of the ACEs and other traumatic experiences that affect too many students involve a toxic combination of danger and unpredictability. Researcher of adverse childhood experiences Robert F. Anda and colleagues (2006) explain that this results in brains on high alert for threats, which can be adaptive in unsafe environments. Feeling unsafe at school makes it very difficult for any student to relax and focus on schoolwork. It can also increase the likelihood of large and challenging responses to what seem like minor provocations (like unexpected changes) for students with more traumatic histories, according to authors Courtney Wiest-Stevenson and Cindy Lee (2016). Working to ensure that all students feel a sense of safety and predictability at school can lower stress levels and help students develop in ways that promote learning.

PERSON AND ENVIRONMENT

It's human nature to fall into the trap of thinking people behave the way they do just because of who they are—their individual skills and characteristics—while failing to see their environment and circumstances shape them. Psychologists call this the *fundamental attribution error* (Berry, 2015). And it's especially common to make this error when we're dealing with challenging behaviors. As educators, we need to be vigilant about asking ourselves not *what's wrong with* individual students but rather *what's missing from the environment* that we can provide to students to enhance their social, emotional, and behavioral success. When we do so, we can better focus on creating a system that rewards students for behaving in positive ways that are consistent with clear expectations.

Research from prevention scientist Celene E. Domitrovich and colleagues (2010) shows that social-emotional skills instruction results in more positive outcomes when combined with such a system. And in this way, we're nurturing a transformative symbiotic relationship: improving school climate supports SEL and improving student social-emotional competence positively affects classroom and school climate (Bear, 2020; Durlak, Domitrovich, Weissberg, & Gullotta, 2015).

How Can Educators Create Safe, Predictable, and Positive Environments?

The following section explores two complementary, evidence-based strategies that schools can use to create safe, predictable, positive environments: positive behavioral interventions and supports (PBIS) and proactive classroom management. Since universal approaches usually do not meet the needs of all students, the text also briefly discusses a more targeted model: multitiered system of supports (MTSS).

POSITIVE BEHAVIORAL INTERVENTIONS AND SUPPORTS

One of the most widely adopted approaches schools use to create safe, predictable, and positive school environments is the PBIS framework. PBIS has research evidence for its effectiveness as well as widely available user guides and tools that can be used to continuously improve outcomes over time. PBIS is a noncurricular approach that gives flexibility to provide for student needs in ways that fit schools' culture, staff, and students (Center on PBIS, 2022). The approach has solid research support; multiple high-quality studies provide strong evidence that universal PBIS reduces student behavior problems that lead to office referrals and suspensions, improves staff and student perceptions of school climate, and reduces teacher-reported social and behavior problems (Bradshaw, 2013; Gage, Whitford & Katsiyannis, 2018; Pas, Hoon Ryoo, Musci, & Bradshaw, 2019).

Too often, our behavioral expectations are culturally loaded and can favor some students over others. Students with backgrounds similar to school staff often have to make less effort to match their behavior to school expectations and norms. For example, educators' perceptions of the three Ds—disrespect, disobedience, and defiance—tend to be culturally loaded and result in unfavorable experiences for students of color, students with disabilities, and other marginalized groups (Owens, 2023). When educators clearly define and teach culturally and developmentally appropriate behavioral expectations, they make it easier for students to understand which behaviors everyone, including the educators themselves, must engage in to help co-create a positive, productive, and peaceful environment. Again, the importance of establishing culturally appropriate behavioral expectations through reaching shared agreements among educators, students, and families is important to creating equitable environments.

Centering the PBIS process around key stakeholders and ensuring that students and families have voice increases engagement and is a safeguard against establishing behavioral expectations that are consistent with one group's cultural lens but inconsistent and potentially harmful to other cultural groups. Representative stakeholders must be directly involved or else their perspectives won't be fully considered and integrated into PBIS. For this reason, we encourage people to seek out resources connected to culturally responsive PBIS. According to educators Tachelle Banks and Festus E. Obiakor (2015), the PBIS system can contribute to equity in schools by making adapting to school smoother for students whose home and community lives might include different norms for behavior than those desired at school.

Reaching shared agreements is best approached through a collaborative, nonhierarchical process (that is, educators come to the table to have students and families co-create things as coequals) that involves communication among the people expected to understand and use the behavioral expectations. The tiered fidelity inventory is a tool commonly used in the implementation of positive behavior intervention and supports (Algozzine et al., 2019). There is a specific section in the inventory that asks educators to think about their own culture and the different cultural backgrounds of their students and families and incorporate student and family voice into the defining the behavioral expectations, discipline procedures, and the problem behaviors that warrant them.

A great suite of practices for creating safe, predictable, positive school environments, PBIS involves educators doing the following.

- **Focusing on positive behavior:** In schools using PBIS, students receive a very clear message about the importance of positive behaviors expected of students throughout the school.
- **Creating a small number of clear, understandable, culturally and developmentally appropriate expectations:** To support the focus on positive behavioral expectations that can be taught, encouraged, and acknowledged, PBIS involves the school community in coming up with a small number of simple expectations that all students and staff learn and know.
- **Explicitly teaching behavioral expectations across natural settings:** A strength of the PBIS approach is the emphasis on teaching students exactly what those expectations look like, sound like, and feel like for the classroom, lunchroom, hallway, playground, bus, sporting events, and so forth. This is essential to ensure that everyone is on the same page, which helps create a predictable environment.
- **Homing in on what students are doing right:** A common pitfall for schools is having too much focus on what students are doing wrong. This results in students getting more negative than positive attention from adults—which is the exact opposite of what creates positive experiences in school for students.

- **Acknowledging and recognizing positive behavior:** In schools using PBIS, the adults create systems and make efforts to acknowledge, recognize, and encourage students who are meeting expectations in ways that fit with their preferences and values. This results in a positive feedback system where students get positive attention for helping to create a safer, more predictable, and positive school environment for everyone, which in turn leads to more positive behavior.

- **Responding effectively to challenging behavior:** PBIS also helps schools respond in consistent and effective ways to perceived unskillful student behavior while avoiding punitive and exclusionary approaches to discipline that derail students' sense of school belonging, undermine engagement, and disproportionately impacting minoritized students. These unforgiving policies and practices not only are unjust but also do not support learning and behavior change (Skiba & Karega Rausch, 2006). Consider how academic mistakes and challenges are typically handled: educators use a problem-solving framework to identify the core skills a student is missing that are driving the problem, and then they select an intervention to address that need. In a similar fashion, the PBIS approach works to identify what may be driving the behavior that is out of line with expectations and looks for solutions that target those root causes. Students still experience consequences for their behavior, but the goal is to create learning opportunities for students that help them be successful rather than focus on punishment.

- **Gathering and using data on behavior and discipline to inform continuous improvement efforts:** PBIS is intended to support continuous learning and improvement so that schools get better over time at creating equitable and positive practices and predictable environments while reducing behaviors that interfere with learning. In PBIS, educators gather and track specific data on behavior and disaggregate those data by student demographics to develop precision statements around for whom and under what conditions the behavior support system is working and not working. These precision statements help inform next steps to create equitable environments for all students rather than environments that most benefit those students who are already doing well.

It's always disheartening to feel like the path forward involves piling on multiple approaches one after the other, each of which makes a separate contribution but requires extra time and effort. The good news is that PBIS and SEL complement and support each other—each makes the other easier and more effective.

Effective SEL means students are improving their social-emotional competence. But students don't necessarily get along and solve problems with peers and make good decisions automatically just because they know how to. People respond to their environment, and students are less likely to display positive behavior in a school or classroom that doesn't encourage and support it. On the other hand, when positive behavioral expectations are clearly spelled out, promoted, acknowledged, and recognized throughout a school, students feel rewarded for putting their social-emotional competence to use and motivated to continue growing their skill set.

Safe, predictable, positive environments support the development of student social-emotional competence. So while creating the right environment using PBIS core practices can establish a proactive and predictable environment that encourages and motivates students to use skills they possess, it also supports the development of student social and emotional skills. Culturally appropriate expectations that are clarified and taught using PBIS practices are more likely to be effective when students have the skills required to meet them. PBIS and SEL support and reinforce each other, and research has shown that when PBIS is integrated with universal SEL, it results in better social, emotional, and behavioral outcomes than when either is done separately (Cook et al., 2015; Domitrovich et al., 2010).

There are numerous resources that are helpful in understanding how to initiate the implementation of PBIS and reach high levels of fidelity, including www.PBIS.org and www.pbisapps.org.

PROACTIVE CLASSROOM MANAGEMENT

Proactive classroom management, according to educator Natalie Rathvon (2008), refers to a set of high-leverage practices that teachers can use to create safe, predictable, and positive environments that promote academic engagement and prevent, rather than react to, behaviors that interfere with learning. Proactive classroom management practices enable teachers to support students in meeting schoolwide behavioral expectations stemming from PBIS, and to respond in constructive ways when students exhibit behaviors inconsistent with the expectations.

Too many teacher training programs fail to adequately teach proactive classroom management strategies, even though they're necessary to create the student engagement and positive behavior that provide the foundation for academic learning, according to educational psychologists Michael Christofferson and Amanda L. Sullivan (2015). Researcher Justin T. Cooper and colleagues (2018) find that over 90 percent of elementary school teachers surveyed say they need more professional development on proactive classroom management, and most postgraduate teacher candidates say they do not feel adequately prepared to manage disruptive behavior in the classroom. Similarly, a survey from the Coalition for Psychology in Schools and Education (2006) showed U.S. teachers across all grade levels said they needed more training in behavioral management and ongoing support in classroom management practices. Too often, new teachers enter the classroom with enthusiasm, great pedagogical theories, and carefully prepared lesson plans only to find themselves overwhelmed by the challenge of keeping students engaged and on task.

Classroom behavior management has historically relied on reactive, as opposed to proactive, strategies. Reactive behavior management puts all the responsibility for meeting classroom expectations on students. It relies on punitive responses to misbehavior (like public reprimands) and exclusionary discipline methods (such as office referral, suspension, or detention). These approaches, according to educators Kelly L. Morrissey, Hank Bohanon, and Pamela Fenning (2010), embarrass or shame students and undermine their sense of belonging. Psychologists Steven G. Little and Angeleque Akin-Little (2008) explain that reactive, punitive discipline can damage student–teacher relationships, increasing disengagement and problem behavior. As an example, some students' problem behavior is driven by a desire to avoid academic work for a variety of reasons. Instead of increasing motivation, engagement, and work, reactive responses focus teacher attention on problem behavior and can result in removal from instruction that inadvertently reinforces the misbehavior (Little & Akin-Little, 2008). But lacking other tools leaves many teachers stuck relying on reactive methods for classroom behavior management despite overwhelming evidence that such strategies are ineffective.

Although it's necessary to have effective strategies for responding to problem behaviors, research from educators Brandi Simonsen and Diane Myers (2015) shows that using proactive classroom management approaches also increases positive, desired behavior while preventing many of the disruptive behaviors that negatively impact the learning environment. Proactive classroom management strategies have been shown to enhance classroom climate, foster positive student–teacher relationships, and prevent classroom problem behavior—all of which are part of creating safe, predictable, and positive environments that promote social-emotional development.

Part of what makes proactive classroom management work so well is that, when done correctly, it produces high levels of academic engagement, and students are rarely engaged and disruptive at the same time. Proactive classroom management is also unique in that teachers can integrate classroom management with academic instruction. Proactive classroom management strategies also target the classroom as a whole rather than focusing on individual students, thereby contributing to a classroom environment that is conducive to learning and student social and emotional development and well-being. The following sections take a detailed look at some specific management strategies teachers can consider when student behavior doesn't meet expectations.

Management Strategies

Multiple proactive classroom management practices (for example, Cook et al., 2017; Evertson & Poole, 2008; Menzies, Lane, Oakes, & Ennis, 2017; and Simonsen & Myers, 2015) have demonstrated effectiveness in promoting academic engagement and reducing classroom problem behaviors through the use of precorrection, opportunities to respond, interspersion of choice, classwide motivation systems, and routines and visual schedules.

Precorrection

Precorrection is a practice that involves reminding students of the behavioral expectations *before* they transition to new settings or tasks. Precorrection is a front-loading strategy that involves anticipating times when students may exhibit behaviors that warrant correction and spending a small amount of time reminding them of or reviewing what is expected and how they can be successful. When applied to academics, precorrection is referred to as *errorless learning*, which means reviewing key information (for example, definitions of unknown words) before the student begins a task (for example, reading a chapter).

Opportunities to Respond

Providing opportunities to respond is among the most widely researched proactive strategies. It involves engaging students academically by integrating regular active student responses to questions or statements. Students may respond verbally, or with gestures or actions, and may do so chorally as a whole class, in pairs, or individually (Cavanaugh, 2013). During instruction, students should not go more than a few minutes without having an active way of responding to the learning material.

Interspersion of Choice

Interspersing choice is a proactive strategy that provides students with opportunities to independently select from two or more options. This strategy aligns what students do with their preferences, which increases engagement in learning. There are different types of available choice options. There are nonacademic choices, like selecting where to sit or what to do during free time, as well as academic choices, such as how to complete the work (video, paper and pencil, computer), where to do the work, who to do the work with, and what work to do (selection from different assignments or tasks). Environments rich with choice tend to have high rates of student academic engagement (Ennis, Lane, & Flemming, 2020; Ennis, Lane, Oakes, & Flemming, 2020).

Classwide Motivation Systems

Most classwide motivation systems involve creating some type of payoff to acknowledge and recognize students for the energy and effort they put into meeting the behavioral expectations of the classroom. Three types of group contingencies that can serve as classwide motivation systems: (1) interdependent, (2) dependent, and (3) intradependent.

1. **Interdependent group contingency, or "All for one":** This classwide motivation system involves having students work in teams or groups to support one another to exhibit well-defined behaviors during a certain period of time. Rather than focusing on individual student behavior, the teacher typically sets a behavioral goal for a group of students (from small group to whole class). The teacher then monitors how students are doing and provides feedback and rewards or incentives to the entire group or team if they are making progress toward the goal. The Good Behavior Game is a well-researched example of the interdependent group contingency strategy (Flower, McKenna, Bunuan, Muething, & Vega, 2014).

2. **Dependent group contingency, or "One for all":** This effective classwide motivation system involves a single student earning something on behalf of the entire class (Little, Akin-Little, & O'Neill, 2015). The teacher identifies specific behaviors they are

looking for and indicates that there is a specific student who has the opportunity to earn something on behalf of the entire class. The identity of the student is not shared with them or the class. Keeping the student unknown has been shown to help promote engagement during times when students may otherwise be motivated to disengage. If the student does not meet the goal for the behavior, the teacher *does not* call the student out but rather indicates that the goal was not met for that day. If the student does meet the goal, the teacher then announces that the class was able to earn the reward based on the student's behavior.

3. **Independent group contingency, or "To each their own":** This classwide motivation system recognizes variability in need among students and aims to tailor a "first, then" plan for individual students who may need additional motivational support. "First, then" plans spell out the behaviors that specific students *first* need to exhibit so they can *then* access a privilege, desired social activity/experience, or reward (van de Pol et al., 2015). Working with the student and family provides ways of ensuring that the "first, then" motivational plans are made to be developmentally and culturally appropriate.

Routines and Visual Schedules

Consistent routines and visual schedules posted in the classroom are critical elements to creating a predictable environment in which students can anticipate what is going to happen, which helps them regulate their behavior. Routines are regular and consistent patterns of activities that are followed on a typical day that help students get in sync. Beginning class with a meeting and ending class with an exit ticket are prime examples of routines that help students anticipate what is going to happen as they transition into and out of the classroom. Visual schedules lay out the details regarding what is going to happen during class, including an intentional mix of activities that students may find more and less preferred. Detailed yet understandable visual schedules combined with prompting students to review the visual schedule helps students meet behavioral expectations.

There are a number of places to obtain resources and support around proactive classroom management practices. Consider the following as a starting point.

- Evidence-Based Intervention Network (https://education.missouri.edu/ebi)

- Comprehensive Integrated Three Tier Model of Prevention (https://www.ci3t.org)
- CharacterStrong On-Demand PD (https://characterstrong.com)

Practices for Progressively Responding to Behavior

Even with a good array of proactive strategies in place to prevent behavioral challenges, there is still a need for effective methods of responding to student behavior that does not meet expectations. This process should be informed by three guiding principles.

First, the process should be geared around effective feedback. On the one hand, effective feedback is a great way to turn a situation into a learning opportunity by signaling what a student did right through specific, concrete, and positive affirmations. Behavior-specific praise is an evidence-based strategy in and of itself that has been shown to create a reinforcing experience that cultivates and maintains behavioral expectations and a positive learning environment (Royer et al., 2019). On the other hand, when situations warrant correction or implementation, behavior-specific feedback is an effective process to help the student to learn.

Second, the process should come from a stance of empathy that seeks to understand the student's perspective before responding. Empathy statements do not involve "however" and "but" phrases. Instead, they attempt to validate the student's perspective or feelings about a situation, which is not the same as agreeing with or endorsing specific behavior. For example, "You seem like you are feeling frustrated and disappointed, because you wanted to finish your science project and now we have to transition to reading. Did I get that right? It's OK to be frustrated. Maybe we can make a plan together to finish your project." When students feel like their perspective is understood, they are more likely to stay in a regulated state and learn from the situation. Students who shut down to an interaction miss out on the learning opportunity and are likely to feel a weaker sense of belonging and connection to the adult who is in charge.

Third, it is important to keep the student in the learning environment and preserve the relationship with the student at all costs, or else our efforts to respond to student behavior may produce more harm than good. To do this, it is important for the adults to learn how to manage their own thoughts and feelings in response to student behavior. It is important for adults to develop strategies to help them pause and get in a regulated state before responding so they can respond in a way that is effective rather than what angry or frustrated thoughts and feelings may be urging. This helps mitigate the impact of implicit bias and ensure that the response is likely to preserve the student's participation in the learning environment and less likely to harm the relationship with the student. Chapter 1 (page 7) provides some strategies to help educators manage emotionally challenging situations. One particularly powerful strategy for progressively responding to behavior is relying on restorative practices.

Restorative practices are valuable and powerful for two reasons. The first is that they provide supportive accountability after a situation has occurred in which a student's behavior has impacted relationships with others. In these situations, students are given support to understand how their behaviors affect others and how they can make things right. Some educators perceive that restorative practices create a weak environment in which they do not hold students accountable. The truth is that the restorative practices model creates a high degree of accountability—the difference from traditional punitive approaches is that they also include a high degree of empathy and support.

The second reason for using restorative practices is that even if an adult responds effectively to a student and holds the student accountable in an empathic and supportive way, there may still be harm done to the relationship with the student. The student may have hurt feelings, may feel like the adult doesn't care about them or want them in class, or may still feel misunderstood. For these reasons, restorative practices also involve adults taking ownership over repairing relationships with students. They do this by reconnecting with the student using restorative communication strategies to repair the relationship with the student. More detail on these strategies can be found in chapter 4 (page 83).

A range of restorative practices can be used to hold students accountable for their behavior when it has negatively affected others or the learning environment, while also creating a compassionate and supportive environment for the student. In this way, students know that even though they made a mistake, they are an accepted and valued member of the school community. Educators can arrange proactive restorative community-building circles or restorative conferences.

- Proactive restorative community-building circles create a positive classroom culture by protecting time for students to connect with one another and have a sense of voice about their future. While frequently used to replace punitive forms of discipline, proactive restorative circles cultivate relationships and provide opportunities for students to learn skills they can use in relationship with one another and to meet the challenges they face.

- Restorative conference is an alternative to punitive discipline that involves holding a student accountable for their behavior in a compassionate and supportive way. There is a misconception that restorative practices "let students get away with their bad behavior." This is not true, as restorative conferences emphasize a high level of accountability by having the student reflect on and learn how their behavior impacted others and what they need to do to make the situation right. While going through this process, the student is unable to access some of the privileges they would otherwise be able to earn.

PROMPT METHOD

The PROMPT method has been studied and found to improve equity in student discipline and result in more positive outcomes for students (Cook, Duong, McIntosh, Fiat, Larson, Pullmann, & McGinnis, 2018). Cook developed the PROMPT method to provide educators with effective strategies for responding to unskillful student behavior in ways that keep students in class and support positive student–teacher relationships. The following describes the strategies in the PROMPT method.

Proximity Control

Proximity control simply means the educator moving to stand near the student (Lewis, Colvin, & Sugai, 2000). The teacher moving to be near the student is itself often enough to reduce perceived problem behaviors. One benefit of proximity control is it can be done without disrupting the flow of instruction because the teacher does not have to speak to or interact with the student.

Redirection Strategies

Teachers can use redirection strategies by asking the student to do something that they are unlikely to refuse to do. This strategy allows the teacher to intervene effectively without having to threaten or warn the student that they are in danger of receiving a disciplinary consequence (Conroy, Sutherland, Snyder, & Marsh, 2008). Redirection can involve simple things like asking the student to collect papers from other students, hand things out to students, sharpen a pencil for you, or run an errand to a nearby classroom.

Ongoing Monitoring

Ongoing monitoring involves impacting a target student's behavior in one of two ways: by providing attention or recognition to other students who are engaging in the desired behavior, or by rewarding the target student with praise when they show behaviors that are close to or in the direction of the desired behavior. Ongoing monitoring utilizes principles of social learning and behavioral shaping and is typically used to address minor problem behavior and avoid escalating challenges that might ultimately result in the student being removed from the learning environment.

Prompt Desired Behavior

Prompting desired behavior is just what it sounds like: giving the student a direct, clear, and short verbal message in a calm and unthreatening way that spells out what the student should be doing (Matheson & Shriver, 2005). Effective prompts should be stated positively, focused on what the student *should* be doing rather than what they should *not* be doing. They should also be short and focused on one specific behavior and should be delivered as a simple statement, not a question. Simply put, an effective prompt is one that states and clarifies the desired behavior the teacher wants instead of the unskilled behavior the student is demonstrating.

Teaching Interaction

The teaching interaction approach is a bit more elaborate than the preceding methods but follows a simple structure that focuses on communicating in an empathic, consistent way designed to create teachable moments out of problem behavior. With this approach, the teacher uses effective communication strategies to help the student learn from the interaction without provoking escalations in behavior. These are the steps involved in a successful teaching interaction:

1. Begin with an empathy question or statement.
2. Label the unskillful behavior.
3. Label the skillful behavior.
4. Give a rationale for the skillful behavior.

5. Set a limit by outlining the choices the student can make and the consequences of each choice.
6. Give the student time and space to arrive at a decision.
7. Check back in to see what choice the student made.

The teaching interaction strategy may take time to learn, but it has real value because it helps teachers avoid unintentionally interacting with students in ways that can harm the student–teacher relationships. An effective teaching interaction does what it says: helps the student learn from the situation without escalating their behavior.

MULTITIERED SYSTEM OF SUPPORTS

Students arrive at school with a variety of needs. In this book, we focus on SEL at the universal (or Tier 1) level: evidence-based supports that all students receive. The MTSS model builds on the foundation of a solid Tier 1 approach. In the MTSS model, all students get universal supports, and then the much smaller number of students who still experience social, emotional, and behavioral struggles are identified and provided with additional support, sometimes referred to as Tier 2 interventions. For an even smaller group of students, Tier 2 interventions are still not sufficient to meet their needs, and more intensive Tier 3 services are required.

The MTSS model does not dictate specific programs and interventions. It provides guidelines for creating environments that effectively respond to all students' needs. MTSS begins with helping schools avoid a focus on individual student deficits by ensuring that all students' basic needs are met. After that foundation has been laid, effective strategies are then used to provide more targeted support to those students who still have additional needs.

MTSS is based on public health models that have been effectively used for decades, and the MTSS approach itself has strong evidence behind it, as researchers Catherine P. Bradshaw, Elise T. Pas, Katrina J. Debnam, and Sarah Lindstrom Johnson (2021) show. It's a framework that helps schools go beyond universal supports and helps them organize their efforts to effectively and efficiently meet all students' academic, social, emotional, and behavioral needs.

An important question is how to decide which students have additional needs beyond universal SEL. A key principle of the MTSS approach is looking at data on students to decide who needs higher levels of support, typically using validated screening tools. We will discuss the topic of universal screening to detect higher student needs in chapter 5 (page 123), which is focused on using data to improve SEL.

It is important to understand that the success of the MTSS system depends on a solid Tier 1 approach that ensures all students daily and consistently have the experiences they need to develop needed skills and feel safe, accepted, and confident as learners in school. Given the intensity of some students' challenges and needs, it's easy for schools to fall into the trap of jumping straight to trying to put out fires with more intensive Tier 2 interventions without first ensuring all students are getting adequate Tier 1 support. Universal SEL is in part a prevention approach that, done effectively, should reduce the number of students requiring more intensive services. Without solid universal SEL in place to help develop the social-emotional competence of the majority of students, far too many students show up on the Tier 2 radar, overwhelming schools' intervention resources. It's like the expensive mistake of building a nice house that keeps needing costly repairs because you neglected to construct a solid foundation. Universal support for all students can meet the needs of many students who might otherwise be referred to more intensive interventions. Universal SEL also contributes to the success of Tier 2 interventions for those students who still need them by providing an SEL foundation on which to build more intensive interventions.

MTSS is an equity-enhancing approach. Equity does not mean all students getting the same thing—it means differentiating supports to ensure everyone receives what they need to be successful. This is as true in SEL and student behavior and well-being as it is in academics. By providing effective universal supports, then using data-driven methods to objectively figure out which students need more and what their specific needs are, schools can ensure their social, emotional, and behavioral initiatives help all students succeed.

The Center on MTSS for Success (https://mtss4success.org) provides schools with a range of resources on the core components of MTSS and how to get started with implementation. Also, the Customized Implementation Supports team at CharacterStrong (www.characterstrong.com) is a group with expertise in partnering with school systems to achieve the successful implementation of integrated models of MTSS that involve combining a continuum of social, emotional, and behavioral supports with academics.

Conclusion

SEL is a developmental process. Creating classroom and school environments that are safe, predictable, and positive is one of the most powerful ways we can support students' healthy social and emotional development. Humans are fundamentally social beings who learn and grow through interactions and relationships with others, and this is especially true for children and adolescents. SEL is too often thought of as simply teaching individual skills, neglecting the essential role that classroom and school environments play in social and emotional development, academic achievement, student behavior, and the well-being of students and adults in schools.

Teaching skills in SEL lessons is necessary but not sufficient on its own. For those skills to become competencies that are applied in real life, they must be practiced and used. One of the most important ways to achieve this is providing students with supportive environments that motivate and reward them for building social-emotional competence. Safe, predictable, and positive environments increase student motivation toward and engagement in positive behavior and academic learning. Solid research shows that one of the primary ways school leaders positively impact academic achievement is through improving school climate.

School and classroom environments are an important equity issue. Intentionally focusing on creating classroom and school environments that are safe, predictable, and positive helps all students increase their social-emotional competence, well-being, and academic success. But creating these types of environments can be especially important for students of color and other students who may be negatively impacted by one-size-fits-all environments focused on compliance and punitive discipline.

Next Steps

What are the important next steps you want to take to maintain or improve the implementation of practices that create a safe, predictable, and positive environment?

Note that your plan should take into account whether you are in a planning phase or already actively implementing effective practices. If implementation has not begun, create a plan to establish motivational readiness to implement. If already implementing, then create a plan to support continuous improvement to reach high-fidelity sustained implementation.

Reflecting on Safe, Predictable, and Positive Environments

Consider the following questions as they relate to your school or district and safe, predictable, positive environments.

- What are you doing in your school or district to assess how safe students feel in school?

- What concrete actions have you taken or can you take to increase your students' sense of predictability in the school environment?

- What steps have you taken or can you take to increase students' experience of school as a positive environment for them?

- How clearly are behavioral expectations taught to students in your school or district?

- How are students recognized and rewarded or reinforced when they work hard to meet those expectations?

- How might you provide opportunities for educators to increase their knowledge and skills around classroom management?

- If your school has not yet identified a core set of practices to implement, how can you select practices that specifically target creating a safe, predictable, and positive environment?

- If your school has already identified a core set of practices, then reflect on whether these practices are being implemented with fidelity and adequately reaching all students in the school. Where is there room for continuous improvement in your efforts to create a safe, predictable, positive environment?

Planning for Safe, Predictable, and Positive Environments

Use the following chart to consider practices to advance safe, predictable, and positive environments. In the space provided, note necessary steps involved in completing each goal as well as key dates to remember aligned with implementation.

Implementation Goal	Necessary Steps	Key Dates
Establish behavioral norms and expectations.		
Teach behavioral norms and expectations applied to each setting and on an ongoing basis.		
Prompt and remind students.		
Recognize and acknowledge students for following behavioral norms and expectations.		
Progressively respond to student behavior with empathy and a restorative approach.		

CHAPTER 4

POSITIVE RELATIONSHIPS

Think back on your school days. Who was your favorite teacher? How did they make you feel? What was your behavior like, how hard did you work, and how much did you learn in their classroom? Amid the hectic day-to-day realities of education, it can be easy to forget that teaching is a human process that is nurtured by positive relationships.

In this chapter, we continue our exploration of the SEL recipe by discussing what characterizes positive relationships, why positive relationships among students as well as between educators and students matter for student outcomes, and how educators can help cultivate both types of positive relationships.

What Are Positive Relationships?

We have all experienced how great it is to have positive relationships with people we spend our days with, and most of us have also experienced how negative relationships can harm our well-being. The positive relationship qualities we are talking about are captured by the key ingredients laid out in chapter 3 (page 53) in our discussion of the kinds of environments that help students thrive: safe, predictable, and positive.

Healthy connections with educators and other students are essential to students' developing a sense of trust, connection, and belonging at school (Sabol & Pianta, 2012). Ideally, we want students to feel confident that their interactions with others in school will be characterized by empathy, consistency, trustworthiness, and unconditional positive regard. We want each student to feel known and cared about as a unique person, and not just seen as one among a group of many. It is through positive relationships that students know that their teachers and peers value them for who they are as members of the school community.

It's valuable to keep in mind that students may not always experience positive relationships as something they either definitively have or do not have. We are all constantly bombarded with cues and signals from all the people who surround us, and it's not always easy to arrive at a solid conclusion about your connections with others. Research has identified "belonging uncertainty" as a serious problem that can interfere with students' academic performance and social and emotional well-being (Cohen, 2022; Walton & Cohen, 2007). Students from groups that may be stigmatized or subject to negative stereotypes are more likely to experience belonging uncertainty. This experience of being unsure whether they belong at their school causes students to constantly scan and monitor their environment, keeping them hyperalert to possible cues that they do not in fact belong. Being in that state takes away from one's ability to be confident and focus on doing one's best.

Why Are Positive Relationships Important?

According to researchers Karine Verschueren and Helma M. Y. Koomen (2012), positive relationships make essential contributions to both academic achievement and healthy social-emotional development. Much of the power of positive relationships with both educators and peers is in helping students feel like they belong to their school community. A sense of belonging, sometimes called *school connectedness*, promotes student academic, social, and emotional success in school and beyond. Students who feel a sense of belonging or connection to their school community have more positive attitudes toward school, are more engaged in academics, are more likely to have better attendance and higher grades and test scores, and are more likely to graduate from high school (Niehaus, Irvin, Rogelberg, 2016; Niehaus, Rudasill, Rakes, 2012). As educator Karen F. Osterman (2000) has shown, they see themselves as more competent, and they have a stronger sense of identity and more motivation to be positive co-contributors to the school's culture and climate. And, crucially important given the rise in student mental health challenges, students who feel connected to their school suffer less emotional distress and fewer thoughts of suicide (Kim, Walsh, Pike, & Thompson, 2020; Langille, Ashbridge, Cragg, & Rasic, 2015; Steiner et al., 2019).

Humans are social beings who depend on meaningful connections with others to develop and function well. Students' social, emotional, behavioral, and even academic success are all powerfully related to the quality of the relationships they experience in school. Neuroscientific research has shown that positive social relationships are necessary for healthy brain development and functioning (Siegel, 2020). Moreover, research from neuroscientists Martin H. Teicher, Jacqueline A. Samson, Carl M. Anderson, and Kyoko Ohashi (2016) reveals that positive relationships with others can help protect or even repair the areas of the brain affected by traumatic experiences. Other research has shown that positive student–teacher relationships and prosocial interactions with peers provide protective emotional and behavioral benefits for children and adolescents, and strong connections with teachers can lower the risk of delinquency and other negative outcomes for students (Sabol & Pianta, 2013; Verschueren & Koomen, 2012).

We all want our students to be fully motivated and engaged in learning, but for many of them, that's difficult because their basic psychological needs for connection and belonging have not been fully met. Imagine spending an entire year in an environment where you don't feel a sense of trust, connection, and belonging with the person in charge or the people around you. You, too, would be less engaged and less responsive. Working to create positive relationships in school is one way we can pay attention to students' basic needs, including their need for authentic social connection. Helping students get their developmental needs met is a wonderful gift to them, but it also lays a crucial part of the solid foundation they need to fully engage in learning and continuously improve in the face of adversity and challenges.

Although all students benefit from safe, reliable connections with peers and adults, positive relationships are especially important for students who have experienced trauma and toxic stress. Educator Jennifer Dods (2013) explains that secure, trusting relationships help reduce stress levels, support healthy development and brain functioning for students, and help students develop the ability to relax, focus, and learn.

Positive relationships are important for health and wellness. But they're also critically important for academic achievement. Positive relationships that cultivate belonging increase student motivation and engagement, improve behavior, decrease violence, buffer students from adversity, and, of course, support social and emotional development (Pianta, Hamre, & Allen, 2012; Walker & Graham, 2021; Wubbels, Brekelmans, Mainhard, den Brok, & van Tartwijk, 2016; Zolkoski, 2019). Relationships strongly impact academic performance, in part through increasing student motivation and engagement. And this is true for students of all ages. Relationships with adults tend to become weaker as students move from early to late elementary and into secondary school. Yet the research shows that those connections become more important as students progress beyond elementary school (Longobardi, Prino, Marengo, & Settanni, 2016). Although young people may seem like they're trying to push both parents and teachers away as they move into adolescence, strong relationships with caring adults are critically important for development and success from childhood through the teenage years.

When we fail to ensure a sense of belonging, it shows in students' attitudes, mindsets, and behavior. Some students lose out on learning by withdrawing or not engaging academically. Curriculum, standards, and tests don't matter if students are not participating in class and investing themselves in learning opportunities. Although we know pedagogy is important, the reality is that students' psychological experience in the classroom strongly affects their motivation and academic performance. And much of what drives the quality of that psychological experience is the relationships students have with their teachers and classmates. One of the learning mindsets that research has identified as particularly important in supporting students' academic behaviors and persistence, and performance on academic tasks, is "I belong in this learning community" (Farrington et al., 2012). We talk more about this in the following pages, but it's important to keep in mind that a sense of belonging in school may be more readily available to some students than others. A sense of belonging is both especially important and often harder to come by for students of color and students from underrepresented groups (LaSalle, Wang, Wu, & Neves, 2020).

Another reason this sense of belonging is so important is that it can help students to embrace a growth mindset. Most educators now know the importance of students having a growth mindset, but they may not be aware that a key piece of that is a willingness to fail in order to get better at things. Being willing to risk failure often depends on trusting you'll be supported and helped rather than judged. Having positive, trusting relationships with their teachers and peers helps students feel safe enough to take the academic and social risks required for learning and growth.

Finally, positive relationships boost teachers' abilities to effectively prevent and respond to challenging student behavior. While some disconnected students tune out, others act out, which disrupts the learning environment and causes stress for teachers and students alike. Research shows that positive student relationships with teachers reduce disruptive behavior (Cook et al., 2018). Without a relationship in place, it is difficult to motivate students to meet behavioral expectations and to constructively correct problem behavior. Imagine trying to motivate behavior change in shoppers you don't know at the grocery store. If you don't have relationships with those people, they are unlikely to give weight to your perspective or input.

How Can Educators Intentionally Cultivate and Support Positive Peer-to-Peer Relationships?

Some of the main outcomes of educators' effective delivery and support of SEL are improved empathy, perspective taking, and social skills among students—all of which make important contributions to positive relationships among peers at school. Many SEL programs also use pedagogical methods focused on peer interaction in ways that promote students getting to know one another, particularly students who might not otherwise interact very much. In addition, relationships among students in a class or school are also affected by class and school climate, which we address in chapter 3 (page 53), on safe, predictable, and positive environments.

So educators who are effectively implementing and supporting SEL are doing a lot to increase positive relationships among students. We also want to highlight two relatively easy-to-implement strategies shown in research studies to support positive peer relationships in both primary and secondary grades: positive peer reporting and classroom meetings.

POSITIVE PEER REPORTING

Positive peer reporting is a class-wide relational practice designed to improve aspects of the peer ecology and climate in classrooms by getting youth to pay more positive attention and provide more positive feedback to one another. Research from psychologists Jillian Murphy and Kimberly Zlomke (2014) has shown that positive peer reporting increases peer acceptance and decreases teacher-reported incidents of disruptive behavior in the classroom.

In positive peer reporting, students work together to earn access to a preferred activity by providing genuine recognition for one or two of their classmates. The students being positively recognized are chosen by the teacher and rotate every couple of days or every week. Positive peer reporting increases positive student relationships in four ways: (1) it involves teaching students how to provide positive praise and recognition to one another, (2) it alters how students pay attention to one another (increasing focusing on positive rather than negative things about classmates), (3) it motivates certain students to behave in ways that earn them more positive peer feedback, and (4) it provides time for building positive relationships and classroom community. Let's look at how to implement positive peer reporting and handle any challenges that accompany it.

Implementing Positive Peer Reporting

Explain to students what they'll be doing. Lay the foundation for success by ensuring students understand how positive peer reporting will work, including what their roles will be, how they'll earn preferred experiences, and how students will rotate through being the recipient of positive feedback.

Work with students to identify the activities or classroom experiences they want to earn as a group. Positive peer reporting involves the whole class earning points every time a student praises and recognizes a peer when the opportunity is provided for them to do so. Decide how many points the class must earn collectively in order to be able to earn access to a preferred classroom activity or experience. Keep track of this over time to tally points and be ready to allow the class to do the activity when they've earned it. Reinforcing experiences for the class can be simple and whimsical. The goal is simply to figure out how students can spend a small amount of time in ways that provide a welcome break from the normal class routine, something that students will find fun and rewarding compared to doing classwork.

Select specific students to be the recipients of praise and recognition for a predetermined amount of time. You can decide how to choose which students will be targeted for praise. They can be chosen randomly so that everyone has an equal chance to receive praise and recognition from peers. You can also focus on certain students who may be in greater need of receiving positive praise and recognition (usually students who appear rejected by peers or engage in negative attention-seeking behavior), but it is still best if you can make it look random, otherwise you run the risk of stigmatizing students. For example, you might mix the higher-needs students with other students who are doing just fine. The students who you select are commonly referred to as the class MVPs, or some other term, to designate them as the individuals the class is going to bring some intentional focus on to show their appreciation for them, for who they are and what they say, do, and achieve in class. Typically, students are the recipients for between two days and a week.

Teach students how to give effective praise and recognition. Use explicit instruction (that is, tell, show, do, and offer feedback) to teach students how effective praise and recognition works. Explain that we can all sometimes see things through "negative glasses," meaning that we focus more on the negative than positive, including in each other. Also explain (or ask students to share about) why receiving words of appreciation from peers is important and valuable. Finally, remind students that sharing genuine appreciation of others is itself an important social-emotional skill that positive peer reporting gives them opportunities to practice.

Students will need to be taught the elements of effective praise and recognition. This can simply be explained, but some teachers create posters that help students understand that the goal is not just praising superficial things like clothing items (for example, "I like your shoes"), but rather, it is focused on recognizing something about who the person is (a personal quality), something they said, something they did, or something they achieved—in a genuine and specific way. Consider the following example.

> *"We are going to be doing something in our class to build a greater sense of appreciation for one another while working on an important skill. This will involve paying close attention to one another to notice positive things about others that each of us would like to praise and recognize. This means we have to figure out what we mean by praise and recognition. Praise means we've noticed something about another person that we want to give them a compliment or shout-out about. When we do it, we need to try to figure out how the person likes to be recognized, we need to really mean it (which means be genuine about it), and we have to be very specific. Praising and recognizing others is like most things—the more we do it, the better we get at it. I'm going to give you some examples of what it looks like to do it well and what it looks like when we don't do it well. Next, you are all going to have a chance to practice doing it."*

Set up positive peer reporting. Here you will need to figure out how long one to two students will be the recipients. Each day, you will remind your class of the one to two students who are the focal students. At the end of every day or class period, you will ask students to raise their hands to offer praise statements about the specific students chosen. Depending on the preference of the recipients, praise can happen publicly or through more private forms like written notes. Students offer genuine and effective praise about something about the person, something they said, something did, or something they achieved. The class earns a point toward earning the group activity or experience each time someone contributes. Research has shown that positive peer reporting is a structured and effective way to increase prosocial interactions and create a more inclusive environment for students (Bowers & Cook, 2017).

Start doing positive peer reporting. Once you've set everything up, it is time to start implementing it with the class. The goal is to stick with it. The research is quite clear that social dynamics and relationships in the class will improve (Murphy & Zlomke, 2014), which means overall academic engagement is likely to increase.

Handling Challenges With Positive Peer Reporting

Ensure praise that students are comfortable with. Students may differ in how they want to give and receive praise. Spend some time when teaching it to learn about how your students prefer to give and receive praise. Keep track of this so when it comes time for students to give and receive praise, it is done in a way that aligns with students' cultural backgrounds and individual needs.

Step in when students undermine the intent. As with any other intervention strategy, students may initially test the limits with positive peer reporting. Sometimes they may make cutting comments about others under the guise of complimenting them (for example, "I want to praise Sally for taking a bath today"). If you find that a student is attempting to undermine the program, meet with them in private. Share your concern that the student is contributing to a negative classroom atmosphere. Remind the student of the disciplinary consequences that await anyone who insults or belittles a classmate. If the student persists in making hurtful comments after your conference, avoid calling on that person to give praise and be sure to enforce appropriate consequences for any negative remarks.

Reteach when students offer praise that is too superficial or vague. You may find students offering praise that is not specifically focused on something about the person or is simply not meaningful. When students struggle to provide authentic praise and recognition to their peers, then it's time for some reteaching. The aim of effective praise is that individuals feel a sense of being appreciated and recognized by others.

It is important to let students know when they are providing effective praise and recognition to their peers and discuss positive examples when they are not.

CLASSROOM MEETINGS

Classroom meetings are a powerful and widely used tool that can enhance connectedness and social-emotional development while building community in the classroom. When introducing the classroom meeting process, let students know that the goal is to create community and connections through helping everyone get to know one another and create a sense of trust and safety in the classroom. Highlight that the meetings will be a time for students, not the teacher, to talk and share.

Classroom meetings are often held with students arranged in a circle where everyone can easily see everyone else. This can be a physical demonstration that the meeting process is intentionally designed to bring out student voices and is a way to facilitate students connecting and communicating with each other. Having students sit in a circle in class meetings is so common that many people refer to the meetings as a "classroom circle" or "circle time."

Everyone should feel respected when they speak in the meeting. Spelling out meeting agreements, or coming up with them as a class, is one way to help create that sense of respect. Another common approach is to use a talking piece. Talking pieces can be anything that is easy to pass from student to student. Many people choose natural objects or something special, but almost anything is fine. The way the talking piece works is that whoever holds it has the floor and everyone knows not to interrupt or talk. This can create a sense of safety or comfort for students, especially ones for whom speaking in front of the class is more difficult. Knowing that peers should not interrupt them when they are holding the talking piece can help embolden students to share with their peers. For this to work, however, the talking-piece process needs to be upheld. The first step is simply reminding students periodically that whoever has the piece should have their attention. But it is common for students, especially early in the process, to interrupt or fail to pay full attention. While the teacher can remind students, it's often more powerful if certain students are assigned the role of checking and reminding peers of the importance of giving whoever has the piece the respect of listening without interruption or side talk.

Sometimes, it's nice to mix things up. A simple way to do this is the popcorn approach. This means when a topic or question is brought up, students raise their hands, and the teacher or an appointed student calls on them one at a time. The popcorn approach can still include a talking piece that gets passed to whomever gets called on, but students should also over time learn to follow the same rules and respect whoever is sharing.

Trust is a key element to the success of a classroom meeting. Keep in mind that trust is created slowly but can be damaged in an instant. It can be helpful to discuss this with students. Without trusting that what is said will be respected by others, students will not feel safe enough to share more personal information. Something that helps build trust early in the meeting process is ensuring students understand they can pass the talking piece and do not need to feel compelled to speak or share. Monitoring how often students pass versus contribute can provide a good measure of the progress of the meeting toward feeling like an emotionally safe place for students. If a lot of students pass, there is probably some work on building trust to be done.

The adage "Go slow to go fast" applies to classroom meetings. Especially early in the process of building your classroom meeting culture, stick to noncontroversial subjects that are fun and easy for students to speak to without much vulnerability. It is usually best to start with simpler and safer topics. Don't expect students (especially secondary students, who often are more self-conscious and aware of peer status) to open up and share personal information early in the meeting process. Starting off with low-risk questions and prompts allows students to slowly gauge how much they can trust their peers and provides opportunities for you to correct inappropriate behavior early. It's important for teachers to keep in mind that they do not know everything happening in students' lives, so it can be unwise to push students to share more than they seem willing to.

One way to generate questions for the group is by having students generate questions that the teacher can choose from. Using questions from students helps them feel ownership of the process and boosts their sense that their thoughts and opinions are valued in classroom meetings. There are many great examples of questions for circle time available on the internet.

A way to bring a little more SEL into meetings is to have a feelings check-in. There are lots of tools available online and in some SEL programs that might be especially helpful for younger students without as much developed emotion vocabulary. Simply going around and having students name a feeling, rate their mood with a number, or other more creative ways to express and share how they're doing can be a great way to start a classroom meeting. Again, expect more honest and in-depth answers as trust in the class grows. When students share that they are not doing well, it is worth considering checking in on them individually to see what's going on. In some cases, a referral to the counselor may be helpful, but often students can benefit from simply sharing and knowing that someone cares. If a student responds in a silly way, it can be best to simply acknowledge them without giving them too much attention.

Students can get excited during the process of setting up the circle, or sometimes the energy level in a class might be a bit much for a calm, focused meeting. In this case, consider calming activities to start the group. Deep slow breathing can be helpful. Another common approach is having students listen without talking and then share the quietest sound they could hear. Some teachers use a chime or other device and ask students to concentrate and then raise their hands or in some way indicate when they can no longer hear the sound.

Finally, many teachers find a closure question to be a nice way to finish a classroom circle. The question can be focused on students' experience of the group that day. An efficient and simple way to close a group like this is to limit students to a word or two to sum up what they thought of the group that day.

How Can Educators Intentionally Cultivate and Support Positive Student-Teacher Relationships?

We know positive relationships between teachers and students are critically important for supporting social-emotional development, positive behavior, and academic achievement. Unfortunately, the data indicate that too many classrooms are characterized by strained relationships that create inequities and unintentionally lead to negative classroom climates (Bottiani, Bradshaw, & Mendelson, 2017; Maldonado-Carreño & Votruba-Drzal, 2011). As discussed in chapter 3 (page 53) in the context of safe, predictable, and positive environments, one cause of this can be reactive and punitive discipline. But even though most teachers know positive relationships with their students are important, very few have been given the training and support they need to learn and intentionally implement concrete strategies to build those relationships. While teacher preparation programs often discuss the value of positive relationships, it's more challenging to equip teachers with concrete strategies and methods to make them happen. Building solid relationships with students is hard. Professional development centered on practical strategies for intentionally building positive relationships can help. In this section, we'll detail the invaluable strategies of the Establish, Maintain, Restore model before discussing how we can leverage this model to successfully navigate the nuances of student–teacher relationships.

USE THE ESTABLISH, MAINTAIN, RESTORE MODEL

One of the authors, Dr. Cook, has developed and researched a suite of concrete methods to intentionally strengthen and maintain strong relationships with students. The model is called Establish, Maintain, Restore (Cook et al., 2018). Research has shown that teachers who received training on Establish, Maintain, Restore liked it and thought the strategies were realistic (Duong et al., 2019). When teachers used the approach, they were able to significantly improve their relationships with students and in turn students' classroom behavior improved—they were less disruptive and more academically engaged (Cook, Coco et al., 2018). One thing we know from research is that students from communities of color are less likely to have positive relationships with their teachers (LaSalle, Wang, Wu, & Neves, 2020). An important part of the evaluation of Establish, Maintain, Restore was that teachers who used the strategies were equally successful at creating relationships with students across different races, socioeconomic statuses, and genders. This means that Establish, Maintain, Restore is an effective strategy for increasing equity in schools by helping to improve relationship quality between teachers and *all* students.

There are three phases of the Establish, Maintain, Restore model, as shown in figure 4.1 (page 95). If you don't have a good relationship with someone, the first step is to *establish* one. But realistically, relationships don't always stay healthy and strong over time by themselves. It takes intentional effort to *maintain* a healthy social connection, whether it be a friendship, romantic partnership, or relationships with colleagues and students. And once you've established a connection and maintained it, even healthy relationships can still hit bumps in the road. If unaddressed, those periodic challenges can cause important connections to start to fray. So the third stage in the model is to put in effort to *restore* the relationship when there's been a misunderstanding, conflict, or other challenge. Establish, Maintain, Restore provides teachers with a deliberate approach that includes common language and concrete practices for intentionally and successfully cultivating positive relationships with students.

Positive Relationships | 95

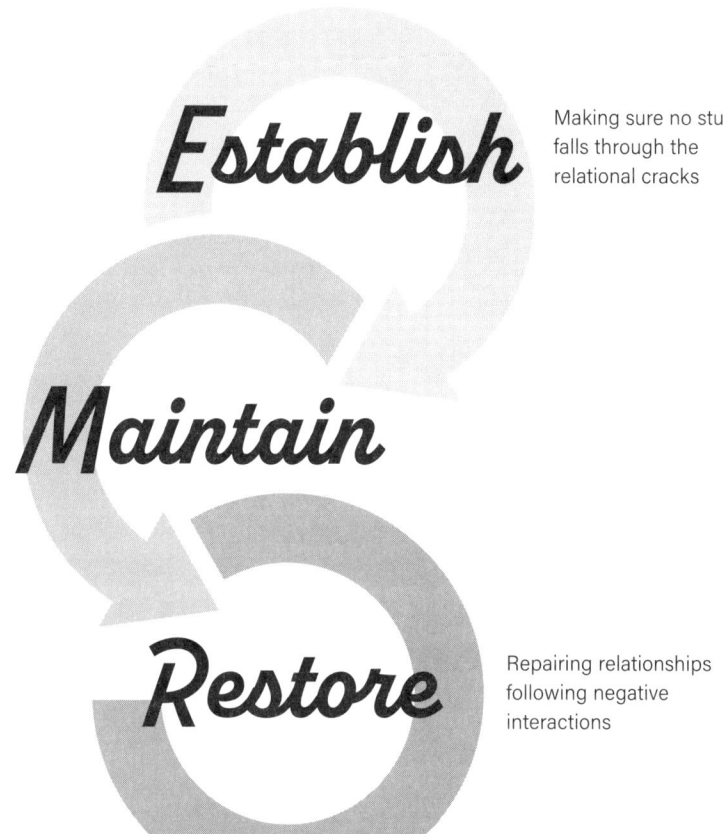

FIGURE 4.1: The Establish, Maintain, Restore model.

Figure 4.2 provides some strategies for each stage of the Establish, Maintain, Restore Model.

Establish Strategies	**Maintain Strategies**	**Restore Strategies**
Banking Time Spend individual time with the student to show that you care and accept who they are as a person.	Five-to-One Maintain a ratio of five positive interactions to every one negative interaction with the student.	Letting Go of the Previous Interaction (Fresh Start) Make it clear that you will not hold on to or bring up the previous interaction.
Gather, Review, and Acknowledge Find an opportunity to acknowledge important information about the student.	Wise Feedback Find opportunities to deliver effective praise that is behavioral specific, contingent, and acknowledges hard work, effort, a strategy, or process used.	Taking Ownership for Part of the Negative Interaction or Problem Let a student know you don't think you handled a situation as well as you would have liked.

FIGURE 4.2: Menu of Establish-Maintain-Restore strategies.   continued →

Positive Greetings at the Door	Check-Ins	Empathy Statement
Deliver positive greetings and farewells on a daily basis to the student using the student's name.	Be deliberate about relationship check-ins to see how things are going and express interests in the student beyond the classroom.	Try to take on the perspective of the student to demonstrate you understand the feeling or motive underlying the behavior.
Two-by-Ten	Responding to Problem Behavior With Empathy	Statement of Care
Spend two minutes a day connecting with the student for ten consecutive days (two weeks).	Deliver empathy statements and make sure the response is proportional to the problem behavior.	Let the student know you still value them as a person after a negative interaction.
Indirect Compliments Through Other Adults	Fun Activities	Collaborative Problem Solving
Convey something positive you noticed about the student to another adult who can pass it on to the student.	Engage in fun activities with the student for the sake of fun and nothing else.	Find a mutually agreeable (win-win) solution.

Visit **go.SolutionTree.com/SEL** *for a free reproducible of this figure.*

Establish Strategies

The goal of the Establish phase is to engage in intentional practices that build positive connections with students that help them feel known and appreciated. This builds a sense of trust, connection, and understanding that creates feelings of belonging. Here are some concrete Establish strategies.

Establish Strategy 1: Banking Time

Banking time is a well-established and well-supported strategy (Pianta & Hamre, 2001). In a nutshell, it involves finding a natural window of time to make intentional efforts to connect one-on-one with a particular student. This could be during independent work time during class, before class if a student happens to show up early, for a few minutes after class, or some convenient time outside normal class time. Given time pressures, teachers can also consider asynchronous ways to connect with and learn about students, such as writing and sharing notes or drawings back and forth. The banking-time metaphor refers to the idea that you have to make deposits before you can make withdrawals. We make withdrawals from the student relationship bank all day, whether by redirecting behavior, encouraging students to tackle difficult work, or providing critical feedback. Banking time is a way to intentionally make deposits so that when we need to make withdrawals, we aren't faced with an empty or overdrawn account.

Once you find or make the time, the basic activity is to engage in *student-centered* conversation using open-ended questions and active listening to learn about the student. It's important to show them you're interested in what they have to say. This is *not* the time to pass judgment, give advice, correct behavior, or deliver instruction. Instead, the goal is to show empathy and work to put yourself in your student's shoes. It can help to preface the conversation by simply explaining that this is something you like to do—to get to know and better understand your students. For some students, this level of one-on-one attention from their teacher can be both new and uncomfortable. We encourage finding simple ways to reduce possible discomfort. This could include asking a student to help you with something in the classroom and then talking while you're engaged in the task together. The goal of banking time is to show students you're interested in who they are as a person as well as to support your ability to have meaningful and relevant ongoing conversations as your relationship develops. Your job is to be a good listener while learning about the student. Closed-ended questions that can be answered with a simple yes or no aren't great for drawing students out. Open-ended questions are better and more likely to help you learn something interesting and keep the conversation going. It's important to use simple active listening strategies like occasionally rephrasing what the student has said to make sure you're following and to let them know you're paying attention and trying to get what they're saying.

Since the goal is to understand more about the student, it can help to use the SEL skill of perspective-taking by trying to put yourself in your students' shoes and imagining what it's like to be them, what life in their world might be like. While some of your students' lives might not be that different from yours, you will not know what life is truly like for them unless you ask. And often, the students you're less likely to connect with easily and naturally have lives very different from how you grew up. Showing them you're interested in learning about their experiences can go a long way toward bridging relational gaps.

What kinds of topics work well for the banking-time strategy? Remember that part of the value of these conversations is giving you information you can use to touch base with students periodically in authentic ways that remind them that you remember things about them, things they're doing, and stuff that's happening in their lives in or outside of school—that you know them as an individual. Examples of topics might be activities they enjoy, information about their family, or their goals or dreams for the future. Banking-time conversations don't need to be overly serious. Remember that at this stage you're still just *establishing* a relationship. Sometimes you'll have to walk the fine line of not actively agreeing with or supporting what they're up to while also not being critical or jumping into your authority figure role. Finally, be thoughtful about when and where you have conversations and when you bring up things students have told you—students may share information with you they would not necessarily want broadcast to their peers or other adults in the school.

Establish Strategy 2: Gather, Review, and Acknowledge

Have you ever had the unpleasant experience of meeting someone several times and having them treat you like they'd never met you before or didn't remember things you discussed with them? Gathering, reviewing, and acknowledging important information about students can help remind them of the efforts you've made to try to understand, know, and remember who they are as individuals. Once you've spent time learning about a student, you can use what you learned later to build and maintain a connection. But realistically, as you learn about more students, you'll be faced with the challenge of keeping track of a bunch of new information on top of everything else you have to do and remember.

Maybe you have the type of memory where nothing gets lost, but for most of us, gathering, reviewing, and acknowledging is a simple way to make banking time more effective. Before you forget what you've learned, find a few moments after a banking-time conversation to just make note of key things you've found out. Then you can periodically quickly refresh your memory down the road, helping you to give individual students the experience of being known in a unique way. Some teachers take the less individualized but often still useful approach of creating a survey to ask students questions at the beginning of the year or quarter about their interests, accomplishments, name and pronouns, life outside school, and other tidbits that can be referenced and acknowledged in later interactions.

Establish Strategy 3: Positive Greetings at the Door

This is a surprisingly powerful and effective Establish strategy that helps build relationships while also allowing you to model everyday social skills for your students and get your class off to a good start. Providing positive greetings at the door entails standing at the door to your classroom and greeting every student individually as they show up and enter the room. People do this in a variety of ways. Using each student's name is important. Make sure to learn and remember how to correctly pronounce students' names. It matters to them. A lot. One of us recently met a middle school student whose fifth-grade teacher mispronounced her name the entire year, a painful and alienating experience she clearly will never forget.

Beyond greeting students by name, some teachers give students a menu of greeting options to choose from such as a handshake, high five, hug, smile, head nod, and so forth. The options are limited only by the creativity of you and your students. We know that physical touch stimulates the hormone oxytocin, which reinforces interpersonal connections and can help promote relaxation, trust, and reduced stress (Ellingsen, Leknes et al., 2016). But not everyone is comfortable with physical contact, so be careful not to make touch a condition for all your students. In general, it's important to be sure students are able to pick what works for them. Also be aware of any school or district policies about appropriate physical contact with students.

This simple strategy has been researched and shown to increase student engagement and reduce disruptive behavior in the classroom (Cook et al., 2018). Positive greetings at the door individualizes and personalizes each student's entry into the classroom, reinforcing belonging and building feelings of connection between teacher and student. It shows each student you're making the effort to notice and acknowledge them and in that way is a simple part of establishing positive relationships. Greeting students at the door is also a great opportunity to let students who have been absent feel like they matter to you by showing that you noticed, you missed them, and you're glad they're back.

Although the main point is simply greeting all students on their way into the classroom, there are two more key components that help make positive greetings at the door most effective and help extend its positive effects into the classroom. One is precorrection—taking the opportunity to reduce possible disruptions or problem behavior by reminding students in a positive way of classroom expectations. For example, brief reminders of the behavioral expectations as students transition into the classroom helps students be more aware of those expected behaviors and so able to regulate their own actions. Precorrection is a more effective approach than reactively correcting students when they exhibit problem behavior. Another aspect of precorrection can be taking a moment with a student you struggled with the day before to specifically remind them both of the classroom expectations and that you're looking forward to them having a good day.

The other component is making sure you set up an entry task that students can get straight to work on in the classroom while you are still out in the hall greeting other students. Positive greetings at the door are not helpful if you connect with each student only to find your class in disarray when you finally walk into the room with the last student. An effective entry task makes it clear what students are expected to do when they enter the class. It's typically something on the board, or projected, that they should get to work on. For younger students, it might be a routine to ensure they put belongings in the right place, gather materials they'll need to get to work when class starts, and so on.

A final important strategy that's related to positive greetings at the door is the use of positive farewells. This can be especially valuable when targeted at specific students you might be making an extra effort to connect with and show you care about. And keep in mind that simply wishing students a good rest of their day can be important, regardless of how they behaved and performed in class. Would you wish your own family members farewell to continue to let them know you care even if you had a misunderstanding or negative interaction? Positive farewells are a great and simple way to show unconditional positive regard.

Establish Strategy 4: Two-by-Ten

Sometimes it can be challenging to find an extended chunk of time to connect with students. One simple Establish strategy is called two-by-ten. Two-by-ten is fairly straightforward but requires some commitment and consistency. The basic approach is to purposefully spend two minutes each day for ten days in a row engaging in conversation with identified students. Make the conversations about getting to know students as people to show that you care about who they are and not just how they perform on tasks and assignments in class. This strategy is typically used with one or two students at a time. Two-by-ten is a simple and focused way to show students that you're invested in connecting with them as a person and getting to know them. The conversational strategies and topics from banking time can all be used for two-by-ten.

Establish Strategy 5: Indirect Compliments Through Other Adults

Directly delivering compliments to a student can sometimes backfire if they don't have a sense of trust and connection with the person doing the complimenting, because the student may feel like the compliment is inauthentic or a backhanded insult. For example, a student whose teacher compliments them for doing well on an assignment could potentially think it means the teacher didn't expect them to do so well—communicating low expectations rather than praise. A more powerful way of complimenting students for things they said, did, or achieved, particularly when you haven't established a relationship with them, is by relaying the compliment through other adults in the student's life. Students are more likely to experience this indirect compliment as genuine. There are multiple other adults who compliments can be indirectly channeled through to show the student you're paying attention to what they say, do, and achieve. Examples include parents or caregivers, an administrator, school counselor, other teacher, or coach or club leader. To use this Establish strategy, find a positive thing you appreciate about a student and tell another adult. You can ask them to tell the student the positive thing they heard about them if necessary.

Maintain Strategies

Relationships don't magically sustain themselves over time just because we've established a good connection. Whether friendships, romantic partnerships, or connections with colleagues and students—all relationships require ongoing, consistent positive interactions to keep them strong and vital.

Maintain Strategy 1: Five-to-One

The primary strategy for *maintaining* healthy, secure relationships with students is to strive for a ratio of five positive interactions for every one negative interaction. Teachers interact with students throughout the day, and when the ratio is skewed toward more negative interactions, relationships weaken. A five-to-one ratio builds and maintains positive connections. To learn more about the research behind the five-to-one ratio, check out the work by John Gottman, one of the foremost experts in relationships (https://www.gottman.com).

This ratio has been shown to be important to preserving relationships in research across multiple arenas. The first research on five-to-one looked at marriages and found that successful marriages that lasted typically had roughly the five-to-one ratio of positive to negative interactions (Gottman, Coan, Carrere, & Swanson, 1998). On the other hand, struggling marriages that ended up breaking apart more often showed ratios closer to one positive to roughly one and a half negative (Gottman & Levenson, 2000). Research on business teams came out similarly. High-performing teams were typically found to fall slightly above the five-to-one ratio while medium-performance teams were closer to two-to-one and low-performance teams were characterized by almost three negative interactions for every one positive (Cunningham & Geller, 2008; Schultz, Milner, Hanson, & Winter, 2011). Research in education has also shown that the five-to-one ratio creates more positive relationships and fewer behavior problems (Cook et al., 2017). However, teachers with weak relationships with students and higher levels of behavior problems were found to engage in *ten* negative interactions for every positive.

In some ways, we can think about positive versus negative interactions a bit like the deposits and withdrawals of banking time. Doling out reprimands or corrections, ignoring bids for attention, imposing punitive discipline, and even rigidly pushing students to focus and be productive can all be experienced as negatives or withdrawals by students. But how on earth does a busy teacher match every correction and reminder to get to work with *five* positive interactions? It's important to make deposits and push on the positive side of the scale through engaging in friendly conversations, offering praise, and asking about weekend activities and new puppies or sports events. But realistically no one can accomplish five of those to match every demand they make of students. The key is to remember that anything students experience as positive counts.

That means smiles, nods, behavior-specific praise, winks, laughter, whole-class compliments, high fives in passing, surprise acts of fun, and any other quick and easy little way to shoot some positivity toward students all fall on the positive side of the scale and can balance out the inevitable negatives. Remember—the goal here is for students to have a positive experience in the classroom and of their teacher, not for every student to get showered in individualized in-depth praise and attention nonstop.

While five-to-one is the key strategy for maintaining positive relationships with all students, it's also important to keep in mind that some students may need it more than others. And, of course, it's also true that some students inevitably receive more negative interactions just based on their behavior in class. Teachers need to be aware of that and make the effort to balance that out with positives if they want to maintain positive relationships with those students. Given that positive relationships reduce disruptive behavior and increase engagement, the extra effort is likely to pay off in a smoother-running classroom, more focused instruction time, and increased student productivity, in addition to all the other benefits of positive relationships.

Keeping track of your ratio of positive to negative interactions with all your students is obviously unrealistic. But there are a few manageable ways to check in on how you're doing. One is to pick a couple of students and keep track of how many of your interactions fall onto which side of the balance. You can keep a running tally in your head, but it might be more accurate and feasible if you have a simple way to keep track. A small tally sheet you carry with you and periodically update is one idea. Teachers have even done things like move popsicle sticks or other items from one pocket to another as a way to see how things add up. Another great way to get actual data and a realistic idea of how you're doing is to have a colleague drop in and simply observe you for a few minutes. It's not hard for someone who's *not* actively teaching to simply mark one side or the other of a balance sheet for a short amount of time. A final approach is to focus less on individual students and more on simply trying to count up and track your interactions with the whole class. The point, of course, is not to get perfect data so much as to simply pay attention to this important aspect of how students experience your classroom and your teaching.

Maintain Strategy 2: Wise Feedback

All students need to know that their teachers have high expectations for them and believe in their ability to grow and develop. Feedback is a natural opportunity to connect with students in a relational way. Without a foundation of high expectations and beliefs, students can easily experience feedback as criticism. The wise part of feedback is to skillfully front-load the feedback you provide about academics or behavior with a relational message that communicates high expectations, high beliefs in the student, and something unique you've observed about them that you appreciate. This practice involves the following five steps.

1. Tell the student about the purpose of the feedback to allay concerns.
2. Deliver a wise message that conveys high expectations and a belief in the student.
3. Communicate something unique and special about the student that you've noticed and appreciate about them.
4. Deliver the feedback to the student to improve behavior or performance.
5. Ask the student if they have any questions or suggestions or need any support.

Maintain Strategy 3: Check-Ins

This easy strategy involves intentionally finding small amounts of time to have short interactions with a student. Check-ins involve simply taking a moment to ask a student how they're doing. This is intended to go beyond how they're doing with classwork to focus on how things are going with them as a person. The goal is to let them know you're interested in them as a person, not just as a student in your class. Check-ins ideally are a chance to express interest in things the student might be involved with or participating in at school. They can even be a chance to chat for a moment about things happening in the student's life outside school, especially if you've used banking time to learn more about them.

Maintain Strategy 4: Responding to Problem Behavior With Empathy

One thing that can help or harm positive relationships once you've established them is how you approach situations that have more potential for negative interactions. In particular, the way you handle instances of problem behavior can have a big impact positively or negatively on your relationships with students. Something that can really help is to employ a key SEL skill: empathy. Ideally, we'd all like to respond to problem behaviors in a way that keeps the student in a calm and receptive state of mind, so that they can learn from the interaction. A great way to make that more likely is to begin with an empathy statement. An empathy statement is all about helping the student feel like you understand (or at least are trying to understand) their perspective and the motive and reason behind their behavior. And this is most effective if you can do it before you address their behaviors. An empathy statement should be delivered in a private, calm, nonthreatening, respectful manner.

Coming up with an empathy statement involves trying to put yourself in your student's shoes and trying to understand what might be underneath or behind their problem behavior. Here's the thing about empathy and perspective-taking, though—it's hard to know for sure what someone else is really experiencing. The good news is that you don't have to get it exactly right for this to count. Kind of like birthday presents, "it's the thought that counts." In other words, all it requires to do this well is show the student that you're interested in and trying to understand their perspective or experience, not that you *know* what they're going through. In the case of responding to problem behavior, you're trying to let them know that you want to understand the reason, motive, emotions, thoughts, or other circumstances that underlie their behavior. Or since they might not know what's driving the behavior, simply how they're feeling or what they're thinking.

There are a couple of simple ways to go about responding to a problem behavior with an empathy statement. The simplest is to just directly ask the student what's going on with them. It can be as easy as asking, "What's up?" Another approach is to do your best to make an educated guess about what's going on with them and then ask to see how on target you are. For example, "It looks like you're really frustrated with this mathematics problem—is that what's going on?"

The full strategy involves more than an empathy statement—that's just the opener that's intended to start the process off on the right foot. After the initial empathy statement, there are five more steps to fully responding to problem behavior with empathy. The full strategy is shown in figure 4.3.

Steps	Description and Examples
Step 1: Make an empathy statement.	Let them know you are trying to understand their experience. For example, "It looks like you're really frustrated with this mathematics problem, is that what's going on?"
Step 2: Label the behavior of concern.	Give them a factual description of what the problem is as you see it. For example, "What you're doing right now is using your phone and it shouldn't be out."
Step 3: Clearly tell them what the alternative behavior is you'd rather they do.	For example, "I'd like you to put your phone away and work on your assignment."
Step 4: Give them the rationale for what you want them to do instead of the problem behavior.	For example, "The reason I'm asking is that I want you to be able to get the assignment done and not have to take it home. Plus, having your phone out can be distracting to other students."
Step 5: Lay out a decisional dilemma for them.	This means outlining the choices they can choose between and the consequences associated with each one, then giving them "Think Time"—a little time and space to come up with a decision (for example, 1–2 minutes). For example, "The way I see it you have three choices. You can keep using your phone, which will result in you losing the privilege of keeping it on you in school. Another choice that you can make that I'm a big fan of is that you can put away your phone and get back to work, and I'll circle back to you to figure out what's bugging you about this assignment and try to make that go away. Or, you can put your phone away, take a brief break to get ready again to focus and do the assignment. I'll come back in a minute to check what choice you want to make. [After 1 minute] So, what choice do you want to make?"
Step 6: Give feedback to the student based on the choice they make.	If the student chooses to continue to exhibit the behavior of concern, follow through by providing additional feedback that you believe will correct the behavior (for example, an in-class disciplinary consequence, offer for the student to take some time away, and so on). If the student chooses the alternative desired behavior, then recognize, acknowledge, and congratulate them on making the good choice.

FIGURE 4.3: Responding to problem behavior with empathy.

*Visit **go.SolutionTree.com/SEL** for a free reproducible version of this figure.*

Maintain Strategy 5: Fun Activities

This strategy is just what it sounds like: engaging in fun activities with the student for the sake of fun and nothing else. It might be tricky to find opportunities or ideas for this strategy, but remember it does not have to be anything elaborate. The key is to come up with simple ideas for engaging with a student in a way that they will find enjoyable. This strategy communicates to a student that you like them and just like any relationship, sharing moments of fun helps keep the connection strong.

There are several different ways educators can integrate fun activities that maintain relationships with students. For example, finding opportunities to play games with students shows that you care about more than just academics. Also, educators can create first-then sequences in the schedule of classroom activities. This involves students first engaging in more challenging and difficult work to then earn access to something fun and preferred. Also, educators can do things like taking class outside or surprising students with something fun to create a fun environment for students.

Restore Strategies

All relationships can hit a rough spot now and then. We don't want everyday challenges like misunderstandings, conflicts, hurt feelings, or arguments to damage relationships we've spent time and energy to create. Even with diligent attention to maintaining relationships with students, we still sometimes have to put in a little work to restore those positive connections. And keep in mind that this is less about having to fix a seriously broken relationship and more about acting quickly to get things back on track or return a relationship to its previously healthy state. When you have used intentional, effective strategies to establish a connection and maintain that relationship over time, you're more likely to be able to work through difficulties with students and restore a healthy connection.

What are some warning signs that you might need to attend to the health of your relationship with a student—that some interaction may have done a little harm? One thing to watch for is changes in a student's behavior. Examples might include changes in how much they make eye contact with you (assuming they made eye contact with you before), if they start ignoring your instructions, argue, debate, or challenge you more than usual, meet your questions with shrugs and nonanswers, or appear more withdrawn in your presence. It's also important to pay attention to signals you might be getting from your own feelings, like if you find yourself getting more annoyed than usual by a student or having some difficulty liking or feeling positive toward a particular student. Sometimes you'll know there's been a negative interaction that means there's a need for some repair, such as engaging in an argument or disagreement, having to remove a student from class—especially if that results in suspension—recognizing that you unintentionally embarrassed a student, experiencing a misunderstanding where you can see that a student takes your constructive feedback personally, or getting negative feedback from a student about you, other teachers, or the school in general.

Once you recognize that something may have harmed your relationship with a student, it's time to engage in an effort at restoration. The Establish, Maintain, Restore model includes five communication strategies that are effective for restoring relationships when they hit a bump in the road. However, successfully repairing a relationship that has suffered some damage is ultimately about the human interaction between teacher and student. None of the Restore strategies will work unless they're delivered by a teacher who is calm, has a handle on their own emotions, and is able to show a student verbally and nonverbally that they are being sincere and genuine. In addition to helping you reconnect with a student, the Restore communication strategies are also an important opportunity to teach by example. Modeling is a powerful way to support student social-emotional development, so bring your best self to the effort so you can help students see how to stay calm in a challenging situation, pay attention to someone else's experience, and communicate in ways that build connection in the midst of difficulty.

The starting point in the Restore process, regardless of which of the five communication strategies you want to use, is to try to put yourself in the student's shoes. How do they perceive the situation or interaction that harmed the relationship? To what extent do they feel like they were treated fairly versus unfairly? Simply taking a moment to try to see the situation from their perspective helps set you up for success. And it also helps inform your choice of which Restore strategy to use. Part of an effective effort to get past a difficult interaction and restore a positive relationship is tailoring your approach to what you know about the student and thinking through which strategy is likely to be the best fit. Use figure 4.4 (page 108) to help you match the right strategy to your student.

Restore Strategy 1: Let Go of the Previous Interaction (Fresh Start)

As you can see from the table, this strategy is best suited to a student you think is likely to believe you aren't going to let go of some problem that happened, that

Restore Communication Strategy	Matching to Student
Let go of the previous interaction (fresh start)	Student who thinks the adult is going to hold a grudge and hold the previous interaction against them
Take ownership for part of the negative interaction or problem	Student who wants to know and hear that there are two sides to every negative interaction and that adults make mistakes, too
Make an empathy statement	Student who wants his or her perspective or feelings understood
Offer a statement of care	Student who thinks you may not want them in class or care for them after the interaction
Collaborate to solve the problem	Student who is strong willed and likes to have a say in identifying a solution

FIGURE 4.4: Matching the restore communication strategy to the student.

Visit *go.SolutionTree.com/SEL* for a free reproducible version of this figure.

you'll hold it against them. A lot of students have experienced this from adults, and it's a natural defensive attitude for many young people. With this strategy, you target that fear and let students know clearly that you won't hold the interaction against them and that you're willing to let it go and start over. Even though it may feel awkward, you can use this repeatedly (as long as you still mean it). Even for students with severe and repeated behavior problems, it will be meaningful for them to know that you won't hold a grudge and aren't going to keep bringing up recent behaviors. This strategy helps communicate to students that you see them as growing and learning, and that mistakes are a learning opportunity, not a sign of who they *really* are. In some ways, this strategy helps you communicate to students that you have a growth mindset about them and their behavior. It shows that you can separate the behavior from the person.

One great thing about this strategy is how quickly you can implement it. Basically, it just involves a short statement to communicate the *letting go* message. For example, "Hey, yesterday was rough, but I'd like to start over today," or "Hey, let's have a fresh start today," or "Yesterday is behind us. I'm thinking today is a do-over for both of us."

Restore Strategy 2: Take Ownership for Part of the Negative Interaction or Problem

This strategy lets a student know you don't think you handled a situation as well as you would have liked. A lot of students are used to adults (in or outside school) never admitting they were wrong or that there might be two sides to a negative interaction. And of course, this strategy works only if you're willing to give up needing to be the unerring, always-right authority figure. But admitting that you could've handled something a little better doesn't have to mean giving away all your power or authority. You can still give and enforce a disciplinary consequence if the student's behavior warrants it, even if you're taking some ownership for the problem. You're still the adult and teacher who is helping the student learn how to take responsibility for their behavior and use more socially acceptable behaviors to get their needs met. But taking ownership is a powerful way to model to students that we are all learning and growing and that adults often make mistakes in how they react to situations and can work to improve how they manage themselves and handle situations.

This strategy has power, especially with the right students, but don't set your expectations too high for how students will respond. For example, students may not spontaneously apologize in response to you taking ownership. They do not have the same level of maturity as adults (and this is not the best time to try to teach that maturity). Nevertheless, this strategy can work to help you and a student get past an interaction that otherwise might damage your relationship.

What does this strategy sound like in practice? Here are a few examples: "Hey, I was thinking about what I said yesterday, and I think I wasn't being fair to you because . . . I'm sorry and I'll try to do better next time." "I wasn't my best self yesterday. I wish I would have been more patient with you and found the time to hear your perspective." "I've told you I'm working on perspective-taking and I feel like I skipped over that when I responded to your request yesterday. I'm going to keep working on that." "When I reflected on what happened yesterday, I realized that I could have prevented things from getting so big by noticing that something wasn't working for you in class. Next time, I'll try to notice, or you can also feel free to let me know if something in class isn't working for you."

Restore Strategy 3: Make an Empathy Statement

Empathy is a core SEL skill that you can apply both to Maintain and Restore relationships with students. Sometimes students' behaviors can be perplexing. We can't always know what's going on with them, and using an empathy statement can be a way to open the door to a conversation about the reasons for their behavior. Some students respond especially well when someone makes the effort to try to understand what they're going through or how they experienced an interaction. Empathy statements are a way to model SEL skills that can help students calm down and become more emotionally aware. When a student feels that you care about and understand how they feel, this may help to restore their trust in you.

The basic message of an empathy statement is that you care about what's going on with a student. The key thing is not whether you accurately read what they're experiencing; it's that you're trying to understand. Given how hard it can be to figure out what some students are feeling or thinking, the best we can do typically is make our best guess and check with the student to see whether what we perceive is a good fit. But it can also be effective to say something simple like "Hey, it looks like you're having a rough day." Empathy statements communicate care, and that can be a simple way to patch up a difficulty. Empathy statements can be particularly powerful if you first jump into the student's shoes to try to understand their perspective and then jump back into your own shoes to imagine what it would be like if you were confronted with similar thoughts and feelings. For example, if the student was bored out of their mind, imagine how you feel when super bored in a long meeting. How likely might you be to engage in avoidance behaviors, such as talking to a peer, using your technology, or doing other work?

Restore Strategy 4: Offer a Statement of Care

Sometimes students will react strongly to a negative interaction, taking it personally and feeling like perhaps you don't care, don't like them, or don't even want them in your class any longer. An explicit statement of care speaks to these feelings. This strategy involves two parts: (1) separating the deed from the doer and (2) identifying personal redeeming qualities or characteristics about the student that you appreciate.

The "separating the deed from the doer" piece is about communicating that the student is more than their behavior. Have you ever lied before or acted rude to someone else? Would you want people to label you as a liar or a fundamentally rude person based on your behavior, or would you want them to try to understand *why* you lied or acted rudely and see you as having intrinsic worth and dignity as a person beyond those behaviors? After taking the first step and directly letting the student know that you still care about and appreciate them, be sure to drive the message home by highlighting some things you genuinely appreciate about them.

This strategy is straightforward if done in a genuine way with real care. Here are a couple of simple examples: "After our interaction yesterday, I want to make sure that you know that I still appreciate you as a person. I value your energy, humor, and the life you bring to class." Or "I wanted to let you know that I still care for you and want you in class. Your behavior yesterday is one thing which I think we can work together to figure out. What I think is cool about you is that you are a natural leader and others look up to you."

Restore Strategy 5: Collaborate to Solve the Problem

The collaborative problem-solving strategy takes a little time and effort on the teacher's part, but it can pay dividends for students who like to have a voice and a say in the matter. Some students react against constantly feeling like adults have all the power and make all the decisions. This can be especially true (and developmentally natural) with adolescents. For these students, having a voice in the conversation and playing a part in figuring out a solution to a problem feels great and goes a long way toward repairing a relationship rift. And collaborative problem solving is a great way to diffuse and avoid a power struggle, saving you stress and annoyance while paving the way to a successful resolution. This strategy by itself can be an effective approach for responding to students with challenging behavior (Pollastri, Epstein, Heath, & Ablon, 2013).

The collaborative problem-solving strategy (shown in figure 4.5, page 112) requires a little planning. You'll need to find an opportunity where you'll have enough time to do the strategy justice based on how challenging you think the process will be for a given student and situation. With some students, there are minor problems that occur regularly and wear away at your relationship over time. This strategy can be an effective alternative to trying to constantly address those challenges each time they pop up by finding the time to address an ongoing issue collaboratively with the student.

GET OUT OF RELATIONSHIP RUTS

Of course, in the real world, relationships are often complicated. You may find yourself consistently in the Restore stage with some students where simply using one of these strategies doesn't solve the problem, or the difficulties keep recurring. To help you and your student get out of a rut, try taking a step back to get more perspective on the situation. It can be helpful to get more information on your student and your relationship with them, and this can help you identify which of the strategies to try moving forward.

First, take a moment to reflect on the current state of the strained relationship you have with the student and what might be making things difficult. Then, to be sure you're in the right frame of mind for constructive thinking, intentionally

Steps	Notes and Examples
Step 1: Engage the student in the process through empathy.	Remember part of the goal is side-stepping a power struggle, and a great way to disarm a potentially conflict-prone student is to start the conversation by letting them know you're thinking about and care about what they're experiencing. An empathy statement is a great way to do that. For example, "You're not doing much of the work in class. I'm sensing you're finding that the work is boring. Is that true? What's up?"
Step 2: Give them your side of the story.	Ask yourself what it is you're concerned about and express that to the student. For example, "I want students to do the work so they can learn and get a passing grade in my class. I like to feel like I've got things handled, and it's hard for me to feel that way when students aren't doing what I'm asking them to do." Again, this strategy is for a student prone to power struggles, so head them off at this point with statements like "I'm not saying you have to . . ." or "Nobody can make you—if you don't want to," and "It's up to you whether . . . ."
Step 3: Invite them to come up with some possible solutions.	Some possible comments are, "Do you have any ideas of how to make class and the work more engaging for you?" or "What other ideas do you have?" You can also share your own ideas with statements like, "Here are some ideas I have . . ." or "I have some ideas that I wanted to share with you to see if you think any of them would work."
Step 4: Agree on and try a solution.	Agree on a solution or idea, try it, and see how it goes—for example, "OK, so we'll work together. I'll do X and you'll do Y. Anything else you need from me to make class work better?"

FIGURE 4.5: Collaborative problem-solving strategy.

*Visit **go.SolutionTree.com/SEL** for a free reproducible version of this figure.*

identify some positive things about the student, things you like or appreciate about them. Next, work to get ahead of the situation a bit by thinking of a future situation where you're likely to encounter some challenge with the student, what you think they'll say or do and how you'd like to react, perhaps even which Restore strategy you think you'll try.

As teachers, we must be realistic about the fact that when there's an ongoing problem with a student, the teacher is one of the two people involved. It can be helpful to double-check yourself. What is your ratio of positive to negative interactions with that student? You might try tracking for a few days or a week to see if you're unintentionally causing problems with too many negatives. Also, we don't react the same to all students, and it's a simple fact that sometimes our unconscious biases play a role in how things go. To counter this possible problem, try to get some objective data on how you're interacting with students you are having more problems with, whether doing your own tracking or by having a peer do a little observation. Sometimes it helps to check our beliefs, perceptions, and feelings about a student and how we're handling them against the facts. Searching for and finding positive, redeeming qualities about the student can be a helpful way of getting out of a rut and changing your perspective and feelings about the student.

Student–Teacher Relationships and Equity

We've discussed the many ways in which having a positive relationship with adults at school benefits students. Positive student–teacher relationships are valuable assets that too often are not distributed equally to all students. For example, roughly 80 percent of teachers in our public schools are white, but over half of students are not (Institute of Education Sciences, 2020). We know from research studies that students of color are less likely to have positive relationships with their teachers than white students, and this difference can translate into less engagement in the classroom and widen gaps in academic performance between white students and students of color (LaSalle et al., 2020). What other characteristics of students affect the likelihood that they'll receive this critical form of support for their social and emotional development and academic achievement? Behavior? Family income? Academic ability? Disability? Gender? Surely it's a rare teacher who discriminates against students intentionally. But we also know now that unconscious bias is widespread, and realistically it can take more intentional effort to build a positive relationship with students you don't naturally connect with. So how can we as teachers check ourselves to pay more careful attention to how well we are connecting with *all* the students we serve?

A simple and effective approach is to use a class roster to identify which students from a class need more relational focus. In this process, you simply go through a list of students one at a time and mark each student with an E, M, or R depending on where you are in the relationship process with them. Have you established a relationship that gives them a sense of trust, connection, and belonging? If so, are you maintaining it? Is your relationship with that student in need of restoring because of a negative interaction? The aim is to focus on the students in the unfavorable relationship states, which are E and R. The goal over time is to move all students into the M state, which means that you have established and are working to maintain healthy, secure relationships with all students.

While teacher reflections on their relationships with students are important and valuable, we can't always know how things look from the student side of the equation. The Student-Teacher Relationship Questionnaire is an easy way to see whether how you perceive your relationship with your students reflects their experience (visit https://t.ly/6iiY1).

Conclusion

Children and youth thrive through positive relationships. For many students, school can be a haven from a difficult world if they are able to feel the gift of positive connections with peers and adults. But the quality of their relationships at school are important for all students. This ingredient is a classic illustration of how factors beyond pedagogy can powerfully affect not only student well-being and development but also behavior and even learning. Positive relationships support all the goals of education.

Relationships are a subjective experience that can be hard to assess from the outside. We cannot rely on students to proactively tell us when they don't feel connected to peers or adults at school. Positive relationships cannot be taken for granted. They are something schools should actively focus on, assess, and work to improve. There are many concrete strategies educators can use to strengthen their connections with students. Given the powerful impact positive relationships have for students as well as classroom and school climate, schools would be well served by working to ensure educators have access to training and resources on ways to cultivate, maintain, and, when needed, restore positive relationships with students.

Next Steps

What are the important next steps you want to take to maintain or improve the implementation of practices that cultivate positive relationships among students?

Note that your plan should take into account whether you are in a planning phase or already actively involved in implementation. If implementation has not begun, create a plan to establish motivational readiness to implement. If actively implementing, then create a plan to support continuous improvement to reach high-fidelity sustained implementation.

Reflecting on Positive Relationships

Consider the following questions as they relate to your school or district and positive relationships.

- How might you go about assessing your students' experiences of their relationships with peers and adults at school?

- How might your school or district leadership communicate to educators that working to create and support positive relationships with students is a priority?

- What practices is your school currently implementing to establish positive student–teacher and peer-to-peer relationships in your school?

- What plans do you have or can you develop to provide educators with support and assistance around practices they can use to focus on and improve their relationships with students?

- If your school has not yet identified a core set of practices to implement, how can you work toward selecting practices that specifically target cultivating positive relationships that lead to belonging and connection?

- If your school has already identified a core set of practices, then reflect on whether these practices are being implemented with fidelity and adequately reaching all students in the school. Where is there room for continuous improvement?

Planning for Positive Relationships

Use the following chart to consider practices to establish, maintain, and restore positive student–teacher relationships. In the space provided, note necessary steps involved in completing each goal as well as key dates to remember aligned with implementation.

Implementation Goal	Necessary Steps	Key Dates
Establish relationships with students who need them the most.		
Maintain relationships through five-to-one positive-to-negative interactions.		
Restore connections with students through skillful communication to repair relationships after a setback.		

The Recipe for Student Well-Being © 2024 Solution Tree Press • SolutionTree.com
Visit **go.SolutionTree.com/SEL** to download this free reproducible.

Notes													
Restore Phase	☐	☐	☐	☐	☐	☐	☐	☐	☐	☐	☐	☐	☐
Maintain Phase	☐	☐	☐	☐	☐	☐	☐	☐	☐	☐	☐	☐	☐
Establish Phase	☐	☐	☐	☐	☐	☐	☐	☐	☐	☐	☐	☐	☐
Student Initials													

The Recipe for Student Well-Being © 2024 Solution Tree Press • SolutionTree.com
Visit **go.SolutionTree.com/SEL** to download this free reproducible.

Student Initials	Establish Phase	Maintain Phase	Restore Phase	Notes
	☐	☐	☐	
	☐	☐	☐	
	☐	☐	☐	
	☐	☐	☐	
	☐	☐	☐	
	☐	☐	☐	
	☐	☐	☐	
	☐	☐	☐	
	☐	☐	☐	
	☐	☐	☐	
	☐	☐	☐	
	☐	☐	☐	
	☐	☐	☐	

The Recipe for Student Well-Being © 2024 Solution Tree Press • SolutionTree.com
Visit **go.SolutionTree.com/SEL** to download this free reproducible.

Restoring Positive Relationships

Teachers need protected time to reflect on their relationships with students and create an action plan for how they will intentionally establish or restore relationships with certain students. Once teachers have identified a subset of students in need of intentional relationship practices from them, they can then use the relationship action plan to formulate how they will implement specific practices to establish or restore relationships with these students.

STEP 1: THE ESTABLISH-MAINTAIN-RESTORE PHASES

Consider the Establish-Maintain-Restore phases of the student–teacher relationship. This framework can help you identify where you are in your relationship with a student and what action to take next.

- **Establish (E):** the initial phase of a relationship when mutual trust, understanding, and connection have not yet been cultivated.
- **Maintain (M):** the phase of a relationship when mutual trust, understanding, and connection are present and there is a need to maintain the relationship through ongoing positive interactions.
- **Restore (R):** the phase of a relationship where a negative interaction has occurred and potentially harmed the relationship, resulting in the need to restore the relationship.

Pause and reflect on your relationship with each student in your class. The ultimate goal, over time, is to move to the Maintain phase with each student so that each student in your class feels a sense of trust, understanding, and connection with you.

Use the following chart to write each student's initials, note which phase of the relationship you're in with that student, and take notes about action steps for developing the relationship. Secondary teachers with multiple classes typically choose one class to start with. To complete this activity as accurately as possible requires some perspective taking by putting yourself in each student's shoes and assessing whether you believe the student feels a sense of trust, feels like you understand them, and feels connected to your class. Students who you mark as being in Establish or Restore are in an unfavorable relationship phase. Each week, you will identify up to three students in the Establish or Restore phases who you will focus on over the course of the next week. Complete student-specific plans for establishing or restoring your relationship with each of the students you identify to focus on over the course of the next week.

STEP 2: EQUITY REFLECTION

The purpose of this part of the reflection is to look for possible inequities in your relationships with students. This can be challenging, but the point is to raise awareness of potential inequities so you can take aligned action. This is not meant to make you feel bad. Through increased awareness, you can move toward creating greater equity for students through intentional efforts to ensure each student has access to a positive relationship with you.

Look over the placement of your students in your relationship chart and then respond to each of the following questions.

1. In what way is race related to where you marked students in the three phases (E, M, and R)? Do you notice any patterns, or is race equally represented across each of the phases?

2. In what way is gender identity related to where you marked students in the three phases (E, M, and R)? Do you notice any patterns, or is gender equally represented across each of the phases?

3. Based on your best understanding of students' background, in what way is socioeconomic status related to where you marked students in the three phases (E, M, and R)? Do you notice any patterns, or is socioeconomic status equally represented across each phase?

4. Can you see any other patterns for which students are in the Establish, Maintain, or Restore phase?

Did you find any potential inequities in your relationship status with students in your chosen class? Consider using this information to inform which students you choose to focus on when developing student-specific game plans.

STEP 3: STUDENT-SPECIFIC RELATIONSHIP GAME PLAN

Focus on up to three students you identified in step 2 as being in the vulnerable relationship phases of Establish or Restore. To complete this step, identify the student, phase of the relationship, practices you want to implement, and how and when you will implement them.

Student 1

Name the student on whom you want to focus.	What relationship phase are you in with this student?	What strategies do you plan on using with this student?	How and when will you implement these strategies?

Student 2

Name the student on whom you want to focus.	What relationship phase are you in with this student?	What strategies do you plan on using with this student?	How and when will you implement these strategies?

Student 3

Name the student on whom you want to focus.	What relationship phase are you in with this student?	What strategies do you plan on using with this student?	How and when will you implement these strategies?

The Recipe for Student Well-Being © 2024 Solution Tree Press • SolutionTree.com
Visit **go.SolutionTree.com/SEL** to download this free reproducible.

CHAPTER 5
SEL CURRICULUM AND INSTRUCTION

Throughout this book, we have laid out the scientific evidence for delivering specific types of support to students to increase their success in school and in life. *Social-emotional learning* is a term that has been widely used to describe this process. The most common way schools directly support the development of the social and emotional competencies students need to thrive is by teaching those skills directly through SEL lessons. The best SEL curricula are designed to accomplish clearly stated goals, and the content of those programs is focused on teaching skills and knowledge shown by research to result in increased well-being, improved school behavior, and higher academic achievement.

Schools are most likely to choose a curriculum that meets their goals and fits with the culture of their school and community by carefully examining program content. Program developers should supply enough information to make it clear what their approach is, and what is and is not included in their SEL lessons.

A critical ingredient to the success of SEL instruction is buy-in. School staff need to believe the program is likely to be effective, easy to deliver, and in line with the school's values. Students need to see themselves in the lessons, experience program content as relevant to their needs and not out of sync with their school culture. And increasingly, the school's parents and community need to see the program as making a valuable contribution to the development and success of their children. Parents need to understand how an SEL program will contribute to their children's growth in ways that they support. Again, the primary aim of most SEL programs is to support students in gaining competencies that help them connect with others, and manage their emotions, behavior, and energy in ways that support academic achievement and success, equipping them to thrive in K–12 and beyond. The reality is that different SEL programs are likely to better fit different schools and communities, and determining that fit is critical to the successful adoption and implementation of an SEL program.

In this chapter, we detail what SEL curriculum and instruction entails, why educators should implement a research-based SEL program, and how educators can choose and best implement research-based SEL curricula and instruction.

What Is SEL Curriculum and Instruction?

While SEL is a fairly new term, societies throughout history have focused on what we today might call educating the whole child. For example, in China over 2,000 years ago, Confucius promoted an education system focused on what could be called moral education, with the primary goal of supporting the development of virtue (Huang, 2011). The ancient Greek philosopher Socrates, who some considered to be the father of education, also saw the promotion of virtue as a primary goal of education (Edmonson et al., 2009). In more modern times, an International Moral Education Congress held multiple meetings throughout Europe in the early twentieth century attended by delegates from at least eighteen different nations (Humanists UK, 2023).

In the United States, there is a long history of school-based programs focused on supporting the nonacademic development of students. This was primarily under the umbrella of "character education" in the earlier part of the twentieth century (Smith, 2013). During the 1980s and 1990s, most nonacademically focused interventions delivered in schools were designed to prevent youth substance use, violence, and delinquency—for example, the Drug Abuse Resistance Education (DARE) program delivered in elementary schools by police officers. Launched in 1983, the DARE program was in up to 75 percent of U.S. elementary schools at its peak. One thing that led to the steep drop in use of that program was solid research from psychologist Donald R. Lynam and colleagues (1999) that showed DARE simply did not work to reduce drug use.

Eventually, people involved in working with and serving youth pushed for moving away from a focus on youth problems and deficits toward more of an emphasis on supporting healthy development. In 1994, a multidisciplinary group of researchers, educators, practitioners, and child advocates with a collective focus on the importance of supporting the social and emotional development and well-being of children and youth came together. That collaboration formed CASEL, still the flagship SEL organization, and created the term *social-emotional learning*. CASEL's vision was for SEL to take place in and support the many goals of schools, as highlighted by its full name: the Collaborative for Academic, Social and Emotional Learning.

From the start, the field of SEL was informed by scientific research, including studies showing that a strong foundation of social-emotional competence was an important driver of school success (for example, Raver, 2002). Among the most significant early research in the SEL field was the 2011 meta-analysis that combined the findings from a wide range of evaluation studies of SEL (Durlak et al., 2011). This study, which combined studies that involved a total of 270,034 K–12 students, found that compared to students who did not receive SEL instruction, students who participated in SEL programs showed significantly improved social and emotional skills and attitudes, improved school behavior, and (perhaps most influential for the spread of SEL) an 11 percentile increase in academic achievement.

The popularity of SEL instruction in schools has grown exponentially in the 21st century, and there has been a big increase in the number and variety of programs, interventions, and even simply ideas available to schools that are branded as SEL. So what *is* and what *is not* effective SEL instruction? Let's take a closer look at the curricular component of comprehensive SEL instruction before exploring what characterizes proven, high-quality SEL programs—they're widely targeted, developmentally differentiated, engaging for students, culturally responsive, user friendly and easy to deliver, pedagogically sound, supportive of generalization, and, of course, backed by research.

BASED ON CURRICULUM, NOT INFUSION

Implementing a carefully developed SEL curriculum is the most common and most proven approach to SEL instruction. An alternative approach is for educators to infuse SEL instruction into their everyday practice rather than deliver prepared SEL lessons. Our view is that this infusion method is not realistic for the majority of educators. The burden on educators with this approach is high. It requires teachers to learn or figure out effective ways to teach students social and emotional skills on the fly in addition to managing everything else happening in a busy classroom. The reality is that few teacher training programs include detailed education in SEL or effective approaches for supporting healthy social and emotional development, and figuring out how to competently weave SEL content into everyday instruction is not a simple challenge. Effective training on do-it-yourself SEL is not widely available.

Although there is scant, if any, research support for it, this approach could work for schools staffed by educators with solid knowledge of effective approaches for delivering SEL and child and youth developmental supports, and adequate time to plan and practice how to infuse SEL into their teaching throughout the school day. For everyone else, we recommend that SEL instruction be guided by a well-designed and developed SEL curriculum.

COMPREHENSIVE, NOT SINGLE TOPIC

As SEL has become more widely embraced in schools, the range of programs and products labeled SEL has expanded to include many interventions too narrowly targeted to warrant that label. While interventions or programs singularly focused on topics like mindfulness, gratitude, and goal setting might be helpful for students, they should not be considered effective approaches to SEL instruction. Supporting the development of social-emotional competence and well-being is a complex challenge that requires providing students with instruction across a wide range of subjects. For example, although it is only one approach to defining the scope of SEL, the CASEL (n.d.b) SEL Framework outlines five broad competencies that SEL programs should work to address: (1) self-awareness, (2) self-management, (3) social awareness, (4) relationship skills, and (5) responsible decision making. Simply addressing one of these topics is not going to advance SEL.

DEVELOPMENTALLY DIFFERENTIATED

In addition to covering a wide range of topics, high-quality SEL programs are designed with students' developmental needs in mind. This applies to both content and delivery. The roots of SEL were in programming for elementary school students. Over time, the field has evolved to include SEL for middle and high schools, but those efforts can sometimes fall into the trap of simply replicating the content and topics found in curricula for younger students (Yeager, 2017). SEL programming for students in the early grades is often focused on teaching basic skills for success in the classroom and school environment, such as listening, focusing attention, following instructions, identifying emotions, sharing, playing with others, and making friends. As students age, their developmental needs change. Social life becomes more complex, emotional challenges may be both more intense and nuanced, and complex problem-solving challenges are increasingly common. By middle and high school, students are likely to need more support with handling stress as well as understanding, preventing, and coping with mental health challenges. Issues such as identity, purpose, and values that are not as relevant for elementary students become more developmentally salient. While SEL at all ages builds life skills that will help students as they mature, secondary SEL programs should also focus on collaboration and teamwork competence to help prepare students for the modern world of work and community involvement.

ENGAGING FOR STUDENTS

To be effective at any age, SEL programs must capture students' interest and get them actively participating with one another and engaging with the curriculum. Lessons at all grades need to feel age appropriate, relevant to the needs and challenges students are facing, culturally responsive, and enjoyable. It doesn't matter how carefully research-based a program is if students don't like the lessons or don't feel like the content speaks to their needs.

Too many programs are guilty of creating lessons that are modeled on or similar to those for younger students, but with an attempt to make them look cooler (Yeager, 2017). By middle, and certainly high school, programs need to acknowledge the increasing need and ability for autonomy and productive collaboration among students. SEL programs for secondary students should involve a lot of student voice and input; support collaborative work in pairs and groups; and provide students with many different options for engaging with and processing lesson content, including talking, writing, drawing, and other creative modalities. Group projects that extend across multiple lessons can create opportunities for students to engage more deeply with program content and connect it with their own lives while at the same time learning and practicing important group work skills.

CULTURALLY RESPONSIVE

One of the challenges facing SEL curricula is that successful programs will be implemented in schools with diverse populations across widely varying communities and neighborhoods. No program can perfectly match the demographics, culture, and background of all the students in any school, much less every school. Thoughtfully designed and developed programs use a wide variety of images, examples, and scenarios so that more students can see themselves or their communities in the program and hopefully find the content and delivery relevant to them. Students often have strongly positive reactions to content where they can see people like themselves represented, especially students for whom that is not the norm.

Opportunities for student voice can be critically important to this topic. Some programs take the approach of providing students with opportunities to incorporate their own examples, stories, or cultural norms into lesson activities, particularly with older students, who may be especially sensitive to lesson content that doesn't fit with their experience. This intentional work to allow lessons to be informed and impacted by student voice can go a long way toward making SEL programming better fit the specific demographics, culture, and everyday reality of a wide variety of students.

USER FRIENDLY AND EASY TO DELIVER

One of the main things that helps make programs more engaging for students is enthusiastic delivery by adults. Programs cannot be effective and engaging if they are onerous to prepare for, confusing to navigate, uninteresting to students, and difficult to deliver smoothly. Students can tell when their teachers are just going through the motions and are not invested or bought into the program. In addition, curricula that are too difficult to teach or require too much preparation time are less likely to be fully delivered or sustained over time. Teacher usability is something educators should look at carefully when considering SEL curricula.

SEL programs are increasingly being delivered digitally, often through the teacher projecting content for the class to work through. But technology problems can sideline even the best lessons, and no teacher wants to be in front of their class struggling to navigate through a poorly designed digital interface.

Educators should consider the following questions as they relate to other usability factors.

- What pedagogical methods are used in a program? Do lessons support student collaboration and engagement, or are teachers likely to be stuck delivering teacher-centric content? Will lessons give students a sense of ownership or cause students to tune out?
- How easy is it for teachers to fully deliver lessons in the time they have? Can the lessons be taught in the amount of time promised,

or will teachers need to rush to get through content or have to cut lessons short?

- How much preparation time is required to effectively deliver lessons? How much protected time, if any, do staff at your school have to prepare for SEL lessons? How well do those two things match up for different programs?

- What kind of training or professional development do program providers offer? At what cost in money and staff time? Offering too little training or expecting too much professional development time from schools are both problematic. Again, the right match for a given school or district is key. How much training does a program recommend to ensure people can competently deliver lessons, and does that match what your school or school system has available?

PEDAGOGICALLY SOUND

Similar to academics, the effectiveness of *what* is taught in SEL programs is strongly dependent on *how* it is taught, and teachers must carefully choose from a number of more and less effective pedagogical strategies. In their research, Joseph A. Durlak, Roger P. Weissberg, and Molly Pachan (2010) identify four elements commonly found in effective SEL programs, captured by the acronym SAFE: (1) sequenced, (2) active, (3) focused, and (4) explicit.

1. **Sequenced:** Improving social and emotional skills is not easy and can rarely be accomplished in one lesson. Sequenced means lessons need to be connected across the scope rather than focus in isolation on one topic after another. Lessons in solid SEL programs typically reinforce and build on each other as the curriculum unfolds across a year as well as grade levels.

2. **Active:** SEL lessons need to be designed so that students are intellectually, emotionally, and even physically engaged with the lessons. How that looks varies widely across grades and topics, but it could include methods such as engaging in whole-class, small-group, and pair discussions; writing and drawing; creating and acting out skits; singing and dancing; and applying lesson content in a variety of ways.

3. **Focused:** Ineffective programs spend a lot of time just "talking about" SEL topics, or may not even be directly focused on SEL. Lessons should be explicitly focused on supporting the development of personal and social skills.

4. **Explicit:** In fact, the final ingredient in this model emphasizes that lessons should explicitly be designed to target specific social and emotional skills. The goals of lessons should be clearly focused on concrete SEL goals.

SEL lessons can be effective only when they build on each other, actively engage students, and focus explicitly on teaching specific social and emotional skills, knowledge, and attitudes shown to benefit student social-emotional competence.

SUPPORTIVE OF GENERALIZATION

Delivering high-quality, developmentally appropriate, and engaging lessons is just the first step in SEL instruction. Another key component is helping students to regularly practice applying the SEL skills they're learning. SEL instruction is about helping students become socially and emotionally *competent*. Competence means students become proficient at applying what they have learned in SEL lessons to a wide variety of challenging situations they encounter in life—*generalizing* their new skills beyond the classroom lesson to real-life challenges and opportunities. SEL is typically taught once a week, and most SEL programs cover a lot of ground, so any given topic may get addressed in only a few lessons in a school year. If we deliver high-quality SEL lessons but don't support students in practicing, improving, and applying the skills they learn, then they are not going to develop the competence they need to effectively use what we teach them.

Unfortunately, many SEL programs fall short on providing teachers with enough user-friendly tools and practices for supporting students' skill development and generalization. Students rarely remember mathematics concepts that they hear about only once and never practice or revisit, so why would we expect them to perfect SEL skills after one or a couple of lessons? In some ways, SEL skills can be more complex to master than many academic skills because students have to learn to adapt them on the fly in all different kinds of often challenging situations. We'll discuss ways teachers can support mastery and generalization of skills more in the How section (page 134).

BACKED BY RESEARCH

We can think of SEL programs from a research-support standpoint as falling into one of three categories: (1) practice based, (2) research based, or (3) evidence based. There are a great many SEL offerings available to schools that are created based on people's practice experience, good ideas, and best intentions. It's hard to say whether these programs will produce positive outcomes for students, because they are not based on any scientific research and have not been evaluated for effectiveness. Programs created with little to no basis in research might work, and they might not—there is no way to tell, short of carrying out a research study. So keep in mind that practice-based SEL programs are at best a gamble.

SEL programs that are research based are typically grounded in a logic model or theory of change that lays out clear long-term outcomes, the short-term goals research says will lead to them, and the content and methods for delivery shown by research as most likely to be effective. Developers should have solid research support for the links between program ingredients and the short-, middle- and long-term outcomes they are targeting. Usually programs have multiple student outcomes that they hope to achieve through helping students develop a variety of social and emotional competencies.

Evidence-based programs are those that have been tested in a rigorous scientific evaluation study and shown to result in positive outcomes for students. The most powerful studies are randomized controlled trials (RCTs), sometimes referred to as the gold standard in program evaluation. These studies randomly assign groups of students to either receive the program or serve as a control group. The benefit of randomly assigning students—similar to flipping a coin—is that all students have an equal chance of being in the intervention or control group. Essentially, it's a way to create treatment and control groups that are as similar as possible, so other things besides the program are less likely to affect the study results. Randomization gives us much more confidence that any positive outcomes the study finds were caused by the program instead of happening by chance or coincidence due to factors like differing student demographics, new school initiatives, or other changes that happened around the same time as the SEL implementation. We can have the greatest confidence that programs with this level of research backing will effectively support student social-emotional competence and positive school and life outcomes.

However, substantial barriers make it difficult to carry out rigorous RCT-type evaluations of programs. Often the biggest is cost. To be scientifically rigorous, the evaluation of a program designed for implementation across a whole school (which includes most SEL programs) requires delivering the program to and collecting data from students in many schools. One carefully designed SEL program evaluation study two of the authors were part of involved more than sixty schools. A study like that costs millions of dollars and takes multiple years, putting it out of reach of programs that are not university based and grant funded or created by organizations that can afford to fund a study of that magnitude. So although results from an RCT are often used to choose programs to recommend, research-based programs that are carefully designed and positively evaluated with less rigorous study designs can still have merit. We recommend that schools look at programs that at least meet the standard of being research based, with a clearly explained logic model or theory of change that includes research-based explanations of how the content of the program should create the outcomes it is targeting.

Why Should Schools Implement a Research-Based Curriculum or Program?

Earlier in the book, we discussed research showing the positive effects of SEL programs. Let's quickly revisit what was learned from two of the largest and best studies. The Durlak and colleagues study published in 2011 showed social and emotional skills, attitudes, and behaviors improved for students who received SEL instruction, and their academic achievement increased by 11 percent compared to students who did not. Research also shows that positive effects of SEL programs last over time. A large-scale study of numerous programs found that more than three years after they received SEL instruction, students continued to academically outperform (by 13.5 percent) students who had not received SEL instruction (Taylor et al., 2017). So one of the main reasons we recommend delivering a research-based, high-quality SEL program is that it is the most likely way to ensure your SEL efforts pay off for your students. Such a program allows for both schoolwide delivery and effective implementation—the keys to ensuring success for *all* students.

SCHOOLWIDE DELIVERY

Using an SEL curriculum makes schoolwide delivery significantly easier. The benefits of delivering SEL schoolwide go beyond simply ensuring that all students get exposed to high-quality instruction. A good SEL program can also make it easier for educators to support the development of student social-emotional competence outside the lessons. Again, direct instruction is only the first step. To really master and learn to skillfully use social and emotional skills, students need reminders to practice and to get feedback when they do. One crucial way high-quality SEL programs do this is by providing both students and educators in the building with *common language* to refer to skills taught in the lessons.

Many of the skills SEL programs teach can help students succeed socially, emotionally, behaviorally, and academically at school. When educators know the skills, tools, methods, and so forth that their students have learned about, it makes it easier for them to support students in getting better at using them when they need them throughout the day and throughout the school. Ideally, students apply their SEL competencies to handle interpersonal challenges outside the classroom at recess, lunch, or in the hallways. Schoolwide delivery of an SEL program makes it possible for educators to cue students to apply skills using terms they know all students understand. It makes it easier for *everyone* in the school to work together to support student growth and success: classroom teachers, counselors, specialists, playground and office staff, and administrators.

Having an SEL program all students receive also makes it easier for educators to explain and take advantage of the potential synergy between the SEL curriculum and other initiatives. For example, research shows positive outcomes for both SEL and positive behavior interventions and supports (PBIS) done alone. But it also shows schools can improve student outcomes beyond the effects of either approach done by itself if they implement both SEL and PBIS at the same time, particularly if they make explicit connections between the two (Cook et al., 2015). PBIS and SEL can be thought of a bit like chocolate and peanut butter—both are good, but they're even better together. PBIS facilitates spelling out clear expectations for student behavior throughout the school (which schools can of course do without PBIS). But many students need SEL instruction to develop the personal and social skills to meet those expectations, especially in the face of challenging situations that involve strong emotions or peer conflicts. Likewise, SEL supports positive student social and emotional development; clear expectations and some amount of positive recognition can help motivate students to put their skills into action.

EFFECTIVE IMPLEMENTATION

Finally, as we discussed earlier, an important reason to choose a high-quality SEL program is that carefully designed and developed programs are not only more effective but also typically easier to deliver. A high-quality SEL program typically undergoes extensive pilot testing to ensure that educators can easily navigate through the materials, that lessons can be finished in the time allotted, and that students find the material and activities engaging, fun, and relevant. As discussed earlier, solid SEL programs should help make it easier for educators to support student social-emotional competence throughout the school and school day. And high-quality SEL programs come with the support educators need, ideally delivered in flexible ways that can meet varied school needs and resources. Video or other asynchronous training and support for educators, readily available implementation and extension ideas, content to help administrators clearly show their support for the program, simple summaries of lessons teachers can quickly review to prep for delivery, and carefully developed culturally relevant family materials all support effective implementation.

Consider the benefits of choosing a research-based SEL curriculum:

- Helps ensure positive outcomes (if implemented as designed)
- Reduces the burden on educators to implement SEL
- Has ready-made, on-demand training materials

How Can Schools Choose an SEL Program?

When choosing a schoolwide SEL program, educators can discover the one that best fits their needs by examining those critical factors discussed earlier in this chapter—namely, school resources, as well as evidence of a given program's effectiveness, developmental and cultural appropriateness, student engagement, and support for generalization. The following sections provide guidance for how to consider these factors in vetting SEL programs.

SCHOOL RESOURCES

When considering SEL programs to adopt, it can be helpful to look at them through a school or district resources lens. The effort and resources that it takes to successfully (and sustainably) implement a program must match the capacity of your school or district.

Examine factors like where lessons could fit in your school's schedule and how much time educators have available to deliver them, whether you can manage the time and potential cost of the training a program requires, and whether the initial and ongoing cost of a program fits your available resources. It is also important to consider how any given SEL program matches the priorities of your school or district and community.

A key question SEL teams need to ask is how much capacity there is for an SEL program given other initiatives and programs. A common challenge for schools is new initiatives getting added each year without others being taken away. Over time, this can cause a problematic initiative overload, which means a program will not be sustainably implemented regardless of initial enthusiasm and support. It's worth taking the time to do an audit of all the initiatives a school or district is pursuing to ensure that there is capacity among staff to put in the time and energy to embrace and fully deliver and support an SEL program.

When vetting an SEL program, consider the following.

- **Financial cost (both initial and ongoing):** There are potentially multiple costs to adopting an SEL program: purchasing lessons, paying for in-person training, and ongoing professional development support. Be sure to look at the big picture and assess possible costs beyond simply purchasing the lessons provided by a program. Most programs are delivered digitally and allow for a renewal process. One benefit a digital format affords is you can try a program and change your mind if lessons don't seem to be a fit or fail to meet your needs.

- **Training and professional development time required:** For many schools, cost is only one consideration when it comes to the training and PD required for effective program implementation. Look carefully at the amount of training a program recommends up front before implementation as well as possible ongoing professional development during the school year. Many programs recommend but do not require training for staff who will implement lessons. While skipping training can make sense given scarce time availability for staff, talk to program providers and try to assess how likely you are to be successful adopting a new SEL program without setting aside time for training. Programs differ widely in the extent to which lessons have been designed and tested for their ease of implementation. The reality is that significant training time is not realistic for many schools; lessons that can be delivered with minimal or no training or prep time may be the best fit in that case. Of course, that requires assessing how likely your staff are to competently deliver lessons without that support. Students can't benefit from lesson content they don't receive, so difficulties in delivering lessons can kill a program's impact.

- **Lesson preparation time:** This is a challenging topic. SEL lessons are different from academic curricula, and it's not always realistic to expect teachers to jump right into delivery without preparation time. On the other hand, many if not most teachers (especially at the secondary level) lack the time to properly prep for delivering each lesson. In many secondary schools, SEL lessons are delivered in classes such as Homeroom that teacher contracts specifically say should not require prep time. A critically important aspect of evaluating possible SEL curricula is understanding the extent to which lessons have been developed with sufficient attention to ease of delivery. Be sure that the time it takes for teachers to competently deliver the program you choose matches the preparation time your staff has available and are likely to put in.

- **Technology requirements:** SEL programs are increasingly being delivered electronically. That means teachers need internet access to work with the lessons and share them with students on their devices. It is worth checking whether, for example, your school has the bandwidth for multiple teachers to access content online at the same time—especially if your schedule means many teachers delivering at the same time.

- **Burden on staff:** This topic relates to the "initiative overload" issue discussed elsewhere. Be wary of your new SEL program being experienced by educators as yet one more thing piled onto an already overflowing plate. Regardless of how valuable SEL could be for your students, they will only benefit if the staff tasked with delivering and supporting a new SEL initiative have the time, energy, and capacity to competently deliver and support lessons. Ideally, the impact of SEL lessons results in easier-to-manage classrooms with students who are more on task for academic instruction, but this payoff typically comes down the road, requiring staff to put in time and effort up front before they see benefits.

- **Capacity of leadership:** SEL programs are like most things in education: more likely to succeed when school and district leadership make it a priority. An SEL initiative's success or failure is strongly influenced by how well it is championed by leadership.

Closely examine the fit between various SEL programs and your school to ensure there is alignment between what successful adoption and implementation really requires and what is sustainably possible in your setting.

EVIDENCE OF EFFECTIVENESS

While we wouldn't say schools should consider *only* programs backed up by positive results from a large-scale RCT evaluation, it's important to look at the research evidence behind any SEL program you're considering. Simply put, you have more reason to think your students will benefit from an SEL program if it has been shown to improve students' social-emotional competence and academic and life outcomes when tested under conditions you can largely replicate. Although randomized control studies are the gold standard, they're not the only research evidence that matters. Quasi-experimental and other studies showing positive effects are worth paying attention to, especially given that conducting an RCT evaluation is financially out of reach for many SEL program developers.

It's worth looking at where program evaluations were conducted and how much like your schools and students the study sample was. It's important to examine how well an SEL program aligns with your particular school, district, and community values, culture, and history. We've talked elsewhere about equity, and this is a place where the rubber meets the road on that essential objective. It's worth looking closely at program materials to see how the content, language, images, examples, and so forth do or do not fit with the culture and background of your students and the population of your community.

An SEL program lives or dies on how educators implement it. Program usability—that is, how easy it is for educators to deliver the program—is a critical program choice variable. SEL programs vary in how realistic their expectations are. Some programs shown to be effective are challenging enough to deliver that most schools can't fully implement them. Then again, it's possible for a program to fail to be substantive enough to be effective. Finding that balance between program rigor and staff time, energy, and commitment is important.

Student engagement is fundamentally important to the effectiveness and success of any SEL curriculum. Realistically, the best judges for this aspect of choosing an SEL program are the students themselves. Careful consideration of SEL programs should include student voice. Having a representative group of students weigh in on how engaging, appropriate, and appealing lessons are during the process of vetting SEL curricula can be a critical way to avoid adopting a program that looks promising to adults but fails to effectively connect with students. This can be especially important at the middle and high school levels, where students can be easily put off by content they feel is talking down to them, not speaking to their needs, or culturally inappropriate.

When vetting an SEL program, consider the following.

- **Research base:** Ask to see research support for both the program's overall effectiveness as well as the specific program ingredients. Why is specific content in the lessons? What are different program ingredients meant to accomplish and how well is that supported by research? Ideally, a program should have a logic model or theory of change that explains what the program's long-term goals are and details the research-based links that show how the specific topics and content covered will lead to those outcomes.

- **Cultural fit:** On the other hand, research findings are unlikely to tell you how any given program will fit with the population you serve and your school, district, or community values and culture. This is where an SEL team, ideally including students, is important. Given the increase in parent concerns over SEL program goals and content, consider including parent representatives in your selection process. Program providers should be able to give you enough access to content for you to assess cultural fit. Keep in mind that your SEL program needs to meet the diverse needs of your students, so work to ensure that programs are examined by a broadly representative mix of students and staff. SEL programs rely on student engagement to be effective. If students do not relate to the content (or even the images and examples used) they may not be engaged enough to benefit. This can be especially true for secondary students.

- **Usability:** Ensure lessons are not complicated and burdensome to deliver. If they require tech skills some teachers lack, if teachers need to put in significant amounts of preparation time to be ready to successfully deliver lessons, and if a program relies on implementers having skills and knowledge that are not universal among educators in the building, the result will be poor implementation, which we know damages program effectiveness.

- **Student engagement:** Does the content encourage student engagement? If students tune out, get bored, feel like lessons don't speak to their needs, are not comfortable with the activities and content, and (realistically) don't find the lessons at least somewhat fun, they won't engage enough with the content to benefit from the lessons. Again, work to involve a diverse group of students in your program vetting process to get diverse perspectives on how engaging and relevant program content will be.

DEVELOPMENTAL APPROPRIATENESS

As the history and roots of SEL are largely in curricula for elementary students, it may come as no surprise that preK–5 is still where the largest number of SEL programs are delivered. Developing SEL content for middle and high school students therefore presents unique challenges that some programs meet better than others. Pay attention to developmental issues in both *form* (how lessons look, what pedagogical methods are used, and what the experience of the lessons is for students and teachers aside from the actual content) and *content* (the skills, knowledge, attitudes, mindsets, and topics programs address).

Development appropriateness is critically important to meeting student needs. Early elementary SEL programs often teach basic skills like sharing, playing fairly, and making friends. By the teen years, student challenges can be more complex. Skills for coping with stress and supporting mental health and well-being become increasingly important topics for SEL programs to address in secondary schools. It's also more appropriate for SEL lessons for high school students, in particular, to focus on thinking about the future, planning, and learning to set and achieve goals. While empathy in elementary grades is often more emotion-focused (how is someone else feeling), it is developmentally appropriate by secondary grades for SEL lessons to focus on improving students' perspective-taking ability, including working to build skills and strategies for putting themselves in others' shoes, and learning and practicing how to gain a greater understanding of the experiences of other students, including those who are different from themselves. High school students are closer to the world of work, and we know that the workplace requires 21st century teamwork skills. A key role of SEL in the upper grades should be helping students develop competency in collaborating successfully with all different types of students.

When vetting an SEL program, consider the following.

- **Developmental differentiation in lesson form:** Ideally, lessons in elementary grades are teacher-led, perhaps providing more opportunities for student discussion and group work in the upper grades. At the middle and high school level, developmentally appropriate lessons make room for more student voice and agency. Lessons for secondary students can get more engagement when students are invited to impact, shape, and apply lesson content to make it relevant to the challenges and opportunities they experience.

- **Developmental differentiation in lesson content:** At the elementary level, especially in the early grades, instruction is appropriately focused on helping students develop basic skills that increase school and peer success. These are the classic SEL topics like listening and attention skills, feelings identification and management, and how to share or play fairly at recess. By upper elementary grades, students should be gaining more complex skills such as interpersonal problem solving. At the middle and high school level, students should ideally be learning some of the neuroscience of how emotions are created and applying content on neuroplasticity to shape how they think about their own and others' ability to improve their emotion management skills. Secondary students should ideally be given opportunities to shape and apply SEL content to their own challenges and goals.

SUPPORT FOR GENERALIZATION

SEL content that is covered in lessons and then never touched on again is unlikely to be effective. Remember, social and emotional *competence* is a primary goal of SEL instruction. One of the most important ways to get to positive outcomes is supporting SEL skill generalization, which is the ability to go beyond simply learning about SEL-related skills, knowledge, and mindsets to being able to skillfully utilize them in daily life, but the reality is that helping teachers scaffold generalization of lesson content is a weakness in many if not most programs. Be sure to examine how different SEL programs go beyond lessons to providing language, examples, and ideas for how schools can support generalization.

When vetting an SEL program, consider the following.

- **Ongoing practice:** Students are less likely to develop skills that are only discussed or taught once a week in a lesson. While most SEL programs primarily create lessons that focus on the teaching of SEL skills, fewer put a lot of attention and time into developing effective ways to help teachers figure out how and when to support student competence development. Ideally, students learn basic skills in lessons, practice them outside those lessons, and receive feedback on their attempts that they can then use to improve. This requires, at a minimum, cueing students to use what's taught in lessons throughout the school day and beyond. As discussed in the section on schoolwide delivery, if all students in a school or grade are getting exposed to similar skills using similar language, educators have an easier time finding ways to cue students to apply the content they are learning. A simple example at the elementary level might be reminding students before recess to practice specific skills they have been learning about playing fairly or handling conflicts, then having a short class discussion when they return to give students an opportunity to discuss their efforts, celebrate their successes, and get help troubleshooting how they might be more skillful the next time a similar challenge arises.

- **Opportunity for self-reflection:** A key way students learn to generalize SEL skills they've learned is by practicing self-reflection. An ideal model for skill acquisition and competence development includes opportunities (with cueing and even coaching) to try new skills followed by individual and group reflection. How did it go? What was successful? How might I get better at this skill? This process is not necessarily something students do automatically. Look to see whether the curriculum provides guidance and support for teachers and other school staff to help students reflect on their attempts to put SEL content into practice and think about both what's working and how they can improve.

How Can Schools Effectively Implement SEL Curriculum and Instruction?

Once a school has identified the best-fit SEL program, leaders can work toward implementation by securing educator buy-in, protecting time for delivery, avoiding initiative overload, offering training and professional development, making the initiative a priority, employing a team approach, ensuring implementation fidelity, and helping to support the content beyond the lessons.

SECURE EDUCATOR BUY-IN

The success of SEL instruction depends on enthusiastic, consistent delivery and support from educators. But adding SEL to teachers' already immense workload is not simply a matter of announcing a new initiative and distributing a program. Sustainable SEL implementation in a school or district depends on leadership support. For educators to put in the time and effort to deliver and support SEL schoolwide over time, it has to be made a clear priority. One place to start is communicating a clear and relevant why that speaks directly to school and district goals as well as teacher priorities. Teachers need to clearly understand the benefits and positive outcomes that a new SEL initiative should bring. We've discussed the many benefits SEL is shown to produce that are relevant here: more student time on task, less disruptive behavior, better relationships among students and between students and adults, and ultimately higher academic achievement. SEL done well should make teachers' jobs easier, not harder.

PROTECT TIME FOR DELIVERY

Even if teachers understand and embrace the why behind SEL, they still need to believe they can deliver it with the time and effort they have available. High-quality SEL curricula are carefully designed and tested to ensure they can be delivered fairly easily by the average teacher without much prep time. But even the easiest program still needs to be delivered somewhere in the schedule and will require set-aside time.

In elementary schools, teachers are often expected to squeeze SEL into their schedule, but it can help if there is an established time during the week that everyone is teaching SEL. This bit of scheduling makes it clear that SEL is a priority and also makes it easy for administrators or others to know when they can observe SEL lesson delivery. In secondary schools, the challenge is different. Although some schools manage to get SEL lessons delivered by teachers during the time scheduled for academic subjects, the reality is that there usually needs to be a set-aside time for SEL in the schedule—often during advisory or homeroom period. Again, making sure to carve out protected time for SEL delivery reduces the burden on teachers while clearly establishing that SEL is a school or districtwide priority. The more barriers and burdens can be reduced, the more likely teachers will see your SEL initiative as something doable that they can buy into.

AVOID INITIATIVE OVERLOAD

In the same vein as protected time, even the most enthusiastic teachers will struggle to embrace delivering SEL if SEL becomes one more thing added to already maxed-out workloads. Avoid the trap of initiative overload, where more and more new curricula, programs, and changes get added without anything being taken away. It's not uncommon for schools, with the best intentions, to keep embracing great new ideas that may really improve learning and other outcomes, all of which add to the complexity of and time demands on teachers' workloads. To realistically set themselves up for success with SEL, some schools and districts may need to identify something they are willing to *cut* before adding something new.

Another factor in initiative overload is staffing changes. High turnover among teachers or building and district leaders is a significant challenge to a school or district. Considering how much stability you have in your staffing is an important part of judging how ready a school or system is for taking on new challenges. If turnover has been high, it might be worth taking a little time to build community and ensure people are capable of handling their current workloads before adding an ambitious SEL program. High rates of turnover can create a need for additional training before new staff can competently implement an SEL program.

These concerns are all in the service of avoiding the attitude of "this too shall pass," common among teachers who have seen countless amazing new programs instituted only to watch them fade out and lose traction when the next exciting thing comes along. Teachers need to know that an SEL program is easy to implement, but they also need to believe it will be supported over the long term. Teachers buy into initiatives they think will last.

OFFER TRAINING AND PROFESSIONAL DEVELOPMENT

One of the best ways to demonstrate that SEL is a priority and increase teacher buy-in can be to make sure everyone involved in delivering a new SEL program gets adequate training and preparation. How SEL lessons are delivered can matter as much as what is actually in the lessons. Program-specific training can equip teachers with the confidence required to feel comfortable with the content, interface, format, and delivery requirements of your chosen SEL program. This typically means training time devoted to giving teachers an overview of the program but also hands-on experience with the lessons and materials. By the end of satisfactory SEL-program-specific professional development, teachers should understand how much and what kind of preparation time they should realistically expect to put in before starting the program and before each individual lesson. They should also have a clear understanding of how to navigate the interface of any digitally delivered programming confidently so they avoid the awful experience of trying to get students interested in content and activities only to get stuck struggling with poorly designed technology.

Professional development for SEL programs should also do more than just address lesson delivery; it should help teachers understand methods and build skills around supporting the generalization and mastery of what is being taught in the lessons. As we've discussed earlier, this is often a weak spot for SEL curricula. It's worth taking this aspect of professional development into consideration when considering both SEL program choice and the training provided to educators. If the program you choose for your school or district does not adequately address how educators should be supporting students in moving from content to competence, it may be worth considering having school or district staff put some time and effort into coming up with approaches to generalization support that connect SEL content with other things happening in your schools (for example, PBIS) and that can provide educators with shared understandings of and shared language for how to carry out this key SEL function.

MAKE IT A PRIORITY

Another aspect of support for SEL implementation is leadership clearly demonstrating that a new SEL initiative is a priority. Teachers may believe in the importance of SEL, but realistically, competing demands often mean that what teachers do reflects perceived administration priorities. Things that are priorities receive time, attention, and resources. And if everything is a priority, nothing is a priority. SEL instruction should be integrated into school and district strategic plans and long-term goals. Showing SEL instruction is a priority can also mean simpler actions like talking about the SEL initiative in morning announcements and making it a topic at staff meetings or a focus of professional learning communities. It is important to make sure the big push, excitement, and support for SEL is not just something that happens at the beginning of the year and then dies out as other priorities take over. SEL programs that are introduced and then left to flourish or languish on their own without ongoing encouragement and prioritization will often simply fade out.

EMPLOY A TEAM APPROACH

The implementation of SEL is most effective when led by a distributed leadership team. A building principal or enthusiastic teacher can't do it on their own. The SEL team is a dedicated group of people who routinely come together with a clear vision and sense of purpose focused on supporting the implementation of SEL in a school. The team's responsibilities include gaining an understanding of where people in the school are with SEL implementation and what they need to be enthusiastic and effective at delivering and supporting the chosen SEL program.

One of the authors, Clay, writes in a blog post about why a dedicated team is essential to successful implementation (Cook, 2019). The advice he shares there about dissemination and implementation teams applies to SEL teams. Making sure the right members are included on the SEL team is critical to successful implementation. Consider the following five guidelines to help schools form effective teams.

1. **The two-pizza rule:** If the team is too large to be fed by two pizzas, then it is too big to effectively problem-solve, strategize, and get work done. A team of six to eight members is ideal.

2. **Representativeness:** The SEL team should represent a diversity of perspectives and include both formal and informal leaders within the building. For example, you might have one or two general education teachers, one special education teacher, support staff (counselor, school psychologist, behavior specialist, and so forth), and building leaders. It can also be useful and important to include students (especially at the secondary level) as well as parents or community members on the team to ensure you have widespread support for your efforts to support student well-being.

3. **Formal leadership:** Include members who have formal, appointed leadership and authority to hold others accountable in the building, such as the principal and deans, assistant principals, or vice principals.

4. **Champions:** Seek out champions of the SEL cause to be on the team. These people fully buy into the purpose underlying the implementation effort and have a high degree of motivation to strategize around and support the uptake and delivery of SEL practices or programming.

5. **Key opinion leaders (KOLs):** It's critical to include the KOLs from various social networks in the building. Because others listen to and respect KOLs, their presence on the team increases implementation success within school buildings. The formal leader who constructs the team must strive to identify KOLs who are connected to the various social networks in the building and who are champions of the cause.

During team meetings, there must be a clear agenda and problem-solving process that results in plans that aim to drive continuous improvement in implementation and support for SEL. This often entails working to put systems of support in place, including by arranging for professional learning opportunities, gathering fidelity data, providing feedback and opportunities for modeling and coaching, offering recognition and acknowledgment of implementation efforts, ensuring protected time for planning and reflection, and creating prompts and reminders to be delivered regularly. The SEL team creates systems of support that are aimed at the adults and focused on what they need to adopt and continuously improve their delivery of SEL curriculum and instruction—all, of course, with the goal of improving outcomes for students.

Based on extensive partnering with schools and districts, CASEL, the leading SEL support and advocacy organization, has come to strongly recommend a team-driven approach to SEL implementation. CASEL provides great content on their website (https://shorturl.at/lKLWX) focused on how to put together and utilize an SEL team to support successful implementation in schools. If you explore the resources they provide, you'll find great guidance on how to create a representative team, ensure team members have specific roles and responsibilities, and create an SEL team that is strong and effective.

ENSURE IMPLEMENTATION FIDELITY

In a nutshell, *implementation fidelity* refers to delivering a program the way it was designed to be done (and ideally the way it was done when tested and shown to be effective). To maximize the impact of an SEL program, educators should pay attention to multiple dimensions of implementation. Failure to achieve high levels of implementation fidelity is a primary reason that programs implemented by schools can fail to result in the same positive outcomes they did when evaluated under carefully controlled conditions.

A fundamental implementation topic is dosage: students cannot benefit from lessons they don't receive. And ideally, students should not just receive all the lessons laid out in a given year but experience them in the correct order. Remember, SEL programs should be based on a clear research-based theory of change that spells out how various components of the curriculum work together to create impact. This synergy is powerful. Most high-quality SEL programs are carefully designed so that lessons build on each other across each grade, as well as from year to year. To pick one example, conflict resolution is a common SEL topic. But students are more likely to be able to succeed at working out problems among themselves if they have first learned some empathy and perspective-taking skills. By the same token, most interpersonal conflicts are emotionally challenging, so SEL lessons on emotion management also contribute to student conflict-resolution success. While picking and choosing only some topics and lessons is tempting, keep in mind that doing so will likely weaken the effects of your SEL curriculum. The same goes with teaching lessons out of order. For some programs, that may not matter, but a carefully developed program will involve lessons that intentionally build on each other across the school year, and switching the order of delivery can therefore be less effective than sticking to the program design.

Although easy-to-deliver SEL lessons are often constructed to minimize the burden placed on teachers, content cannot simply stand on its own. High-quality implementation of SEL content, much like effective academic instruction, requires enthusiastic delivery. Teachers communicate how they feel about SEL through their attitude and approach to delivery. Students are less likely to be engaged and take SEL seriously if they think their teacher does not believe it is important and is not convincingly supportive of what is being taught in SEL lessons.

SUPPORT CONTENT BEYOND LESSONS

We know students don't build competence simply from short lessons on SEL topics. Teaching a skill needs to be followed up by reminders to try it out and, ideally, feedback on one's efforts. However, most SEL programs focus almost entirely (and perhaps understandably) on the part of SEL instruction that takes place during a specific set-aside class time and that can be delivered through a lesson script or template. Supporting the generalization of the content taught in lessons can be more complex because it needs to be done throughout the school day, often outside the classroom, and not necessarily at preplanned times or in scripted ways.

There is a fairly straightforward method or formula for supporting the practice of SEL skills outside lessons. The first step is to cue or remind students when there is a good opportunity to put an SEL skill into practice. Sometimes that can be done at routine times during the day, such as before going to lunch for elementary students, or when working in groups for secondary students. Other times, SEL skills are most useful when challenging moments arise, such as peer conflicts in the classroom or situations where a student becomes upset. Either way, it can be helpful to have clear language that teachers across a school can use to cue students. This shared language makes it possible for different staff in a school to cue students in consistent and familiar ways that don't need explaining each time and don't require students to match different cues to the same skill. Some lessons for preschool, kindergarten or early elementary students teach students specific gestures to accompany skill instruction that can be used as reminders. For example, the Second Step program teaches Skills for Listening to young students, and each piece is taught in part through gestures or hand signals that teachers can use to cue students without needing to disrupt the flow of teaching by cueing them out loud.

Schools can do more than cue and encourage students to use SEL skills throughout the day. This is where the synergy between SEL instruction and clear classroom and school expectations comes into play. In PBIS, for example, students learn and are rewarded for following clearly specified behavioral expectations. If those behaviors matched how students naturally behaved all the time, they wouldn't be needed. Sometimes students simply need a clear understanding of what's expected. But even when that is in place, students are sometimes unable to skillfully control their behavior or manage their emotions in ways needed to meet behavioral expectations. That is where SEL can be especially useful. Many of the skills and competencies taught in SEL lessons can help students make conscious decisions about how they behave and make it easier for them to match their behavior to what's expected and rewarded. So if a school and classroom has clearly established and taught norms, adults can utilize those expectations as opportunities to cue students to practice and improve on their SEL skills. For example, a student who returns to class upset about something that happened at recess might benefit from being cued to use a deep breathing or other calm down skill they've learned to enable them to return their focus to classroom work.

Finally, parents are important partners in successful SEL, particularly around helping students to put what they're learning in SEL lessons into action, turning the skills they've learned into competencies through supported trial and error at home and beyond. Communication with families around SEL is critical. Information should be sent home that explains your SEL initiative, the reasons for it, what your goals are for student outcomes, and specific material that explains what educators are covering and students are learning in SEL lessons. Ideally, family materials can help support conversations at home about how to get better at using and applying the SEL content to daily challenges. It can be helpful for families to understand that you view them as important partners in the process of supporting healthy child and youth development and preparing students to succeed socially, emotionally, and academically.

Conclusion

To most effectively and sustainably teach social-emotional competence to students, most schools and districts will be best served by carefully choosing a well-designed SEL curriculum. While it may be possible for educators to infuse SEL instruction throughout the school day on their own, there is little research to support that approach, and we don't think it's a realistic option for the vast majority of schools. High-quality SEL programs are created through extensive translation of research on child and youth development, based on effective instructional design principles, and thoroughly piloted and shown to be easy to use for teachers and engaging for students.

Simply choosing an SEL program or initiative is not the first step in SEL instruction. Schools need to realistically assess the resources available for SEL implementation, including money to purchase curricula and training, class time for delivery, staff availability for planning and supporting the SEL initiative, and administration commitment to ensure the effort is given adequate ongoing support and prioritization.

Educators need to understand why SEL is important and how it fits into the larger goals and plans for their school and district. They also need to know there is protected time blocked out for SEL rather than feel like it's one more thing for them to somehow shoehorn into an already full schedule. Educators need to be trained and supported so they feel ready to teach and support SEL. And it needs to be clear that your SEL efforts are going to be supported over the long term as opposed to becoming one more program that is introduced with excitement and fanfare only to fade away before the year is done.

The process of choosing the right SEL program is worth careful consideration. There are resources, discussed in this chapter, for searching out and comparing programs. Curricula need to be vetted for developmental fit with the age of your students and for cultural fit with your community and student population. Program providers must offer training and professional development adequate to the challenge of preparing teachers to be confident in their ability to teach lessons. Lessons must be easy enough to deliver that virtually all teachers can feel able to successfully teach them. That includes being able to access lessons, which increasingly means schools need to evaluate the level of usability of digital platforms.

High-quality SEL programs are based on research. That means you should be able to review a logic model or theory of change that shows solid research links between long-term program outcomes, medium-term changes that should happen for students, and the specific content and methods used in the lessons. Ideally there should be solid research documenting that an SEL program has been evaluated under something like real-world conditions and shown to produce the kinds of positive outcomes the program claims to target.

Finally, student engagement is really where the rubber meets the road in SEL curricula. Do students find lessons enjoyable? Students need to willingly participate, whether that means participating in pair, group, and or class discussions or drawing, writing, or engaging with materials in other creative ways. Students should feel like the content speaks to them and addresses real issues, struggles, and needs they experience.

Next Steps

What are the important next steps you want to take to maintain or improve the implementation of SEL curriculum and instruction that supports students to acquire and apply competencies?

Note that your plan should take into account whether you are still planning for implementation or already actively implementing an SEL program. If implementation has not begun, create a plan to ensure staff are motivated and ready to implement. If actively implementing a curriculum, then create a plan to support continuous improvement in the quality and consistency with which lessons are implemented across the school.

Reflecting on SEL Curriculum and Instruction

Consider the following questions as they relate to your school or district and positive relationships.

- What curriculum and instructional practices is your school currently implementing to teach students specific social-emotional competencies?

- If you don't already have an SEL program in place, how do you plan to include those criteria in your process of looking at and choosing an SEL curriculum?

- What can you do (or have you done) to support educator buy-in for implementing an SEL program?

- What are some ways you can work to ensure that educators follow up on lessons by supporting the development and application of SEL skills and competencies throughout the school and school day?

- What steps can you take to make sure educators are universally delivering your SEL program to all students in your school or district?

- How might you build gathering information on implementation (reach, fidelity, quality) into your SEL program efforts?

- Where is there room for continuous improvement in your SEL instruction?

Planning for SEL Curriculum and Instruction

Use the following chart to consider practices to advance SEL and curriculum instruction. In the space provided, note necessary steps involved in completing each goal as well as key dates to remember aligned with implementation.

Implementation Goal	Necessary Steps	Key Dates
Select a curriculum that is shown to be effective *and* is feasible to implement and sustain over time.		
Make sure the curriculum's scope and sequence align with the needs of your students and are developmentally and culturally appropriate.		

The Recipe for Student Well-Being © 2024 Solution Tree Press • SolutionTree.com
Visit **go.SolutionTree.com/SEL** to download this free reproducible.

Intersperse student choice in instructional practices.		
Provide students opportunities to respond and engage with the learning material.		
Employ generalization practices that support students to apply what they learn beyond the lessons.		

CHAPTER 6

ASSESSMENT

Simply put, assessment is about understanding what you are doing and how well it is working. If you don't see the results you hope for, assessment can help you figure out why. Failing to collect assessment data on your SEL efforts is like driving at night with your headlights off—you might get where you're going, but your chances are greatly improved if you can see where you are and whether the direction you are heading leads to your destination.

SEL is not magic. Simply buying a program or trying a new strategy does not guarantee success. Both effective practice and, perhaps most important, ongoing improvement require data. But just like buying an SEL program doesn't necessarily ensure outcomes, gathering data without a clear plan costs time and effort without ensuring students are getting the support they need and that the time and money put into SEL is paying off.

In this chapter, we discuss the role of our final ingredient, assessment, in supporting the success of your SEL work. We'll cover what SEL assessment entails; why it's important; and how educators can conduct the assessment, gather assessment data, and home in on specific ingredients of instruction and the larger SEL recipe in their review.

What Is SEL Assessment?

SEL assessment refers to collecting data that schools can use to improve their support for students' development of social-emotional competence and well-being. Assessment takes time and resources, and it should be guided by identifying clear ways you'll use the results to drive concrete actions to improve outcomes for students. For an SEL assessment initiative to be successful, it should be driven by a well-thought-out plan. This often takes the form of a theory of action (see American Institutes for Research, 2019). A theory of action can be thought of as an if-then statement that clearly lays out the purpose of your SEL assessment efforts. It should spell out the following.

- **What will be measured:** If you have an SEL program with solid research support, you might focus on measuring the quality and quantity of teacher implementation and the level of student engagement. On the other end of the spectrum, you may have specific outcomes you are pursuing (like improved class or school climate, increased student sense of belonging, increased time on task, or fewer disruptions in class) and your assessment may be focused on assessing progress toward those goals.

- **How that will be done:** Your assessment plan or theory of action should spell out exactly how you will gather data on your chosen topics. The most common approach is through teacher and student surveys, but in some cases, observations can provide valuable information. For bigger-picture outcomes such as disciplinary referrals, schools may choose to simply access the information they already collect.

- **How the assessment findings will be processed and used to inform action:** The biggest pitfall to avoid is putting time and money into SEL assessment that doesn't yield actionable insights into how to improve your SEL practice and SEL-related outcomes for students. Ideally, your assessment plan should include specifying how you will address any problems or shortfalls you discover. Efforts you make to react to assessment findings can inform the next steps. For example, poor implementation of lessons may lead to additional support and professional development from program providers or in-house experts. If you're delivering lessons well, but you aren't seeing the behavior changes you're hoping for, you might explore possible problems with student engagement, lack of support for generalization, or even consider switching to a new program. Your plan should spell out specific ways you will respond to what your assessment shows.

WHAT TO ASSESS

SEL-related assessment can help you gather useful data on two basic concerns: (1) what you're doing, including how well you're doing it, and (2) how your SEL efforts are impacting students. Our advice is to initially, and perhaps even primarily, focus on the first of these—that is, use an assessment process to clearly understand exactly what is being done to incorporate the SEL ingredients previously laid out in this book: SEL for adults; safe, predictable, and positive environments; positive relationships; and SEL curriculum and instruction.

All the SEL ingredients have strong evidence to support their effectiveness. Ensuring you're doing a good job of following the recipe and providing high-quality support to students across the ingredients is the key to producing positive results. This means focusing SEL assessment on providing a clear picture of what is and isn't being done to address each of the SEL ingredients. Ideally, this information can then be used to improve the quality, and therefore impact, of what is happening in your school or district around each of the ingredients to effective SEL laid out in this book. We will go into more detail on measuring the various ingredients in the how section of this chapter.

SEL assessment is often framed as simply being about measuring students' social and emotional skills. This may be because this focus on discrete skills seems to make SEL assessment analogous to ways assessment is used in academic instruction. However, there can be shortfalls to focusing your assessment efforts primarily on SEL skills.

The SEL skills approach to assessment doesn't cover many of the key ingredients of effective SEL and fails to fully capture the goals of most SEL instruction. SEL curricula typically go beyond teaching skills to also trying to change or instill attitudes, knowledge, mindsets, values, and norms. In addition, all the SEL ingredients laid out in this book are included because we know they support successful student development. Measuring student social and emotional skills alone is not an effective way to understand, for example, the effectiveness and impact of providing SEL support to educators. Safe, predictable, and positive environments are intended in part to help support student development of social and emotional skills, but measuring those skills doesn't necessarily help you to understand the actual quality of the environments students are experiencing and how and where you might work to improve them. The same applies to positive student relationships with teachers and peers. While the right kinds of environments and relationships make it more likely students will be able to learn, practice, and develop fluency with social and emotional skills, they are also intended to produce other important outcomes, such as a greater sense of belonging among students. As discussed in chapters 3 and 4 (page 53 and 83) on environments and relationships, a solid sense of belonging provides students with many valuable aspects of social and emotional well-being that are unlikely to be captured when just measuring discrete skills.

We suggest that before spending time and energy measuring student outcomes, including SEL skills, schools are better served by assessing the implementation of the foundational components of SEL they are delivering. This typically means collecting implementation-focused data that captures information about the uptake and fidelity of delivery of core SEL practices. Essentially, this approach to assessment is focused on learning who's doing how much of what and how well. For example, to gain insights into how to improve direct SEL instruction, your assessment work would likely be focused on measuring teacher buy-in, how many teachers are delivering how many lessons, the fidelity of program delivery, and levels of student engagement. Assuring that your students are receiving the full dose (with high-quality delivery) of your chosen curriculum should come before looking into measuring possible program outcomes.

As another example, the only way SEL curricula contribute to the development of student social and emotional skills and competence is if students actively engage with lessons. And we know that students are unlikely to take lessons seriously without enthusiastic delivery by educators. One of the positive outcomes of SEL for adults is that it can help teachers to better understand on a personal level the content they'll be teaching in SEL lessons, which increases their confidence and buy-in. Assessing levels of teacher buy-in, student engagement, and fidelity of delivery can provide critically important, actionable information on where to target improvements. Similarly, data can be gathered on the full range of SEL ingredients, and that information can then be used to ensure students are truly getting the SEL support they need before time and money are spent looking at outcomes, such as changes in SEL skills.

If you're confident that you're adequately addressing your chosen SEL ingredients and making improvements in them where needed, then it may be appropriate and useful to also assess outcomes, including but not limited to SEL skills. Most SEL programs have short-, medium-, and long-term goals, including things like improvements in student sense of connectedness and belonging, student well-being, growth mindsets, and student behavior and academic achievement in addition to discrete SEL skills. Whatever SEL program you choose should be able to specify the outcomes you should focus on to determine the program's effects on your students. In addition, the SEL ingredients laid out in this book have their own assessable outcomes to help you gauge progress. For example, the quality and quantity of student relationships with both peers and adults in the building can be assessed through student surveys. The same goes for gauging classroom and school climate.

SCREENING

One additional assessment topic we want to touch on is using validated screening instruments—most commonly surveys—to ensure you're able to identify students who have needs that your universal SEL efforts aren't meeting. Screening is a form of assessment that helps schools provide early identification and intervention for students with emerging mental health needs. An extensive discussion of this topic is beyond the scope of this book given our focus on universal SEL, but screening is nonetheless an important part of supporting all students' social and emotional development, well-being, and academic achievement.

This use of assessment is linked to the MTSS model described in chapter 3 (page 53). As discussed there, not all student needs are fully met by universal SEL. While well-planned and well-implemented universal SEL meets the needs of most students and reduces the number of students who require additional support, it's important to provide for the social and emotional development and well-being of all students. For some, this means more intensive, targeted interventions. Figuring out who those students are and what interventions are most appropriate can be facilitated through universal use of screening tools. Although only perhaps 20 percent of schools use validated screening tools for this purpose (Herman et al., 2021), there are important reasons why a more formal screening process can help improve how you meet the needs of struggling students.

One of the primary advantages of screening tools is that they can be used to identify students who have what psychologists often call *externalizing* or *internalizing challenges* (Olivier, Morin, Langlois, Tardif-Grenier, & Archambault, 2020). *Externalizing* difficulties are often easy to spot because the term refers to students whose internal difficulties manifest through obvious behaviors that can make learning challenging for students. On the other hand, students with internalizing difficulties can easily be missed. There are students with serious social and emotional needs who fly under the radar because they keep their challenges to themselves and are often able to meet behavioral expectations in a classroom and school setting.

Many available screening tools have been validated through research studies and shown to be high quality. Schools should choose screening tools that have research support. Here are some examples.

- The Social, Academic, and Emotional Behavior Risk Screener, available from Illuminate Education (www.illuminateed.com). This is a brief rating scale that teachers can complete on their students from kindergarten to twelfth grade. The tool has nineteen questions and provides information on internalizing and externalizing behaviors as well as student social competence.
- The Devereux Student Strengths Assessment-Mini (DESSA-Mini) allows you to rate SEL competencies in K–8 students. It can be completed by educators, mental health professionals, or caregivers who regularly interact with the student. The DESSA-Mini is made up of eight questions and can be scored manually or using a digital scoring software. Additional tools are available to help schools compare pre- and postassessments and to allow you to generate reports at the individual, classroom, and school levels.
- The short form of the Social Emotional Assets and Resilience Scales™ is an SEL screening tool for K–12 students. It has twelve questions, is completed by teachers, and focuses on students' strengths, specifically problem-solving, interpersonal, and coping skills.

For more information and guidance on how to carry out screening-based assessment, we recommend "Best Practices in Social, Emotional, and Behavioral Screening: An Implementation Guide," which can be found online (https://smhcollaborative.org/universalscreening).

Why Is SEL Assessment Important?

Perhaps the most powerful reason for engaging in SEL assessment is that it provides the foundation for data-based decision making around SEL. But it can also be an effective way to demonstrate commitment to an SEL initiative. Sayings like "What gets measured gets treasured" and "What gets assessed gets addressed" are common in education because they reflect the value of assessment for clarifying and communicating priorities. Ongoing leadership support is key to the sustainable success of any new initiative in schools (Grissom, Egalite, & Lindsay, 2021).

Assessing the quality and impact of SEL efforts communicates that school or district leadership values SEL. Carefully conducted assessment can also show SEL is a serious endeavor by using the resulting data to drive improvements—especially when the effectiveness of those improvements are then examined through further assessment. In this way, SEL assessment can fuel an effective data-based continuous improvement process for SEL (McKown & Herman, 2020).

Assessment can also be a tool for understanding the extent to which students experience your SEL instruction as engaging and how well adults are striving to encourage and support students in developing the skills taught in lessons throughout the school day. Gathering assessment data on all the key comprehensive SEL ingredients covered in this book can provide actionable information that points toward clear areas where schools can focus on improving their support for student social-emotional competence and well-being.

Another important reason to engage in SEL assessment efforts is that solid data can provide insights beyond just how students are doing on average and what kinds of support they are receiving overall. Disaggregating data is the process of going beyond looking at what's happening for all students by breaking the information down to enable comparisons across different groupings of students (National Forum on Education Statistics, 2016). This might be by gender, grade, race or ethnicity, status as an English learner, disciplinary history, or any other distinction you think will yield meaningful insights. Successful efforts to meet the needs of all students through comprehensive SEL requires looking at data that can tell you who is and is not benefiting from your SEL efforts. Disaggregating data can provide important information that identifies easy-to-miss holes in the delivery and impact of your SEL initiative and can highlight ways to improve outcomes for all students in your school or district. It is important for universally delivered SEL to meet the needs of as many students as possible so that the number of students needing additional support does not overwhelm school resources. Disaggregating data can help you identify ways that your SEL efforts can be strengthened in part to ensure the success of the more intensive supports some students need.

How Can Schools Conduct SEL Assessment?

In this section, we'll detail the necessity of a distributed leadership team for SEL assessment, as well as explore the options schools have for carrying out the assessment plan: paying for it or doing it themselves.

SEL TEAM

Once you've made a carefully considered SEL assessment plan, collecting data is only the beginning of the process. That information must then be examined, interpreted, and used to make decisions. The full SEL assessment process is most effectively carried out by a dedicated distributed leadership team who engages in strategic decision making and action planning around the implementation of key SEL ingredients. Part of the team's job is to help maintain a focus on improving SEL efforts while avoiding staff burnout and initiative overload. The team supports the collection and use of data on your chosen SEL ingredients to monitor how things are going; problem-solve barriers to implementation across different ingredients; and develop, prioritize, and enact action plans that include strategies for improvement. See chapter 5 (page 123) for more information on creating an SEL team.

For additional resources on how to successfully develop and use a team approach, visit:

- CASEL, Guide to Schoolwide SEL (https://schoolguide.casel.org/focus-area-1a/create-a-team)
- A Primer for Continuous Improvement in Schools and Districts (www.edc.org/sites/default/files/uploads/primer_for_continuous_improvement.pdf)
- How School Teams Use Data to Make Effective Decisions: Team-Initiated Problem Solving (https://shorturl.at/vyABI)

APPROACHES TO SEL ASSESSMENT: PAY OR DO IT YOURSELF

Schools have a choice between paying an external organization to provide assessment services or carrying out the process themselves. For those with the resources, conducting SEL assessment yourself is feasible. But as mentioned earlier, the time and expertise required to carry out high-quality SEL assessment is often beyond what schools or districts are capable of or willing to prioritize. If the cost is manageable for your school or district, we recommend finding a high-quality provider to work with. Fortunately, an increasing number of companies are available that can make SEL assessment relatively quick and low burden. The best SEL assessment service providers use carefully developed high-quality surveys, make data collection fairly simple, and provide easy-to-understand reports that make it possible for educators to dive in and work to determine what the data say about their students and their SEL practices.

An important part of planning for SEL assessment is to examine the amount of burden different approaches require. Tackling assessment yourself will likely involve more burden in multiple ways. This approach requires significant staff time to investigate assessment options, determine priorities, and make and carry out a plan, as well as decide how those tasks will be carried out by administration and SEL team members. Student and staff surveys are probably the most commonly used tools for SEL assessment, but finding, choosing, or developing those surveys takes significant expertise that schools and districts may or may not possess. The best surveys are short, targeted, and research validated. Professional assessment services can often provide streamlined assessment tools and processes that are hard for districts to duplicate. Many of the top organizations (for example, Panorama Education, www.panoramaed.com) allow you to collect data from students digitally or through paper surveys, which are then very quickly processed into readily understandable reports. The well-designed surveys created by top assessment organizations allow you to collect targeted and meaningful data on topics you choose in a fairly streamlined and time-efficient process that, again, is only possible to duplicate if your school or district possesses staff with significant assessment related expertise and resources.

A key burden consideration in SEL assessment is the time and effort involved in examining the data you generate and figuring out what it means for your SEL work. This part of the assessment process is strongly impacted by how the collected data is compiled and presented. Another way paying for assessment services reduces burden is at this point of making sense out of what the collected data say and mean for your SEL efforts moving forward. The best assessment providers summarize your data in ways that are easy to understand and provide many different options for diving in deeper. For example, Panorama Education makes it easy to disaggregate your data to look at SEL outcomes across specific groups by gender, grade, race and ethnicity, and other meaningful variables. They also, for an extra fee, make it easy to upload archival data on topics like attendance, disciplinary referrals, or special education status, which you can then use to further disaggregate your data and drill into the experiences of specific groups of students.

How Can Schools Gather SEL Assessment Data?

In this section, we discuss a few ways to gather data related to SEL: establishing a comparison, consulting administrative records, and disseminating surveys.

ESTABLISH A COMPARISON

Implementation of new approaches, such as student–teacher relationship practices or SEL lesson delivery, can be measured fairly simply. However, for many of the possible types of data you might choose to focus on, it will be possible to make sense out of your findings only if you have something to compare your data to. Typically, SEL assessment data (especially around SEL outcomes) is difficult to interpret by itself because there are no set standards that apply across schools and populations. The best way to know what a given finding means is to have relevant comparison data from your own setting. Whether you're examining data on student sense of belonging, behavior or skills, teacher buy-in, school climate, or other SEL variables, you're most likely to be able to make sense out of that data by comparing it to some kind of baseline. Without that baseline, you can't tell if what you're finding shows your efforts are paying off or failing to make a difference.

However, one of the challenges of assessment is that a lot of things related to SEL naturally vary across each school year from fall to spring. So, while it's natural to take the approach of simply measuring SEL variables in the fall and then looking at data collected in spring to see what effect your efforts are having, that approach can result in misleading information. An intervention study conducted by researchers Adriana Sum Miu and David S. Yeager (2015) concludes a lot of what we might measure around SEL is likely to change across the school year even without any focused SEL efforts: Students often start the year in a bit of a honeymoon phase that includes better outcomes than what we see as the year progresses and students face interpersonal challenges and conflicts. The problem is it's hard to know how variables would have changed without your SEL efforts, so it's difficult to determine SEL impacts from a fall-to-spring comparison. Miu and Yeager's intervention study (2015) measured a large impact on student depression across the ninth-grade year. The data showed that students who received the intervention had no change in their level of depression across the year. While that may not seem like a success, it in fact was, because the students who did not receive the intervention showed a 40 percent *increase in depression* from fall to spring (Miu & Yeager, 2015). Without understanding the natural changes in student depression from fall to spring, a school implementing that intervention might see the lack of improvement as an indication the program didn't work.

Although it's challenging to do so, avoid putting too much stock in single-year assessment results. Multi-year data collection allows you to, for example, look at specific times of the year and compare them to data gathered at those times in previous years, offering insight into trends that aren't visible in single-year assessments. One useful approach to help you avoid misleading fall-to-spring comparisons is to compare data from similar times of the year, such as looking at data from spring one year compared to the same data from the previous spring. This effectively cancels out the impact of the natural changes that might occur during the school year and allows you to make clearer judgments on the meaning of the SEL data you collect.

CONSULT ADMINISTRATIVE RECORDS

One of the more straightforward and least expensive and demanding ways to look at some data relevant to SEL is by examining information most schools and districts already collect. However, it is important to keep in mind that different outcomes from effective SEL are likely to show up over varying timelines. Let's say you adopt an SEL program with a logic model or theory of change that says a strong focus on improving relationships among students through program content will lead to an increased sense of belonging, which then results in better behavior and attendance, and ultimately improves student academic engagement and academic achievement. While grades are readily available to schools, that outcome is only likely to occur slowly over time as the earlier pieces of the program theory of change improve. Given the program theory of change we briefly laid out, you would be likely to see changes in school data on attendance and disciplinary referrals before improvements in grades.

In this example, examining data on truancy and behavior should show program effects (if there are any) sooner than looking at changes in grades. And to flesh out the example further, if you were able to assess possible changes in student sense of belonging, that might help you make sense out of changes or lack of changes in the school level attendance and behavior data. If you found increased student sense of belonging as well as some effects on attendance, for example, that would provide support for the SEL program you chose because it follows how the program was intended to work.

DISSEMINATE SURVEYS

Surveys are the most common way to gather SEL assessment information from both students and teachers (and sometimes other educators and school staff). These surveys most commonly consist of multiple-choice questions but also sometimes include open-ended questions. The key difference to keep in mind is that the answers to multiple-choice questions can all be aggregated and made easy to look at and understand, whereas open-ended questions result in individually written responses that can't be merged into data points and must be read one by one—making this approach time-consuming and particularly difficult to use with larger numbers of respondents. However, open-ended survey questions (or even data from focus groups or student interviews) can be used as a preliminary process for identifying specific issues that you then decide to gather more objective data on through surveying larger numbers of students with multiple-choice questions.

Surveys can assess a wide range of SEL-related topics. In particular, surveys (both student and teacher) can assess student SEL skills, as well as more complex or intermediate SEL-related factors like teacher buy-in and student engagement with SEL lessons, student emotion understanding, sense of safety and belonging, quality of peer relationships, classroom and school climate, and SEL implementation.

Creating good surveys is harder than it might appear, and the best surveys are created by experts who specialize in survey development. Ideally, survey tools are tested before being widely used. A characteristic typically required of high-quality surveys is what's called *validity*. Validity refers to how well a survey measures what it is intended to. Assessing SEL is not as concrete as assessing mathematics knowledge, for example. SEL surveys often measure somewhat complex concepts like belonging, empathy, social skills, and engagement—referred to by researchers as *constructs*. The typical approach to measuring constructs is to use multiple questions that are all intended to assess the same topic from different angles. Where this complicates the process of using surveys is that if each targeted SEL construct requires multiple questions, then surveys can quickly become long and time-consuming. To some extent, using surveys involves tradeoffs between survey accuracy and length. Students have varying attention spans when it comes to surveys, and teachers have limited classroom time for delivering student surveys and are hard pressed for time outside class to complete surveys themselves. High-quality assessment providers work to create accurate surveys of manageable length.

SEL assessment commonly includes teachers completing surveys about their students. Teachers typically have good familiarity with their students, being with them all day in elementary grades, and usually daily in secondary grades. In particular, teacher surveys are one of the only ways to get information about students too young to competently fill out surveys themselves—typically below third grade. However, teachers are best at rating observable student behaviors. They are much less able to accurately report on students' internal experiences, thoughts, and feelings. And it is important to consider the amount of burden imposed by teacher surveys. Asking a teacher to fill out individual surveys about each of their students can be a time-intensive chore added to an already overfilled workload. The use of teacher surveys should be strategic, including by trying to use that method infrequently and targeting a limited number of survey topics.

Another challenge with gathering SEL data through teacher surveys on students is that it is common for teachers, like everyone else, to have unconscious biases that impact how they view and report on students. Different teachers may report differently on the same student. One source of bias is the halo effect caused when teachers' ratings of students on one topic is impacted by other characteristics of the student. For example, teacher rating of students' impulsivity and executive function can be different depending on their classroom behavior (Álvarez-García, García, & González-Castro, 2014).

Beginning at roughly third grade, most students are able to fill out surveys about themselves and their own classroom and school experiences. Student surveys have the advantage of generating information directly from students, as opposed to indirectly through assessing what the teacher thinks is going on with their students. Among other benefits, gathering survey data directly from students makes it more feasible to learn about their internal experiences that are not necessarily visible to an observer, such as emotional state and attitudes, and on SEL-related topics such as empathy, self-awareness, and mindset. However, student surveys obviously require class time to complete and generate much larger datasets that can be more difficult to process than teacher surveys if a school or district is doing its own data processing.

Both student and teacher surveys can be done digitally or by hand on paper surveys. Obviously digital data collection makes surveys easier to process, especially with larger numbers of respondents. But many companies that provide surveys still include the option of paper surveys that can be mailed back and then scanned and processed rapidly.

How Can Schools Assess SEL Ingredients?

Each of the ingredients to our SEL recipe is backed by research that shows its importance and impact. Since the ingredients can make a difference by themselves as well as when combined, it can be a good idea to specifically assess each of the five ingredients. Obviously not all schools will be implementing all the ingredients, but assessments targeted at the ones you are supporting can tell you how well things are going and give you insight into how to improve that particular strategy.

SEL FOR ADULTS

Adults' social-emotional knowledge and competence help provide a solid foundation for SEL for students and is something that can be measured and that can provide clear, actionable information on how to boost your SEL efforts. The effectiveness of SEL support for adults can be assessed through surveys that gather information on adults' own SEL knowledge and skills as well as their sense of self-efficacy regarding delivering SEL programming to students. The goal is to assess foundational factors related to educator well-being such as psychological safety and belonging, feelings of being a valued and appreciated member of the school, emotional well-being, and collective efficacy. It is also possible to measure factors that undermine adult well-being and performance, such as burnout and mental health difficulties.

SAFE, PREDICTABLE, AND POSITIVE CLASSROOM AND SCHOOL ENVIRONMENTS

As stated previously, when conducting assessments, it is first important to identify the student outcomes that should be improved by specific SEL ingredients. The byproducts of a safe, predictable, and positive environment are students who feel safe, report that they are clear about behavior expectations and norms, and are more likely to be in a regulated state where they show behaviors that are consistent with agreed-on norms and expectations. These outcomes can be measured through school administrative data such as behavior disciplinary incidents, since safe, predictable, and positive environments lead to fewer behaviors that require disciplinary responses. Student surveys can also be used to gather data on the degree to which students feel safe, understand the behavioral expectations and norms, and can anticipate what will happen, when, and why. Teacher surveys can be used to gather information on how well students are able to regulate their behavior in ways that are consistent with the norms and expectations of class.

POSITIVE RELATIONSHIPS WITH TEACHERS AND PEERS

Positive relationships amount to interactions, and perceptions based on those interactions, that result in outcomes for students like a sense of belonging and connection to school. Positive relationships can be measured via walkthrough or observational tools that operationalize positive interactions and rate the degree to which those positive interactions are happening. Greetings, positive affirmations, skillful conflict resolution, and invitations to others to join a group or activity are all examples of positive interactions. Positive relationships are more commonly and simply measured via student and educator perception surveys that include specific items that capture feelings of belonging, acceptance, and inclusion based on how others in school treat them.

SEL INSTRUCTION

The best SEL program in the world can easily fail if poorly implemented. Implementation is a multicomponent process, and assessment needs to be targeted across multiple aspects of implementation for you to understand just what is going right and wrong with how your SEL program is delivered. One of the authors worked at an SEL company where the prevailing belief was that when schools bought the program, delivery was rough the first year then improved each year; it seemed that ideal implementation always took time to roll out schoolwide. Once the company gathered data on implementation across multiple schools, they realized that belief was false. The reality was just the opposite: the data revealed that implementation was best (though not necessarily great) the first year after the curriculum was purchased then declined each year after that. By year three, rather than excellent implementation across whole schools, the lessons were no longer being taught in many classrooms. In this section we detail elements of a successful and usable assessment of how an SEL program is delivered.

A school or district can choose a powerful, well-thought-out SEL program that still fails to produce results because of weak implementation. Assessing the implementation of SEL initiatives provides a critical foundation for making sense out of all other SEL assessment data. Unless you really know what is being done and how, you cannot meaningfully use other assessment data to inform practice improvements. The best programs will fail if poorly implemented, and implementation data on the range of SEL ingredients provide some of the most clearly actionable information that can be gained through SEL assessment.

Assessment of implementation involves paying close attention to whether SEL programming and interventions are being delivered as designed and planned, in ways that are likely to promote meaningful changes in outcomes of interest. Monitoring implementation by gathering data allows schools to course correct when necessary and adapt to challenges as they arise. It's easy to jump past gathering implementation data to focus on student SEL skills or other social and emotional outcomes. The problem is that without data on implementation, there's no way to understand what's causing the problem if students don't respond to the SEL programming or interventions put in place. It could be that the SEL curriculum selected wasn't a good fit, did not match what the students needed, or wasn't an effective program for other reasons. But it could also be that an effective and appropriate program was chosen but failed to help students because it was poorly implemented. In order to draw reasonable conclusions about the effectiveness of SEL programming and what changes may need to happen, school leaders must consider three aspects of implementation: (1) adoption, (2) reach, and (3) fidelity.

Adoption

Adoption refers to uptake and reflects the number and proportion of people who start delivering a given program or practice once they have received training. For example, it unfortunately is not terribly uncommon for SEL curricula to be bought at the district or school level and distributed to teachers (perhaps without enough being done to ensure buy-in), only to find that halfway through the school year lessons are simply not getting delivered in many classrooms. Adoption is typically estimated by looking at the number of people expected to implement the program or practice compared to the number of people implementing. Having a designated time for SEL lessons makes it easy to stop into classrooms and see who is and is not delivering lessons. Other options for assessing adoption include talking to or surveying students or surveying teachers.

Schools should move on to assessing other aspects of implementation only once they have achieved adequate levels of adoption.

Reach

Program reach is an implementation topic closely related to adoption. *Reach* simply refers to the proportion of students who are receiving SEL. Similar to adoption, this is typically a simple process of figuring out how many students are getting SEL supports (which usually means in how many classrooms lessons are being taught) compared to how many they are intended to reach. For many schools, it can be tricky to figure out where, when, and how to deliver SEL lessons. For example, some schools use counselors to teach SEL. In that case, it may be that your counselor or counselors are fully engaged in delivering lessons (high adoption) but do not have the time to ensure all the classrooms get all the lessons in a curriculum (a reach problem). Or at the secondary level, SEL lessons may be delivered by all the teachers in a given subject, such as health, that not all students take, which of course means you'll have problems with reach.

Fidelity

Once an SEL program or practice has been successfully adopted, with a solid plan to reach all students, then it becomes important to assess the fidelity of implementation—how closely to how it was designed the program is being delivered.

High-quality SEL programs and practices are carefully designed and studied to ensure they maximize impact on students. Those studies are typically done in ways that ensure high fidelity of implementation, which means your best chance at getting those outcomes for your students is ensuring the program is also delivered with fidelity in your school or district.

There are multiple aspects of fidelity of implementation that can be worth assessing. One common problem is that students don't receive all the lessons in a curriculum, or dosage. Another fidelity issue is that lessons can get taught out of order or changed in some way. Implementation quality (how well, how clearly, and how enthusiastically lessons are taught) can also have impacts on the effectiveness of SEL programming.

One thing that can strongly affect the quality of lesson delivery (and be measured) is teacher buy-in. Students know when their teacher thinks something is valuable and important. And they can also tell when someone is just going through the motions but doesn't necessarily believe in the importance of SEL, doesn't think teaching it should really be part of their job, or is simply lacking the training needed to effectively deliver the SEL content. Thus, one way to assess implementation quality can be through student surveys focused on questions like how enthusiastic their teacher is about SEL lessons and how important students think their teacher thinks the lessons are.

STUDENT ENGAGEMENT

The only way SEL curricula contribute to the development of student social and emotional skills and competence is if students are actively engaged with the lessons—and that means more than just participation. They need to feel like the material is enjoyable, relevant to them and their life challenges, and developmentally and culturally appropriate. This is another aspect of assessment that relies on student surveys. Simple questions can be used aimed at understanding the extent to which students enjoy lessons, think they are valuable, think they address issues and concerns in their lives, feel like they are represented in the images and examples in the lessons, and the extent to which they actively participate in various aspects of lessons such as discussions, groups work, and so on.

Conclusion

SEL assessment helps schools understand what SEL supports students are receiving and what difference the supports are making. The SEL assessment topic is complex, and success requires thoughtful and informed planning. Your assessment efforts should be guided by a clear understanding of what you want to measure and how that data will be used to strengthen the SEL supports you provide to students. SEL assessment is best planned and led by a distributed leadership team that represents the school community. Schools need to think about the various forms of burden imposed by assessment and choose an assessment plan that matches available resources. For assessment to make a positive contribution to your SEL efforts, you should have a clear vision that ensures you collect actionable data to help you understand your school or district's SEL needs, provides data on exactly what is being done and how, and illuminates specific actions that can be taken to continually improve the delivery and positive impact of the full range of SEL ingredients.

Next Steps

What are the important next steps you want to take to maintain or improve assessing the effectiveness of your SEL program?

Reflecting on Assessment

Consider the following questions as they relate to your school or district and assessment of your SEL program.

- What SEL data does your school routinely gather to monitor the impact of implementation efforts and spur continuous improvement?

- If data are being collected, how are the data used to inform decisions and drive continuous improvement?

- What is your if-then statement that captures your theory of action for SEL assessment in your school or district? If you haven't yet developed one, do so now.

- How does your theory of action spell out what you will measure, how that will be done, and how the findings of your assessment will be put into action to support and improve your SEL efforts?

- What screening assessment tool are you using to identify students who need additional support beyond Tier 1 universal SEL?

- Write about the distributed leadership SEL team that is planning and guiding your SEL assessment efforts. If you don't yet have a team in place, brainstorm next steps for establishing this team and its efforts.

Planning for SEL Assessment

Consider the following practices to advance SEL assessment.

Implementation Goal	Necessary Steps	Key Dates
Survey data from staff and students regarding their experience of the school climate. Includes outcomes like belonging, sense of safety, positive and negative emotions, and self-efficacy.		
Use a validated tool to proactively identify students who need additional support and evaluate the overall health of Tier 1 supports in your school.		
Assess whether specific SEL practices are being delivered as planned and in a way that increases the probability of positive outcomes for students.		

Reviewing Resources for SEL Assessment

Consider the following resources to support you in assessing your SEL program.

- **CASEL resources:** The Collaborative for Social and Emotional Learning (CASEL) is the flagship organization in the SEL field. They provide a variety of assessment-related information and resources, including:
    - Student Social and Emotional Competence Assessment (https://casel.org/casel-gateway-student-sel-competence-assessment)
    - Assessment Tools (https://casel.org/state-resource-center/assessment-tools)
    - Making SEL Assessment Work (https://casel.org/making-sel-assessment-work)
    - Selecting SEL Assessments That Are Rigorous, Reasonable, and Relevant (https://casel.org/events/sel-assessments-aperature-webinars)
- **Choosing and Using SEL Competency Assessments:** Like the CASEL SEL Assessment Guide, this resource from The RAND Corporation focuses on what schools and districts need to know to assess SEL competencies. It provides a wealth of information and links related to both planning and assessment tool choice from an SEL competency assessment lens (visit https://measuringsel.casel.org/pdf/practitioner-guidance.pdf).
- **RAND Education Assessment Finder:** The RAND Education Assessment Finder is a web-based tool that provides information about assessments of K–12 students' interpersonal, intrapersonal, and higher-order cognitive competencies. Practitioners, researchers, and policymakers can use it to explore what assessments are available, what they are designed to measure, how they are administered, what demands they place on students and teachers, and what kinds of uses their scores support (visit www.rand.org/education-and-labor/projects/assessments.html).
- **Panorama for Social-Emotional Learning:** Panorama Education is one of the top commercial providers of comprehensive SEL-related assessment services. They offer a comprehensive menu of surveys schools can choose from. Panorama provides both digital and paper options for survey completion, both of which are processed rapidly to ensure schools have usable results quickly. Their data dashboard

allows educators with no special expertise to quickly and easily examine their data in a variety of ways including different ways of representing data (graphs, tables, and so on). The Panorama dashboard is powerful because educators can easily disaggregate data—for example, looking at any given outcome by grade level, race, sex, and so forth to see whose needs are and are not getting met. For an additional fee, schools and districts can also have Panorama integrate their archival data on topics like attendance, grades, and office disciplinary referrals into the SEL-specific data they collect as another lens for examining SEL data (visit www.panoramaed.com/social-emotional-learning-sel).

- **xSEL Labs:** xSEL is an assessment provider that offers surveys that cover student social-emotional skills, climate ("how students see the conditions of learning"), and educator SEL belief, competency, and implementation data. xSEL Labs provides scalable systems to assess students' SEL development (visit https://xsel-labs.com).

- **Are You Ready to Assess Social and Emotional Learning and Development?** This resource from the American Institutes of Research provides a concise and useful primer on how to approach SEL assessment (visit www.air.org/sites/default/files/SEL-Ready-to-Assess-Stop-2019.pdf).

EPILOGUE

As educators, we are tasked with helping our children and youth to become strong, caring, successful adults. Our students of today need to become the capable friends, parents, neighbors, workers, and community members of tomorrow. SEL is truly about creating a positive future through educating the whole student. In this book, we've tried to provide concrete, practical, research-backed strategies schools can use to fully support the social, emotional, behavioral, and academic growth and success of all students.

Child and youth development happens at home, in neighborhoods, and across communities. But school is where students spend their days. To fully support the healthy development of students, we need to create the right kind of environments for them to spend those days in, support positive relationships with the people they are surrounded by at school, and teach the nonacademic knowledge, skills, and attitudes that fuel school and life success. Part of the reason for our recipe is that none of those ingredients stand alone; they all support one another. Positive relationships help provide a foundation for safe, predictable, positive environments and vice versa. The climates in classrooms and schools are inextricably linked to the connections among students and between students and adults. Students' abilities to both meet behavioral expectations and contribute to a positive environment as well as make friends and treat other students well are key targets of SEL lessons. Careful assessment helps schools understand both the quality of their SEL efforts as well as their impact.

Education is a human process driven by the skills, knowledge, and well-being of educators. That's why addressing SEL for the adults in schools is a fundamental part of a comprehensive and effective approach to SEL. We know that teaching is among the most stressful professions, and like their students, educators deserve to get the support they need to cope with challenges and be resilient. For student social and emotional development to be supported throughout every school day (not just in a short weekly lesson), educators need to do more than follow a scripted SEL lesson. They need to gain a personal understanding of the skills and competencies we want to teach students. SEL for adults improves teachers' abilities to create the environments and relationships students need to thrive, teach and support SEL lessons, and enhance their own well-being.

Though each is effective, none of the ingredients of our comprehensive SEL recipe are quick fixes. The challenge, and key to success, is consistently working toward lasting, sustainable implementation. This requires both strong, focused leadership and solid school staff buy-in and support. How well the ingredients are delivered can be as important as what ingredients you choose. Assessment can help you gauge progress over time in how much of and how well each of the ingredients are being implemented. Ideally, that information is then used as part of a continuous improvement effort that results in increasing benefits for students over time. Ultimately the success of SEL is cumulative, not something that can be quickly accomplished in a single burst of enthusiasm. Schools and districts that are successful at providing effective SEL make it a central part of their mission and a lasting priority.

REFERENCES AND RESOURCES

Abrams, Z. (2023). Kids' mental health is in crisis. Here's what psychologists are doing to help. *American Psychological Association Monitor on Psychology*, *54*(1), 63. Accessed at www.apa.org/monitor/2023/01/trends-improving-youth-mental-health on August 28, 2023.

AEI-Brookings Working Group on Poverty and Opportunity. (2015, December 3). *A good education is important to achieving the American dream.* Washington, DC: The Brookings Institution. Accessed at www.brookings.edu/research/a-good-education-is-important-to-achieving-the-american-dream on October 12, 2022.

Algozzine, B., Barrett, S., Eber, L., George, H., Horner, R., Lewis, T., et al. (2019). *School-wide PBIS tiered fidelity inventory*, version 2.1. OSEP Technical Assistance Center on Positive Behavioral Interventions and Supports. Accessed at www.pbis.org on October 2, 2023.

Allen, K., Kern, M. L., Vella-Brodrick, D., Hattie, J., & Waters, L. (2018). What schools need to know about fostering school belonging: A meta-analysis. *Education Psychology Review*, *30*(1), 1–34.

Álvarez-García, D., García, T., & González-Castro, P. (2014). Halo effect of student misbehavior on teacher ratings of impulsivity and other executive function deficits. In M. C. Olmstead (Ed.), *Psychology of impulsivity: New research* (pp. 21–31). Hauppauge, NY: Nova Science.

Alzahrani, M., Alharbi, M., & Alodwani, A. (2019). The effect of social-emotional competence on children academic achievement and behavioral development. *International Education Studies*, *12*(12), 141–149.

American Institutes for Research. (2019). *Are you ready to assess social and emotional learning and development?* Accessed at www.air.org/sites/default/files/SEL-Ready-to-Assess-Stop-2019.pdf on October 26, 2022.

Anda, R. F., Felitti, V. J., Bremner, J. D., Walker, J. D., Whitfield, C., Perry, B. D., et al. (2006). The enduring effects of abuse and related adverse experiences in childhood. *European Archives of Psychiatry and Clinical Neuroscience, 256*(3), 174–186.

Ayduk, Ö., & Kross, E. (2010). From a distance: Implications of spontaneous self-distancing for adaptive self-reflection. *Journal of Personality and Social Psychology, 98*(5), 809–829.

Baker, J. A., Grant, S., & Morlock, L. (2008). The teacher-student relationship as a developmental context for children with internalizing or externalizing behavior problems. *School Psychology Quarterly, 23*(1), 3–15.

Banks, T., & Obiakor, F. E. (2015). Culturally responsive positive behavior supports: Considerations for practice. *Journal of Education and Training Studies, 3*(2), 83–90.

Baumeister, R. F., & Leary, M. R. (1995). The need to belong: Desire for interpersonal attachments as a fundamental human motivation. *Psychological Bulletin, 117*(3), 497–529.

Bear, G. G. (2020). *Improving school climate: Practical strategies to reduce behavior problems and promote social and emotional learning.* New York: Routledge.

Becker, K. D., Bradshaw, C. P., Domitrovich, C., & Ialongo, N. S. (2013). Coaching teachers to improve implementation of the good behavior game. *Administration and Policy in Mental Health, 40*(6), 482–493.

Berry, Z. (2015). Explanations and implications of the fundamental attribution error: A review and proposal. *Journal of Integrated Social Sciences, 5*, 44–57.

Bingham, G. E., & Okagaki, L. (2012). Ethnicity and student engagement. In S. L. Christenson, A. L. Reschly, & C. Wylie (Eds.), *Handbook of research on student engagement* (pp. 65–95). Secaucus, NJ: Springer Science + Business Media.

Black, W. W., Fedewa, A. L., & Gonzalez, K. A. (2012). Effects of "safe school" programs and policies on the social climate for sexual-minority youth: A review of the literature. *Journal of LGBT Youth, 9*(4), 321–339.

Blank, C., & Shavit, Y. (2016). The association between student reports of classmates' disruptive behavior and student achievement. *AERA Open, 2*(3).

Bloomfield, M. A. P., McCutcheon, R. A., Kempton, M., Freeman, T. P., & Howes, O. (2019). The effects of psychosocial stress on dopaminergic function and the acute stress response. *eLife, 8*, Article e46797.

Bottiani, J. H., Bradshaw, C. P., & Mendelson, T. (2017). A multilevel examination of racial disparities in high school discipline: Black and white adolescents' perceived equity, school belonging, and adjustment problems. *Journal of Educational Psychology, 109*(4), 532–545.

Bottiani, J. H., Duran, C. A. K., Pas, E. T., & Bradshaw, C. P. (2019). Teacher stress and burnout in urban middle schools: Associations with job demands resources, and effective classroom practices. *Journal of School Psychology, 77*, 36–51.

Bowers, F., Cook, C.R., Jensen, M.E., Snyder, T., & Mchearern, A. (2017). Generalization and maintenance of positive peer reporting intervention for peer-rejected youth. *International Journal of Behavioral Consultation, 4*, 230–247.

Bradshaw, C. P. (2013). Preventing bullying through Positive Behavioral Interventions and Supports (PBIS): A multitiered approach to prevention and integration. *Theory Into Practice, 52*(4), 288–295.

Bradshaw, C. P., Koth, C. W., Thornton, L. A., & Leaf, P. J. (2009). Altering school climate through school-wide Positive Behavioral Interventions and Supports: Findings from a group-randomized effectiveness trial. *Prevention Science, 10*(2), 100–115.

Bradshaw, C. P., Pas, E. T., Debnam, K. J., & Johnson, S. L. (2021). A randomized controlled trial of MTSS-B in high schools: Improving classroom management to prevent EBDs. *Remedial and Special Education, 42*(1), 44–59.

Brasfield, M., Lancaster, C., & Yonghong, X. (2019). Wellness as a mitigating factor for teacher burnout. *Journal of Education, 199*(3), 166–179.

Brauner, C. B., & Stephens, C. B. (2006). Estimating the prevalence of early childhood serious emotional/behavioral disorders: Challenges and recommendations. *Public Health Reports, 121*(3), 303–310.

Bronfenbrenner, U. (1992). Ecological systems theory. In R. Vasta (Ed.), *Six theories of child development: Revised formulations and current issues* (pp. 187–249). Philadelphia, PA: Kingsley.

Bryant, G., Crowley, S., & Davidsen, C. (2020, July). *Finding your place: The current state of K–12 social emotional learning*. Boston: Tyton Partners. Accessed at https://d1hzkn4d3dn6lg.cloudfront.net/production/uploads/2020/07/Finding-Your-Place_The-Current-State-of-K-12-Social-Emotional-Learning.pdf on June 9, 2023.

Cacioppo, J. T., Ernst, J. M., Burleson, M. H., McClintock, M. K., Malarkey, W. B., Hawkley, L. C., et al. (2000). Lonely traits and concomitant physiological processes: The MacArthur social neuroscience studies. *International Journal of Psychophysiology, 35*(2–3), 143–154.

Carrell, S. E., Hoekstra, M., & Kuka, E. (2018). The long-run effects of disruptive peers. *American Economic Review, 108*(11), 3377–3415.

CASEL Guide to Schoolwide SEL – SEL Team. Accessed at https://schoolguide.casel.org/focus-area-1a/create-a-team on August 23, 2023.

CASEL Program Guide. (2023). Accessed at https://pg.casel.org on August 31, 2023.

Cavanaugh, B. (2013). Performance feedback and teachers' use of praise and opportunities to respond: A review of the literature. *Education & Treatment of Children, 36*(1), 111–137.

Center on PBIS. (2022). Supporting and responding to students' social, emotional, and behavior needs: Evidence-based practices for educators (version 2). Center on PBIS, University of Oregon. Accessed at https://global-uploads.webflow.com/5d3725188825e071f1670246/626c27c785879e08c1a7c8ea_Supporting%20and%20Responding%20to%20Students%E2%80%99%20Social%2C%20Emotional%2C%20and%20Behavioral%20Needs.pdf on September 7, 2023.

Center on the Developing Child at Harvard University. (n.d.). *Toxic stress derails healthy development* [Video file]. Accessed at https://developingchild.harvard.edu/resources/toxic-stress-derails-healthy-development on September 6, 2021.

Chaparro, E. A., Horner, R., Algozzine, B., Daily, J., & Nese, R. N. T. (April 2022). How school teams use data to make effective decisions: Team-initiated problem solving (TIPS). Center on PBIS, University of Oregon. Accessed at https://assets-global.website-files.com/5d3725188825e071f1670246/62506d7cebcf8d5172182bb1_How%20School%20Teams%20Use%20Data%20to%20Make%20Effective%20Decisions-%20Team-Initiated%20Problem%20Solving%20(TIPS)%20(1).pdf on September 11, 2023.

Christofferson, M., & Sullivan, A. L. (2015). Preservice teachers' classroom management training: A survey of self-reported training experiences, content coverage, and preparedness. *Psychology in the Schools, 52*(3), 248–264.

Coalition for Psychology in Schools and Education. (2006, August). *Report on the teacher needs survey*. Washington, DC: American Psychological Association & Center for Psychology in Schools and Education.

Cohen, G. L. (2022). *Belonging: The science of creating connection and bridging divides*. New York: W. W. Norton & Company, Inc.

Cohen, J., Espelage, D., Twemlow, S. W., Berkowitz, M. W., & Comer, J. P. (2015). Rethinking effective bully and violence prevention effects: Promoting healthy school climates, positive youth development, and preventing bully-victim-bystander behavior. *International Journal of Violence and Schools 15*, 2–40.

Collaborative for Academic, Social, and Emotional Learning. (n.d.a). CASEL Program Guide. Accessed at https://pg.casel.org on September 24, 2023.

Collaborative for Academic, Social, and Emotional Learning. (n.d.b). Fundamentals of SEL. Accessed at https://casel.org/fundamentals-of-sel on September 13, 2022.

Collaborative for Academic, Social, and Emotional Learning. (n.d.c). *What is the CASEL framework?* Accessed at https://casel.org/fundamentals-of-sel/what-is-the-casel-framework on September 13, 2022.

Collaborative for Academic, Social, and Emotional Learning. (n.d.d). *Student Social and Emotional Competence Assessment.* Accessed at https://casel.org/casel-gateway-student-sel-competence-assessment on September 23, 2023.

Collaborative for Academic, Social, and Emotional Learning. (n.d.e). *Assessment tools.* Accessed at https://casel.org/state-resource-center/assessment-tools on September 23, 2023.

Collaborative for Academic, Social, and Emotional Learning. (n.d.f). *Making SEL assessment work.* Accessed at https://casel.org/making-sel-assessment-work on September 23, 2023.

Collaborative for Academic, Social, and Emotional Learning. (n.d.g). *Selecting SEL assessments that are rigorous, reasonable, and relevant.* Accessed at https://casel.org/events/sel-assessments-aperature-webinars on September 23, 2023.

Colvin, G., Sugai, G., Good, R. H., & Lee, Y. Y. (1997). Using active supervision and precorrection to improve transition behaviors in an elementary school. *School Psychology Quarterly, 12*(4), 344–363.

Conroy, M. A., Sutherland, K. S., Snyder, A. L., & Marsh, S. (2008). Classwide interventions: Effective instruction makes a difference. *TEACHING Exceptional Children, 40*(6), 24–30.

Cook, C. (2019, October 8). No successful implementation without a dedicated team. IM4 Blog. Accessed at https://im4education.com/blog/Need-Dedicated-Team on September 11, 2023.

Cook, C. R., Coco, S., Zhang, Y., Fiat, A. E., Duong, M. T., Renshaw, T. L., et al. (2018). Cultivating positive teacher-student relationships: Preliminary evaluation of the Establish–Maintain–Restore (EMR) method. *School Psychology Review, 47*(3), 226–243.

Cook, C. R., Duong, M. T., McIntosh, K., Fiat, A. E., Larson, M., Pullmann, M. D., & McGinnis, J. (2018). Addressing discipline disparities for Black male students: Linking malleable root causes to feasible and effective practices. *School Psychology Review, 47*(2), 135–152.

Cook, C. R., Fiat, A. E., Larson, M., Daikos, C., Slemrod, T., Holland, E. A., et al. (2018). Positive greetings at the door: Evaluation of a low-cost, high-yield proactive classroom management strategy. *Journal of Positive Behavior Interventions, 20*(3), 149–159.

Cook, C. R., Frye, M., Slemrod, T., Lyon, A. R., Renshaw, T. L., & Zhang, Y. (2015). An integrated approach to universal prevention: Independent and combined effects of PBIS and SEL on youths' mental health. *School Psychology Quarterly, 30*(2), 166–183.

Cook, C. R., Grady, E. A., Long, A. C., Renshaw, T., Codding, R. S., Fiat, A., & Larson, M. (2017). Evaluating the impact of increasing general education teachers' ratio of positive to-negative interactions on students' classroom behavior. *Journal of Positive Behavior Interventions, 19*, 67–77.

Cook, C. R., Thayer, A. J., Fiat, A., & Sullivan, M. (2020). Interventions to enhance affective engagement. In A. L. Reschly, A. J. Pohl, & S. L. Christenson (Eds.), *Student engagement: Effective academic, behavioral, cognitive, and affective interventions at school* (pp. 203–237). New York: Springer.

Cooper, J. T., Gage, N. A., Alter, P. J., LaPolla, S., MacSuga-Gage, A. S., & Scott, T. M. (2018). Educators' self-reported training, use, and perceived effectiveness of evidence-based classroom management practices. *Preventing School Failure: Alternative Education for Children and Youth, 62*(1), 13–24.

Corcoran, R. P., Cheung, A. C. K., Kim, E., & Xie, C. (2018). Effective universal school-based social and emotional learning programs for improving academic achievement: A systematic review and meta-analysis of 50 years of research. *Educational Research Review, 25*, 56–72.

Côté-Lussier, C., & Fitzpatrick, C. (2016). Feelings of safety at school, socioemotional functioning, and classroom engagement. *Journal of Adolescent Health, 58*(5), 543–550.

Crum, A. J., Akinola, M., Martin, A., & Fath, S. (2017). The role of stress mindset in shaping cognitive, emotional, and physiological responses to challenging and threatening stress. *Anxiety, Stress, and Coping, 30*(4), 379–395.

Cunningham, T. R., & Geller, E. S. (2008). Organizational behavior management in health care: Applications for large-scale improvements in patient safety. In: K. Henriksen, J. Battles, M. A. Keyes, & M. L. Grady (Eds.), *Advances in patient safety: New directions and alternative approaches* (Vol. 2: Culture and Redesign). Rockville (MD): Agency for Healthcare Research and Quality (US). Accessed at www.ncbi.nlm.nih.gov/books/NBK43716 on September 8, 2023.

Darling-Hammond, L., & Cook-Harvey, C. M. (2018, September). *Educating the whole child: Improving school climate to support student success.* Palo Alto, CA: Learning Policy Institute.

Davidson, K. (2016). Employers find "soft skills" like critical thinking in short supply. *Wall Street Journal.* Accessed at https://www.wsj.com/articles/employers-find-soft-skills-like-critical-thinking-in-short-supply-1472549400 on September 13, 2023.

Deming, W. E. (n.d.). PDSA Cycle. Accessed at https://deming.org/explore/pdsa on September 5, 2023.

DePaoli, J. L., Atwell, M. N., Bridgeland, J. M., & Shriver, T. P. (2018, November). *Respected: Perspectives of youth on high school and social and emotional learning.* Chicago: CASEL.

De Pry, R. L., & Sugai, G. (2002). The effect of active supervision and pre-correction on minor behavioral incidents in a sixth grade general education classroom. *Journal of Behavioral Education, 11*(4), 255–267.

Diliberti, M. K., Schwartz, H. L., & Grant, D. (2021). *Stress topped the reasons why public school teachers quit, even before COVID-19.* Santa Monica, CA: RAND Corporation. Accessed at www.rand.org/pubs/research_reports/RRA1121-2.html on January 1, 2023.

Dineen, J. N., Chafouleas, S. M., Briesch, A. M., McCoach, D. B., Newton, S. D., & Cintron, D. W. (2022). Exploring social, emotional, and behavioral screening approaches in U.S. public school districts. *American Educational Research Journal, 59*(1), 146–179.

Doan, S., Steiner, E. D., Pandey, R., & Woo, R. (2023). *Teacher well-being and intentions to leave: Findings from the 2023 State of the American Teacher survey.* Santa Monica, CA: RAND Corporation. Accessed at www.rand.org/pubs/research_reports/RRA1108-8.html on September 24, 2023.

Dods, J. (2013). Enhancing understanding of the nature of supportive school-based relationships for youth who have experienced trauma. *Canadian Journal of Education, 36*(1), 71–95.

Domitrovich, C. E., Bradshaw, C. P., Greenberg, M. T., Embry, D., Poduska, J. M., & Ialongo, N. S. (2010). Integrated models of school-based prevention: Logic and theory. *Psychology in the Schools, 47*(1), 71–88.

Duong, M. T., Pullmann, M. D., Buntain-Ricklefs, J., Lee, K., Benjamin, K. S., Nguyen, L., & Cook, C. R. (2019). Brief teacher training improves student behavior and student-teacher relationships in middle school. *School Psychology, 34*(2), 212–221.

Durlak, J. A., Domitrovich, C. E., Weissberg, R. P., & Gullotta, T. P. (Eds.). (2015). *Handbook of social and emotional learning: Research and practice.* New York: Guilford Press.

Durlak, J. A., Weissberg, R. P., Dymnicki, A. B., Taylor, R. D., & Schellinger, K. B. (2011). The impact of enhancing students' social and emotional learning: A meta-analysis of school-based universal interventions. *Child Development, 82*(1), 405–432.

Durlak, J. A., Weissberg, R. P., & Pachan, M. (2010). A meta-analysis of after-school programs that seek to promote personal and social skills in children and adolescents. *American Journal of Community Psychology, 45*(3–4), 294–309.

Dweck, C. S. (2016). *Mindset: The new psychology of success* (Updated ed.). New York: Random House.

Eccles, J. S., & Roeser, R. W. (2011). School and community influences on human development. In M. H. Bornstein & M. E. Lamb (Eds.), *Developmental science: An advanced textbook* (pp. 571–643). Psychology Press.

Edmondson, A. C., & Lei, Z. (2014). Psychological safety: The history, renaissance, and future of an interpersonal construct. *Annual Review of Organizational Psychology and Organizational Behavior, 1*, 23–43.

Edmonson, S. L., Tatman, R., & Slate, J. R. (2009). Character education: An historical overview. *International Journal of Educational Leadership Preparation, 4*, 159.

Ellingsen, D. M., Leknes, S., Løseth, G., Wessberg, J., & Olausson, H. (2016). The neurobiology shaping affective touch: Expectation, motivation, and meaning in the multisensory context. *Frontiers in Psychology, 6*, 1986.

Emmons, R. A., Froh, J., & Rose, R. (2019). Gratitude. In M. W. Gallagher & S. J. Lopez (Eds.), *Positive psychological assessment: A handbook of models and measures* (2nd ed., pp. 317–332). Washington, DC: American Psychological Association.

Ennis, R. P., Lane, K. L., & Flemming, S. C. (2020). Empowering teachers with low-intensity strategies: Supporting students at-risk for EBD with instructional choice during reading. *Exceptionality, 29*, 1–19.

Ennis, R. P., Lane, K. L., Oakes, W. P., & Flemming, S. C. (2020). Empowering teachers with low-intensity strategies to support instruction: Implementing across-activity choices during third-grade reading instruction. *Journal of Positive Behavior Interventions, 22*(2), 78–92.

Evertson, C. M., & Poole, I. R. (2008). Proactive classroom management. In T. L. Good (Ed.), *21st century education: A reference handbook* (pp. 131–139). Thousand Oaks, CA: SAGE.

Farrington, C., Porter, S., & Klugman, J. (2019, October). *Do classroom environments matter for noncognitive aspects of student performance and students' course grades?* [Working paper]. University of Chicago Consortium on School Research. Accessed at https://consortium.uchicago.edu/publications/do-classroom-environments-matter-for-noncognitive-aspects-of-student-performance-and-students-course-grades on October 10, 2022.

Farrington, C. A., Roderick, M., Allensworth, E., Nagaoka, J., Keyes, T. S., Johnson, D. W., & Beechum, N. O. (2012). *Teaching adolescents to become learners: The role of noncognitive factors in shaping school performance: A critical literature review.* Chicago: University of Chicago Consortium on Chicago School Research.

Fekete, E.M., Deichert, N.T. A brief gratitude writing intervention decreased stress and negative affect during the COVID-19 pandemic. *Journal of Happiness Studies, 23*, 2427–2448 (2022).

Flower, A., McKenna, J. W., Bunuan, R. L., Muething, C. S., & Vega, R. (2014). Effects of the good behavior game on challenging behaviors in school settings. *Review of Educational Research, 84*(4), 546–571. https://doi.org/10.3102/0034654314536781

Fredricks, J. A., Reschly, A. L., & Christenson, S. L. (Eds.). (2019). Interventions for student engagement: Overview and state of the field. In J. A. Fredricks, A. L. Reschly, & S. L. Christenson (Eds.), *Handbook of student engagement interventions: Working with disengaged students* (pp. 1–11). Cambridge, MA: Academic Press.

Fredricks, J. A., Ye, F., Wang, M.-T., & Brauer, S. (2019). Profiles of school disengagement: Not all disengaged students are alike. In J. A. Fredricks, A. L. Reschly, & S. L. Christenson (Eds.), *Handbook of student engagement interventions: Working with disengaged students* (pp. 31–43). Cambridge, MA: Academic Press.

Furlong, M. J., You, S., Renshaw, T. L., O'Malley, M. D., & Rebelez, J. (2013). Preliminary development of the Positive Experiences at School Scale for elementary school children. *Child Indicators Research, 6*(4), 753–775.

Furlong, M. J., You, S., Renshaw, T. L., Smith, D. C., & O'Malley, M. D. (2014). Preliminary development and validation of the Social and Emotional Health Survey for secondary students. *Social Indicators Research, 117*(3), 1011–1032.

Gaab, J., Rohleder, N., Nater, U. M., & Ehlert, U. (2005). Psychological determinants of the cortisol stress response: The role of anticipatory cognitive appraisal. *Psychoneuroendocrinology, 30*(6), 599–610.

Gage, N. A., Whitford, D. K., & Katsiyannis, A. (2018). A review of schoolwide positive behavior interventions and supports as a framework for reducing disciplinary exclusions. *The Journal of Special Education, 52*(3), 142–151.

Gottman, J. M., Coan, J., Carrere, S., & Swanson, C. (1998). Predicting marital happiness and stability from newlywed interactions. *Journal of Marriage and the Family, 60*(1), 5–22.

Gottman, J. M., & Levenson, R. W. (2000). The timing of divorce: Predicting when a couple will divorce over a 14-year period. *Journal of Marriage and the Family, 62*(3), 737–745.

Greater Good Science Center. (n.d.). *Positive staff relationships: Why are they important?* Accessed at https://ggie.berkeley.edu/school-relationships/positive-staff-relationships/#tab__2 on September 6, 2021.

Greenberg, M. T., Brown, J. L., & Abenavoli, R. M. (2016). Teacher stress and health: Effects on teachers, students, and schools. University Park, PA: Edna Bennett Pierce Prevention Research Center, The Pennsylvania State University.

Greenberg, M. T., Domitrovich, C. E., Weissberg, R. P., & Durlak, J. A. (2017). Social and emotional learning as a public health approach to education. *The Future of Children, 27*(1), 13–32.

Grissom, J. A., Egalite, A. J., & Lindsay, C. A. (2021). "How principals affect students and schools: A systematic synthesis of two decades of research." New York: The Wallace Foundation. Accessed at www.wallacefoundation.org/principalsynthesis on September 11, 2023.

Herman, K. C., Reinke, W. M., Thompson, A. M., Hawley, K., Wallis, K., & Stormont, M., et al. (2021). A public health approach to reducing the societal prevalence and burden of youth mental health problems: Introduction to the special issue. *School Psychology Review, 50*(1), 8–16.

Huang, F., & Anyon, Y. (2020). The relationship between school disciplinary resolutions with school climate and attitudes toward school. *Preventing School Failure: Alternative Education for Children and Youth, 64*(3), 212–222.

Huang, Y. (2011). Can virtue be taught and how? Confucius on the paradox of moral education. *Journal of Moral Education, 40*(2), 141–159.

Hughes, K., Bellis, M. A., Hardcastle, K. A., Sethi, D., Butchart, A., Mikton, C., et al. (2017). The effect of multiple adverse childhood experiences on health: A systematic review and meta-analysis. *The Lancet Public Health, 2*(8), Article e356–e366.

Humanists UK. (2023, September 8). First International Moral Education Congress. Accessed at from https://heritage.humanists.uk/moral-education-congress on September 8, 2023.

Hunzicker, J. (2010, June). *Characteristics of effective professional development: A checklist* (ED510366). ERIC. Accessed at https://files.eric.ed.gov/fulltext/ED510366.pdf on June 9, 2023.

Institute of Education Sciences. (2020). *Race and ethnicity of public school teachers and their students*. U.S. Department of Education. Accessed at https://nces.ed.gov/pubs 2020/2020103/index.asp on December 5, 2022.

Irvin, M. J., Meece, J. L., Byun, S., Farmer, T. W., & Hutchins, B. C. (2011). Relationship of school context to rural youth's educational achievement and aspirations. *Journal of Youth and Adolescence, 40*(9), 1225–1242.

Jennings, P. A., & Greenberg, M. T. (2009). The prosocial classroom: teacher social and emotional competence in relation to student and classroom outcomes. *Review of Education Research, 79*, 491–525.

Johnson, L. R. (2016). Editorial: How fear and stress shape the mind. *Frontiers in Behavioral Neuroscience, 10*, 24.

Jones, E. E., & Harris, V. A. (1967). The attribution of attitudes. *Journal of Experimental Social Psychology*, *3*(1), 1–24.

Jones, S. M., & Kahn, J. (2017, September 13). *The evidence base for how we learn: Supporting students' social, emotional, and academic development*. Washington, DC: Aspen Institute.

Joyce, B., & Showers, B. (2002). *Student achievement through staff development* (3rd ed.). Alexandria, VA: ASCD.

Kariou, A., Koutsimani, P., Montgomery, A., & Lainidi, O. (2021). Emotional labor and burnout among teachers: A systematic review. *International Journal of Environmental Research and Public Health*, *18*(23), 12760.

Kidd, C., Palmeri, H., & Aslin, R. N. (2013). Rational snacking: Young children's decision-making on the marshmallow task is moderated by beliefs about environmental reliability. *Cognition*, *126*(1), 109–114.

Kim, J., Walsh, E., Pike, K., & Thompson, E. A. (2020). Cyberbullying and victimization and youth suicide risk: The buffering effects of school connectedness. *The Journal of School Nursing*, *36*(4), 251–257.

King, K., Yahya, D., & Mahfouz, J. (2022, November 29). Six self-care practices for school leaders. Greater Good Science Center. Accessed at https://greatergood.berkeley.edu/article/item/six_self_care_practices_for_school_leaders on September 5, 2023.

Kirk, E. R., Becker, J. A., Skinner, C. H., Fearrington, J. Y., McCane-Bowling, S. J., Amburn, C., et al. (2010). Decreasing inappropriate vocalizations using classwide group contingencies and color wheel procedures: A component analysis. *Psychology in the Schools*, *47*(9), 931–943.

Kobau, R., Seligman, M. E., Peterson, C., Diener, E., Zack, M. M., Chapman, D., & Thompson, W. (2011). Mental health promotion in public health: perspectives and strategies from positive psychology. *American Journal of Public Health*, *101*(8), e1–e9.

Korpershoek, H., Canrinus, E. T., Fokkens-Bruinsma, M., & de Boer, H. (2020). The relationships between school belonging and students' motivational, social-emotional, behavioural, and academic outcomes in secondary education: A meta-analytic review. *Research Papers in Education*, *35*(6), 641–680.

Kretlow, A. G., Cooke, N. L., & Wood, C. L. (2012). Using in-service and coaching to increase teachers' accurate use of research-based strategies. *Remedial and Special Education*, *33*(6), 348–361.

Kross, E. (2021). *Chatter: The voice in our head, why it matters, and how to harness it*. New York: Crown.

Langille, D. B., Asbridge, M., Cragg, A., & Rasic, D. (2015). Associations of school connectedness with adolescent suicidality: Gender differences and the role of risk of depression. *Canadian Journal of Psychiatry, 60*(6), 258–267.

La Salle, T. P., Wang, C., Wu, C., & Neves, J. R. (2019). Racial mismatch among minoritized students and white teachers: Implications and recommendations for moving forward. *Journal of Educational and Psychological Consultation, 29*(3), 314–343. doi:10.1080/10459880.2019.1662821

La Salle, T. P, Wang, C., Wu, C., & Rocha Neves, J. (2020). Racial mismatch among minoritized students and white teachers: Implications and recommendations for moving forward. *Journal of Educational and Psychological Consultation, 30*(3), 314–343.

Lenzi, M., Sharkey, J., Furlong, M. J., Mayworm, A., Hunnicutt, K., & Vieno, A. (2017). School sense of community, teacher support, and students' school safety perceptions. *American Journal of Community Psychology, 60*(3–4), 527–537.

Levy, D. J., Heissel, J. A., Richeson, J. A., & Adam, E. K. (2016). Psychological and biological responses to race-based social stress as pathways to disparities in educational outcomes. *American Psychologist, 71*(6), 455–473.

Lewis, T. J., Colvin, G., & Sugai, G. (2000). The effects of pre-correction and active supervision on the recess behavior of elementary students. *Education and Treatment of Children, 23*(2), 109–121.

Li, S., Sheng, Y., & Jing, Y. (2022). How social support impacts teachers' mental health literacy: A chain mediation model. *Frontiers in Psychology, 13*, 851332. doi:10.3389/fpsyg.2022.851332

Lieberman, M. D., Eisenberger, N. I., Crockett, M. J., Tom, S. M., Pfeifer, J. H., & Way, B. M. (2007). Putting feelings into words: Affect labeling disrupts amygdala activity in response to affective stimuli. *Psychological Science, 18*(5), 421–428.

Little, S. G., & Akin-Little, A. (2008). Psychology's contributions to classroom management. *Psychology in the Schools, 45*(3), 227–234.

Little, S. G., Akin-Little, A., O'Neill, K. (2015). Group contingency interventions with children—1980–2010: A meta-analysis. *Behavior Modification, 39*(2): 322–341.

Logan-Greene, P., Green, S., Nurius, P. S., & Longhi, D. (2014). Distinct contributions of adverse childhood experiences and resilience resources: A cohort analysis of adult physical and mental health. *Social Work in Health Care, 53*(8), 776–797.

Longobardi, C., Prino, L. E., Marengo, D., & Settanni, M. (2016). Student-teacher relationships as a protective factor for school adjustment during the transition from middle to high school. *Frontiers in Psychology, 7*, 1988.

Losada, M., & Heaphy, E. (2004). The role of positivity and connectivity in the performance of business teams: A nonlinear dynamics model. *American Behavioral Scientist, 47*(6), 740–765.

Lynam, D. R., Milich, R., Zimmerman, R., Novak, S. P., Logan, T. K., Martin, C., et al. (1999). Project DARE: No effects at 10-year follow-up. *Journal of Consulting and Clinical Psychology, 67*(4), 590–593.

Maas, J., Schoch, S., Scholz, U., Rackow, P., Schüler, J., Wegner, M., & Keller, R. (2022). School principals' social support and teachers' basic need satisfaction: The mediating role of job demands and job resources. *Social Psychology of Education, 25*, 1545–1562.

MacDonald, G., & Jensen-Campbell, L. A. (Eds.). (2011). *Social pain: Neuropsychological and health implications of loss and exclusion.* Washington, DC: American Psychological Association.

Mahfouz, J., King, K., & Yahya, D. (2022, September 6). "Five ways to support the well-being of school leaders." Greater Good Science Center. Accessed at https://greatergood.berkeley.edu/article/item/five_ways_to_support_the_wellbeing_of_school_leaders on September 5, 2023.

Mahoney, J. L., Durlak, J. A., & Weissberg, R. P. (2018). An update on social and emotional learning outcome research. *Phi Delta Kappan, 100*(4), 18–23.

Making Caring Common. (2021, February). *Loneliness in America: How the pandemic has deepened an epidemic of loneliness and what we can do about it.* Harvard Graduate School of Education. Accessed at https://mcc.gse.harvard.edu/reports/loneliness-in-america on February 24, 2023.

Maldonado-Carreño, C., & Votruba-Drzal, E. (2011). Teacher-child relationships and the development of academic and behavioral skills during elementary school: A within- and between-child analysis. *Child Development, 82*(2), 601–616.

Malloy, J. M., Bohanon, H., & Francoeur, K. (2018). Positive behavioral interventions and supports in high schools: A case study from New Hampshire. *Journal of Educational and Psychological Consultation, 28*(2), 219–247.

Maslach, C., & Leiter, M. P. (2016). Burnout. In G. Fink (Ed.), *Stress: Concepts, cognition, emotion, and behavior* (pp. 351–357). London: Elsevier Academic Press.

Mather, M. (2010). *U.S. children in single-mother families.* Population Reference Bureau. Accessed at www.prb.org/wp-content/uploads/2010/05/05152010-single-mother families.pdf on July 6, 2023.

Matheson, A. S., & Shriver, M. D. (2005). Training teachers to give effective commands: Effects on student compliance and academic behaviors. *School Psychology Review, 34*(2), 202–219.

Maxwell, S., Reynolds, K. J., Lee, E., Subasic, E., & Bromhead, D. (2017). The impact of school climate and school identification on academic achievement: Multilevel modeling with student and teacher data. *Frontiers in Psychology, 8,* 2069.

McKown, C., Herman, B. (2020). *SEL Assessment to Support Effective Social Emotional Learning Practices at Scale.* Edna Bennett. Pierce Prevention Research Center, Penn State University. Accessed at https://prevention.psu.edu/wp-content/uploads/2022/09/PSU-SEL-Assessment-Brief.pdf on August 22, 2023.

Menzies, H. M., Lane, K. L., Oakes, W. P., & Ennis, R. P. (2017). Increasing students' opportunities to respond: A strategy for supporting engagement. *Intervention in School and Clinic, 52*(4), 204–209.

Merrell, K. W. (2011). *Social and emotional assets and resilience scales (SEARS).* Lutz, FL: Psychological Assessment Resources.

Merrell, K. W., Cohn, B. P., & Tom, K. M. (2011). Development and validation of a teacher report measure for assessing social-emotional strengths of children and adolescents. *School Psychology Review, 40*(2), 226–241.

Mischel, W., & Metzner, R. (1962). Preference for delayed reward as a function of age, intelligence, and length of delay interval. *Journal of Abnormal and Social Psychology, 64,* 425–431.

Miu, A. S., & Yeager, D. S. (2015). Preventing symptoms of depression by teaching adolescents that people can change: Effects of a brief incremental theory of personality intervention at 9-month follow-up. *Clinical Psychological Science, 3*(5), 726–743.

Moffett, L., Flannagan, C., & Shah, P. (2020). The influence of environmental reliability in the marshmallow task: An extension study. *Journal of Experimental Child Psychology, 194,* Article 104821.

Moffitt, T. E., Arseneault, L., Belsky, D., Dickson, N., Hancox, R. J., Harrington, H., et al. (2011). A gradient of childhood self-control predicts health, wealth, and public safety. *Proceedings of the National Academy of Sciences of the United States of America, 108*(7), 2693–2698.

Moore Partin, T. C., Robertson, R. E., Maggin, D. M., Oliver, R. M., & Wehby, J. H. (2009). Using teacher praise and opportunities to respond to promote appropriate student behavior. *Preventing School Failure: Alternative Education for Children and Youth, 54*(3), 172–178.

Morrissey, K. L., Bohanon, H., & Fenning, P. (2010). Positive behavior support: Teaching and acknowledging expected behaviors in an urban high school. *TEACHING Exceptional Children, 42*(5), 26–35.

Murphy, J., & Zlomke, K. (2014). Positive peer reporting in the classroom: A review of intervention procedures. *Behavior Analysis in Practice, 7*(2), 126–137.

Murphy, M. C., & Zirkel, S. (2015). Race and belonging in school: How anticipated and experienced belonging affect choice, persistence, and performance. *Teachers College Record, 117*(12), 1–40.

Murray, C., & Pianta, R. C. (2007). The importance of teacher-student relationships for adolescents with high incidence disabilities. *Theory Into Practice, 46*(2), 105–112.

Murthy, V. (2023, May 3). New surgeon general advisory raises alarm about devastating impact of epidemic of loneliness and isolation in the United States. Accessed at www.hhs.gov/about/news/2023/05/03/new-surgeon-general-advisory-raises-alarm-about-devastating-impact-epidemic-loneliness-isolation-united-states.html on September 6, 2023.

Naglieri, J. A., LeBuffe, P. A., & Shapiro, V. B. (2011a). *The Devereux Student Strengths Assessment—Mini (DESSA-Mini): Assessment, technical manual, and user's guide.* Charlotte, NC: Apperson.

Naglieri, J. A., LeBuffe, P., & Shapiro, V. B. (2011b). Universal screening for social-emotional competencies: A study of the reliability and validity of the DESSA-mini. *Psychology in the Schools, 48*(7), 660–671.

National Center for Education Statistics. (2023). Characteristics of public school teachers. Condition of Education. U.S. Department of Education, Institute of Education Sciences. Accessed at https://nces.ed.gov//programs/coe/indicator/clr on September 6, 2023.

National Center on Safe Supportive Learning Environments (n.d.). School climate improvement. Accessed at https://safesupportivelearning.ed.gov/school-climate-improvement on September 23, 2023.

National Forum on Education Statistics. (2016). Forum Guide to Collecting and Using Disaggregated Data on Racial/Ethnic Subgroups. (NFES 2017-017). U.S. Department of Education. Washington, DC: National Center for Education Statistics.

National Scientific Council on the Developing Child. (2020). Connecting the brain to the rest of the body: Early childhood development and lifelong health are deeply intertwined. Working Paper No. 15. Cambridge, MA: Center on the Developing Child at Harvard University.

Newman, J., & Dusenbury, L. (2015). Social and emotional learning (SEL): A framework for academic, social, and emotional success. In K. Bosworth (Ed.), *Prevention science in school settings: Complex relationships and processes* (pp. 287–306). New York: Springer.

Niehaus, K., Irvin, M. J., & Rogelberg, S. (2016). School connectedness and valuing as predictors of high school completion and postsecondary attendance among Latino youth. *Contemporary Educational Psychology, 44–45*, 54–67.

Niehaus, K., Rudasill, K. M., & Rakes, C. R. (2012). A longitudinal study of school connectedness and academic outcomes across sixth grade. *Journal of School Psychology, 50*(4), 443–460.

Niolon, P. D. (n.d.). Preventing and Addressing ACEs in CDC's Injury Center [slide deck]. Centers for Disease Control and Prevention. Accessed at www.miace.org/wp-content/uploads/2023/06/Kenote-Dr.-Niolon.CDC_.pdf on August 21, 2023.

Oberle, E., & Schonert-Reichl, K. A. (2016). Stress contagion in the classroom? The link between classroom teacher burnout and morning cortisol in elementary school students. *Social Science and Medicine, 159*, 30–37.

Office of Juvenile Justice and Delinquency Prevention. (2023, April 18). Poverty status of children by family structure. Statistical Briefing Book. Accessed at www.ojjdp.gov/ojstatbb/population/qa01203.asp?qaDate=2021 on September 5, 2023.

Office of the Surgeon General (2022). *Framework for workplace mental health and well-being.* Accessed at www.hhs.gov/surgeongeneral/priorities/workplace-well-being/index.html on September 23, 2023.

Olivier, E., Morin, A. J. S., Langlois, J., Tardif-Grenier, K., & Archambault, I. (2020). Internalizing and externalizing behavior problems and student engagement in elementary and secondary school students. *Journal of Youth and Adolescence, 49*(11), 2327–2346.

OSEP. (2012). Positive Behavioral Interventions and Supports: What is school-wide PBIS? Accessed at https://www.pbis.org on November 23, 2022.

Osterman, K. F. (2000). Students' need for belonging in the school community. *Review of Educational Research, 70*(3), 323–367.

Owens, J. (2023). Seeing behavior as black, brown, or white: Teachers' racial/ethnic bias in perceptions of routine classroom misbehavior. *Social Psychology Quarterly, 86*(3), 298–311.

Panorama for Social Emotional Learning (n.d.a). Accessed at www.panoramaed.com/social-emotional-learning-sel on September 23, 2023.

Pas, E. T., Hoon Ryoo, J., Musci, R. J., & Bradshaw, C. P. (2019). A state-wide quasi-experimental effectiveness study of the scale-up of school-wide Positive Behavioral Interventions and Supports. *Journal of School Psychology, 73*, 41–55.

Peetz, C. (2023). Kids' declining mental health is the 'crisis of our time,' surgeon general says. *Education Week.* Accessed at www.edweek.org/leadership/kids-declining-mental-health-is-the-crisis-of-our-time-surgeon-general-says/2023/04 on September 28, 2023.

Perou, R., Bitsko, R. H., Blumberg, S. J., Pastor, P., Ghandour, R. M., Gfroerer, J. C., et al. (2013). Mental health surveillance among children—United States, 2005–2011. *MMWR Supplements*, *62*(2), 1–35.

Pianta, R., & Hamre, B. (2001). *Banking time: Preschool relationships enhancement project: Pre–K manual*. Charlottesville, VA: Center for Advanced Study of Teaching and Learning.

Pianta, R. C., Hamre, B. K., & Allen, J. P. (2012). Teacher-student relationships and engagement: Conceptualizing, measuring, and improving the capacity of classroom interactions. In S. L. Christenson, A. L. Reschly, & C. Wylie (Eds.), *Handbook of research on student engagement* (pp. 365–386). New York: Springer.

Pollastri, A. R., Epstein, L. D., Heath, G. H., & Ablon, J. S. (2013). The collaborative problem solving approach: Outcomes across settings. *Harvard Review of Psychiatry*, *21*(4), 188–199.

Provasnik, S., & Dorfman, S. (2005, June). *Mobility in the teacher workforce* (NCES 2005–114). U.S. Department of Education, National Center for Education Statistics. Washington, DC: U.S. Government Printing Office.

Rathvon, N. (2008). *Effective school interventions: Evidence-based strategies for improving student outcomes* (2nd ed.). New York: Guilford Press.

Raver, C. C. (2002). Emotions matter: Making the case for the role of young children's emotional development for early school readiness. *Social Policy Report*, *16*(3), 1–20.

Reinke, W. M., Stormont, M., Herman, K. C., & Newcomer, L. (2014). Using coaching to support teacher implementation of classroom-based interventions. *Journal of Behavioral Education*, *23*(1), 150–167.

Romer, N., von der Embse, N., Eklund, K., Kilgus, S., Perales, K., Williams Splett, J., et al. (2020). *Best practices in universal social, emotional, and behavioral screening: An implementation guide* (Version 2.0). Accessed at https://smhcollaborative.org/universalscreening on August 5, 2022.

Royer, D. J., Lane, K. L., Dunlap, K. D., & Ennis, R. P. (2019). A systematic review of teacher-delivered behavior-specific praise on K–12 student performance. *Remedial and Special Education*, *40*(2), 112–128.

Ruiz, L. D., McMahon, S. D., & Jason, L. A. (2018). The role of neighborhood context and school climate in school-level academic achievement. *American Journal of Community Psychology*, *61*(3–4), 296–309.

Ryan, A. M., & Patrick, H. (2001). The classroom social environment and changes in adolescents' motivation and engagement during middle school. *American Educational Research Journal*, *38*(2), 437–460.

Sabol, T. J., & Pianta, R. C. (2012). Recent trends in research on teacher-child relationships. *Attachment and Human Development*, *14*(3), 213–231.

Sabol, T. J., & Pianta, R. C. (2013). Relationships between teachers and children. In I. B. Weiner (Ed.), *Handbook of psychology* (2nd ed., Vol. 7, 199–211). Hoboken, NJ: Wiley.

Salzman, C. D., & Fusi, S. (2010). Emotion, cognition, and mental state representation in amygdala and prefrontal cortex. *Annual Review of Neuroscience*, *33*, 173–202.

Schaeffer, K. (2022). "Just over half of U.S. public schools offer mental health assessments for students; fewer offer treatment." Pew Research Center. Accessed at www.pewresearch.org/short-reads/2022/08/10/just-over-half-of-u-s-public-schools-offer-mental-health-assessments-for-students-fewer-offer-treatment on August 28, 2023.

Schirf, E., & Serapiglia, A. (2017, November). Identifying the real technology skills gap: A qualitative look across disciplines. *Information Systems Education Journal*, *15*(6), 72–82.

Schonert-Reichl, K. A. (2017). Social and emotional learning and teachers. *The Future of Children*, *27*(1), 137–155.

Schultz, I., Milner, R., Hanson, D., & Winter, A. (2011). Employer attitudes towards accommodations in mental health disability. 10.1007/978-1-4419-0428-7_17.

Sebastian, J., Allensworth, E., & Huang, H. (2016). The role of teacher leadership in how principals influence classroom instruction and student learning. *American Journal of Education*, *123*(1), 69–108.

Sege, R. D., & Harper Browne, C. (2017). Responding to ACEs with HOPE: Health outcomes from positive experiences. *Academic Pediatrics*, *17*(7), S79–S85.

Shakman, K., Bailey, J., Breslow, N. (2017). A primer for continuous improvement in schools and districts. Education Development Center. Accessed at www.edc.org/sites/default/files/uploads/primer_for_continuous_improvement.pdf on August 23, 2023.

Shapiro, V. B., Kim, B. K. E., Robitaille, J. L., & LeBuffe, P. A. (2017). Protective factor screening for prevention practice: Sensitivity and specificity of the DESSA-Mini. *School Psychology Quarterly*, *32*(4), 449–464.

Shea, C. M., Jacobs, S. R., Esserman, D. A., Bruce, K., & Weiner, B. J. (2014). Organizational readiness for implementing change: A psychometric assessment of a new measure. *Implementation Science*, *9*, Article 7.

Shek, D. T., Dou, D., Zhu, X., & Chai, W. (2019). Positive youth development: current perspectives. *Adolescent Health, Medicine and Therapeutics*, *10*, 131–141.

Short, N. A., Boffa, J. W., Clancy, K., & Schmidt, N. B. (2018). Effects of emotion regulation strategy use in response to stressors on PTSD symptoms: An ecological momentary assessment study. *Journal of affective disorders, 230,* 77–83.

Siegel, D. J. (2013). *Brainstorm: The power and purpose of the teenage brain.* New York: Tarcher/Penguin.

Siegel, D. J. (2020). *The developing mind: How relationships and the brain interact to shape who we are* (3rd ed.). New York: Guilford Press.

Simonsen, B., & Myers, D. (2015). *Classwide positive behavior interventions and supports: A guide to proactive classroom management.* New York: Guilford Press.

Skaalvik, E. M., & Skaalvik, S. (2018). Job demands and job resources as predictors of teacher motivation and well-being. *Social Psychology of Education, 21.* 1251–1275.

Skiba, R. J., Arredondo, M. I., & Williams, N. T. (2014). More than a metaphor: The contribution of exclusionary discipline to a school-to-prison pipeline. *Equity and Excellence in Education, 47*(4), 546–564.

Skiba, R. J., & Karega Rausch, M. (2006). Zero tolerance, suspension, and expulsion: Questions of equity and effectiveness. In C. M. Evertson & C. S. Weinstein (Eds.), *Handbook of classroom management: Research, practice, and contemporary issues* (pp. 1063–1089). New York: Routledge.

Smith, B. H. (2013). School-based character education in the United States. *Childhood Education, 89*(6), 350–355.

Steiner, R. J., Sheremenko, G., Lesesne, C., Dittus, P. J., Sieving, R. E., & Ethier, K. A. (2019). Adolescent connectedness and adult health outcomes. *Pediatrics, 144*(1), Article e20183766.

Stichter, J. P., Lewis, T. J., Whittaker, T. A., Richter, M., Johnson, N. W., & Trussell, R. P. (2009). Assessing teacher use of opportunities to respond and effective classroom management strategies: Comparisons among high- and low-risk elementary schools. *Journal of Positive Behavior Interventions, 11*(2), 68–81.

Swathi, J. (n.d.). Teacher-student relationship questionnaire (TSRQ) rating scale: A student survey parameters strongly agree agree disagree strongly disagree. Accessed at www.academia.edu/6810648/Teacher_Student_Relationship_Questionnaire_TSRQ _Rating_Scale_A_Student_Survey_Parameters_Strongly_agree_Agree_Disagree _Strongly_disagree on August 23, 2023.

Suldo, S. M., & Doll, B. (2021). Conceptualizing youth mental health through a dual-factor model. In P. J. Lazarus, S. Suldo, & B. Doll (Eds.), *Fostering the emotional well-being of our youth: A school-based approach* (online ed., pp. 3–20). Oxford University Press. Accessed at https://academic.oup.com/book/28758/chapter -abstract/235123664?redirectedFrom=fulltext on August 31, 2023.

Surkalim, D. L., Luo, M., Eres, R., Gebel, K., van Buskirk, J., Bauman, A., & Ding, D. (2022). The prevalence of loneliness across 113 countries: systematic review and meta-analysis. *BMJ, 376*, e067068. doi:10.1136/bmj-2021-067068

Taylor, C., Dollard, M. F., Clark, A., Dormann, C., & Bakker, A. B. (2019). Psychosocial safety climate as a factor in organisational resilience: Implications for worker psychological health, resilience, and engagement. In M. F. Dollard, C. Dormann, & M. Awang Idris (Eds.), *Psychosocial safety climate: A new work stress theory* (pp. 199–228). New York: Springer.

Taylor, R. D., Oberle, E., Durlak, J. A., & Weissberg, R. P. (2017). Promoting positive youth development through school-based social and emotional learning interventions: A meta-analysis of follow-up effects. *Child Development, 88*(4), 1156–1171.

Taylor, S. E. (2012). Tend and befriend theory. In P. A. M. Van Lange, A. W. Kruglanski, & E. T. Higgins (Eds.), *Handbook of theories of social psychology* (pp. 32–49). Thousand Oaks, CA: SAGE.

Teicher, M. H., Samson, J. A., Anderson, C. M., & Ohashi, K. (2016). The effects of childhood maltreatment on brain structure, function and connectivity. *Nature Reviews Neuroscience, 17*(10), 652–666.

Thakkar, M. M., Sharma, R., & Sahota, P. (2015). Alcohol disrupts sleep homeostasis. *Alcohol* (Fayetteville, N.Y.), *49*(4), 299–310.

Urdan, T., & Schoenfelder, E. (2006). Classroom effects on student motivation: Goal structures, social relationships, and competence beliefs. *Journal of School Psychology, 44*(5), 331–349.

van de Pol, J., Volman, M., Oort, F., & Beishuizen, J. (2015). The effects of scaffolding in the classroom: support contingency and student independent working time in relation to student achievement, task effort and appreciation of support. *Instructional Science, 43*, 615–641.

Verschueren, K., & Koomen, H. M. Y. (2012). Teacher-child relationships from an attachment perspective. *Attachment and Human Development, 14*(3), 205–211.

Voight, A., Hanson, T., O'Malley, M., & Adekanye, L. (2015). The racial school climate gap: Within-school disparities in students' experiences of safety, support, and connectedness. *American Journal of Community Psychology, 56*(3-4), 252–267.

Walker, M. (2018). *Why we sleep: Unlocking the power of sleep and dreams*. New York: Scribner.

Walker, S., & Graham, L. (2021). At risk students and teacher-student relationships: Student characteristics, attitudes to school and classroom climate. *International Journal of Inclusive Education, 25*(8), 896–913.

Walton, G. M., & Cohen, G. L. (2007). A question of belonging: Race, social fit, and achievement. *Journal of Personality and Social Psychology*, *92*(1), 82–96.

Wang, M.-T., & Degol, J. L. (2016). School climate: A review of the construct, measurement, and impact on student outcomes. *Educational Psychology Review*, *28*(2), 315–352.

Watts, T. W., Duncan, G. J., & Quan, H. (2018). Revisiting the marshmallow test: A conceptual replication investigating links between early delay of gratification and later outcomes. *Psychological science*, *29*(7), 1159–1177.

Weinberg, A. (2022, September 2). 4 essential guidelines for mentors. Edutopia. Accessed at www.edutopia.org/article/4-essential-guidelines-mentors on September 5, 2023.

Weiner, B. J., Lewis, C. C., & Sherr, K. (Eds.). (2023). *Practical implementation science: Moving evidence into action*. New York: Springer.

Weissberg, R. P., & O'Brien, M. U. (2004). What works in school-based social and emotional learning programs for positive youth development. *The Annals of the American Academy of Political and Social Science*, *591*, 86–97.

Weissbourd, R., Batanova, M., Lovison, V., & Torres, E. (2021). *Loneliness in America*. Harvard University. Accessed from https://mcc.gse.harvard.edu/reports/loneliness-in-america on August 21, 2023.

Wiest-Stevenson, C., & Lee, C. (2016). Trauma-informed schools. *Journal of Evidence-Informed Social Work*, *13*(5), 498–503.

Will, M. (2020, April 7). The success of social-emotional learning hinges on teachers. *Education Week*. Accessed at www.edweek.org/leadership/the-success-of-social-emotional-learning-hinges-on-teachers/2020/04 on September 5, 2023.

Wong, Y. J., Owen, J., Gabana, N. T., Brown, J. W., McInnis, S., Toth, P., & Gilman, L. (2018). Does gratitude writing improve the mental health of psychotherapy clients? Evidence from a randomized controlled trial. *Psychotherapy Research*, *28*(2), 192–202.

World Health Organization. (n.d.). Mental health. Accessed at www.who.int/news-room/fact-sheets/detail/mental-health-strengthening-our-response on August 31, 2023.

Wubbels, T., Brekelmans, M., Mainhard, T., den Brok, P., & van Tartwijk, J. (2016). Teacher-student relationships and student achievement. In K. R. Wentzel & G. B. Ramani (Eds.), *Handbook of social influences in school contexts: Social-emotional, motivation, and cognitive outcomes* (pp 127–142). New York: Routledge.

xSEL Labs (n.d.). Accessed at https://xsel-labs.com on September 23, 2023.

Yazzie-Mintz, E. (2007). *Voices of students on engagement: A report on the 2006 high school survey of student engagement.* Accessed from www.semanticscholar.org/paper/Voices-of-Students-on-Engagement%3A-A-Report-on-the-Yazzie-Mintz/504fce0c038d6cf1206d67566d54ebe1df8d0d2d on September 21, 2023.

Yeager, D. S. (2017). Social-emotional learning programs for adolescents. *The Future of Children, 27*(1), 73–94.

Yeager, D. S., Hanselman, P., Walton, G. M., Murray, J. S., Crosnoe, R., Muller, C., et al. (2019). A national experiment reveals where a growth mindset improves achievement. *Nature, 573*(7774), 364–369.

You, S., Furlong, M., Felix, E., & O'Malley, M. (2015). Validation of the social and emotional health survey for five sociocultural groups: Multi-group invariance and latent mean analyses. *Psychology in the Schools, 52*(4), 349–362.

Zolkoski, S. M. (2019). The importance of teacher-student relationships for students with emotional and behavioral disorders. *Preventing School Failure: Alternative Education for Children and Youth, 63*(3), 236–241.

INDEX

A

academic achievement
    motivation and engagement and, 60
    positive relationships and, 84, 85–86
    safe, predictable, and positive environments and, 59, 62–63, 79
    social-emotional learning and, 2, 12–14, 125, 132

active learning, 28

administrative records, consulting, 165. *See also* assessments/SEL assessment

adoption of programs, 170

adverse childhood experiences (ACEs), 15, 16, 17, 64. *See also* trauma-informed practices

"all for one" motivation systems, 71. *See also* motivation

assessments/SEL assessment
    about, 155
    assessing SEL ingredients, 167–171
    comprehensive SEL and, 12
    conclusion, 172
    conducting SEL assessments, 161–163
    gathering SEL assessment data, 163–167
    importance of SEL assessment, 160–161
    next steps, 172
    reproducibles for, 173–177
    screening and, 159–160
    SEL ingredients, 8, 9
    what is SEL assessment, 155–160
    what to assess, 157–159

B

banking time, 96–98, 102. *See also* establish strategies

behavior. *See also* classroom management; discipline; positive behavioral interventions and supports (PBIS)
    positive relationships and, 87
    practices for progressively responding to behavior, 73–75
    prompting desired behavior, 76
    responding to positive behavior with empathy, 104–105

behavioral well-being, 14–15. *See also* well-being

belonging. *See also* positive relationships
    belonging uncertainty, 84
    exclusionary discipline and, 69
    impact of, 11, 86
    school connectedness and, 84–85

bias, 167

Bruce, K., 22

bullying, 54

buy-in
    implementing comprehensive SEL, 22–25
    SEL assessment and, 158
    SEL curriculum and instruction and, 142

C

care/caring, offering a statement of care, 110–111
character education, 124
check-ins, 103–104. *See also* maintain strategies
choice and management strategies, 71. *See also* proactive classroom management
classroom management. *See also* behavior; discipline; proactive classroom management
    positive greetings at the door and, 99
    practices for progressively responding to behavior, 73–75
    predictability and, 58
    redirection strategies and, 75–76
    social-emotional learning and, 14
classroom meetings, 91–93
classwide motivation systems, 71. *See also* motivation
closed-ended questions, 97
coaching and implementing comprehensive SEL, 28. *See also* professional development
collaborating to solve the problem, 111, 112. *See also* restore strategies
Collaborative for Academic, Social, and Emotional Learning (CASEL)
    formation of, 125
    resources, 146, 162, 176
    SEL competencies, 126
color wheel, 58
continuous improvement and implementing comprehensive SEL, 25–26
co-rumination, 46–47
cultural responsiveness and SEL programs, 127–128, 138

D

data
    disaggregating data, 161
    how can schools gather SEL assessment data, 163–167
Devereux Student Strengths Assessment-Mini (DESSA-Mini), 160
differentiation and SEL curriculum and instruction, 126–127, 140
discipline. *See also* behavior
    equity and, 18, 63, 79
    five-to-one strategy and, 102
    positive behavioral interventions and supports and, 67
    proactive classroom management and, 69
    PROMPT method and, 75–77
    restorative practices and, 74–75
disrespect, disobedience, and defiance (three D's), 65
Drug Abuse Resistance Education (DARE), 124

E

educational equity, 18. *See also* equity
educator well-being, 34–36. *See also* well-being
emotional exhaustion, 37
emotional intelligence, 34
emotional labor, 37
emotional regulation, 14
emotional well-being, 14–15. *See also* well-being
emotions, reining in one's emotions, 43–44. *See also* social-emotional learning (SEL)
empathy
    academic achievement and, 13–14
    educator well-being and, 35
    making an empathy statement, 109–110
    practices for progressively responding to behavior, 73
    responding to positive behavior with, 104–105
    teaching interaction approach and, 76
engagement
    equity-focused practices and, 19
    impact of SEL on, 13

positive greetings at the door and, 99
positive relationships and, 86
safe, predictable, and positive environments and, 60
SEL assessment and, 158, 171
SEL curriculum and instruction and, 127, 139
environmental impact on the person, 64
environmental support. *See also* safe, predictable, and positive environments
educator well-being and, 35–36
supporting SEL for adults in schools, 39–42
equity
academic achievement and, 13–14
multitiered system of supports and, 78
safe, predictable, and positive environments and, 63
SEL and equity-focused practices, 18–19
student-teacher relationships and, 113–114
errorless learning, 70
essential competencies, 34–35
Esserman, D., 22
Establish, Maintain, Restore model
about, 94–95
establish strategies, 96–101
maintain strategies, 101–106
menu of Establish-Maintain-Restore strategies, 95–96
restore strategies, 106–111
student-teacher relationships and equity and, 113–114
establish strategies. *See also* Establish, Maintain, Restore model
about, 96
banking time, 96–98
gather, review, acknowledge, 98
indirect compliments by other adults, 100–101
positive greetings at the door, 98–100
two-by-ten, 100
expectations, 24, 58, 65
externalizing challenges, 159

F

feedback
and implementing comprehensive SEL, 26–27
performance-based feedback, 27
practices for progressively responding to behavior, 73
wise feedback, 103
fidelity
implementing comprehensive SEL and, 26–27
SEL assessment and, 158, 171
five-to-one, 101–103. *See also* maintain strategies
fun activities, 106. *See also* maintain strategies
fundamental attribution error, 64

G

gather, review, acknowledge, 98. *See also* establish strategies
gender, percentage of male versus female teachers in U.S. public schools, 55
getting out of relationship ruts, 111–113. *See also* positive relationships; relationships
gratitude, practicing, 45
growth mindset, 61

H

habits and psychological safety, 42
halo effect, 167

I

implementation fidelity, 146–147
indirect compliments by other adults, 100–101. *See also* establish strategies
initiative overload, 143
internalizing challenges, 159

interspersion of choice, 71. *See also* proactive classroom management

introduction
    about well-being, 1
    book overview, 4–6
    comprehensive approach to student well-being, 1–2
    role of social-emotional learning, 2–4

J

Jacobs, S., 22

K

key opinion leaders (KOL), 146

L

letting go of the previous interaction (fresh start), 107–108. *See also* restore strategies

M

maintain strategies. *See also* Establish, Maintain, Restore model
    about, 101
    check-ins, 103–104
    five-to-one, 101–103
    fun activities, 106
    responding to positive behavior with empathy, 104–105
    wise feedback, 103

making an empathy statement, 109–110. *See also* empathy; restore strategies

marshmallow test, 56–57

Masten, A., 2

matching the restore communication strategy to the student. *See* restore strategies

meditation, 43

mental health
    comprehensive approach to student well-being and, 1–2
    definition of, 2

mentorship, 39. *See also* positive relationships; relationships

mindfulness, 43

mindsets, 61

modeling, 42

motivation
    classwide motivation systems, 71
    positive relationships and, 86
    safe, predictable, and positive environments and, 60

multitiered system of supports (MTSS), 77–78, 159. *See also* safe, predictable, and positive environments

O

offering a statement of care, 110–111. *See also* restore strategies

"one for all" motivation systems, 71–72. *See also* motivation

ongoing monitoring, 76. *See also* classroom management

open-ended questions, 97, 165–166

opportunities to respond, 70–71. *See also* proactive classroom management

P

peer relationships. *See also* positive relationships; relationships
    classroom meetings and, 91–93
    positive peer reporting, 87–91
    SEL assessment and, 168–169

percentage distribution of teachers in U.S. public schools by race, 56

percentage of male versus female teachers in U.S. public schools, 55

performance-based feedback, 27. *See also* feedback

person, impact of environment on the, 64

perspective-taking
    banking time and, 97
    empathy and, 104
    SEL for adults and, 35, 37
    social-emotional learning and, 139, 147
    taking ownership for part of the negative interaction or problem and, 109

positive behavioral interventions and supports (PBIS), 65–68, 133. *See also* safe, predictable, and positive environments

positive expectations, 24. *See also* expectations

positive farewells, 100

positive greetings at the door, 98–100. *See also* establish strategies

positive peer reporting. *See also* peer relationships
    about, 87–88
    handling challenges with, 90–91
    implementing, 88–90

positive relationships. *See also* relationships
    about, 83
    comprehensive SEL and, 11
    conclusion, 114
    educator well-being and, 34–35
    importance of, 84–87
    next steps, 114
    peer-to-peer relationships, intentionally cultivating and supporting positive, 87–93
    reproducibles for, 115–122
    SEL assessment and, 157, 168–169
    SEL for adults and, 38
    SEL ingredients, 8, 9
    student-teacher relationships and equity, 113–114
    student-teacher relationships, intentionally cultivating and supporting positive, 93–113
    what are positive relationships, 83–84

positivity, 58–59. *See also* safe, predictable, and positive environments

poverty and equity-focused practices, 18–19

praise and recognition, 88–90

precorrection, 70, 99. *See also* proactive classroom management

predictability, 56–58. *See also* safe, predictable, and positive environments

proactive classroom management. *See also* classroom management
    about, 68–70
    management strategies, 70–73
    practices for progressively responding to behavior, 73–75

professional development
    choosing SEL programs and, 135–136
    implementing comprehensive SEL and, 25–26
    implementing SEL curriculum and instruction and, 143–144
    self-care and, 41
    training and coaching for SEL implementation, 27–28

PROMPT method, 75–77. *See also* safe, predictable, and positive environments

prompting desired behavior, 76

proximity control, 75

psychological safety
    environmental support and, 35–36
    habits and, 42
    neurological impacts of safety and, 54–55

purpose, strategies to improve adult stress coping and well-being, 44. *See also* SEL for adults

R

race, percentage distribution of teachers in U.S. public schools by race, 56

reach, SEL assessment and, 170

readiness, definition of, 22

redirection strategies, 75–76. *See also* classroom management

relationships. *See also* positive relationships
    creating opportunities for connection, 40
    fostering genuine connection with teachers, 39
    getting out of relationship ruts, 111–113
    practices for progressively responding to behavior and, 73–74

relationship skills, 33, 126
safe, predictable, and positive environments and, 60
social support and, 46–47
trauma and toxic stress and, 17
reproducibles for
planning for positive relationships, 117–119
planning for safe, predictable, and positive environments, 82
planning for SEL curriculum and instruction, 153–154
planning for SEL for adults, 50
planning for SEL practices, 32, 175
reflecting on assessment, 173–174
reflecting on positive relationships, 115–116
reflecting on safe, predictable, and positive environments, 80–81
reflecting on SEL curriculum and instruction, 151–152
reflecting on SEL for adults, 49
reflecting on the SEL recipe, 30–31
restoring positive relationships, 120–122
reviewing research-based strategies for educators to improve stress coping and resilience, 51–52
reviewing resources for SEL assessment, 176–177
resilience
positive relationships and, 15
SEL for adults and, 10, 37–38
shifting one's stress mindset and, 45
sleep and, 46
resources
choosing SEL programs, 134–137
and implementing comprehensive SEL, 26
responding to positive behavior with empathy, 104–105. *See also* maintain strategies
responsible decision making, 126

restorative practices, 74–75. *See also* classroom management
restore strategies. *See also* Establish, Maintain, Restore model
about, 106–107
collaborating to solve the problem, 111, 112
letting go of the previous interaction (fresh start), 107–108
making an empathy statement, 109–110
matching the restore communication strategy to the student, 108
offering a statement of care, 110–111
taking ownership for part of the negative interaction or problem, 108–109
routines and visual schedules, 58, 72–73

S

SAFE (sequenced, active, focused, and explicit), 129–130
safe, predictable, and positive environments. *See also* environmental support
about, 53
comprehensive SEL and, 10
conclusion, 79
creating, 64–78
importance of, 59–64
multitiered system of supports and, 77–78
next steps, 79
positive behavioral interventions and supports and, 65–68
proactive classroom management and, 68–75
PROMPT method and, 75–77
reproducibles for, 80–82
SEL assessment and, 157, 168
SEL for adults and, 38
SEL ingredients, 8, 9
what kinds of environments support SEL, 54–59

Index | 209

safety, 54–56. *See also* safe, predictable, and positive environments
school connectedness, 84–85. *See also* belonging
screening, 159–160. *See also* assessments/SEL assessment
SEL assessment. *See* assessments/SEL assessment
SEL curriculum and instruction
    about, 123–124
    buy-in and, 142
    choosing/how can schools choose, 134–141
    comprehensive range of, 126
    comprehensive SEL and, 11–12
    conclusion, 149–150
    cultural responsiveness and, 127–128
    curriculum and infusion and, 125–126
    delivery, protecting time for, 142–143
    delivery, schoolwide, 132–133
    delivery, user friendly and easy to deliver, 128–129
    developmental appropriateness, 139–140
    developmentally differentiated, 126–127
    engagement and, 127
    evidence of effectiveness, 137–139
    generalization and, 130, 140–141
    implementation fidelity and, 146–147
    implementation/how can schools effectively implement, 142–149
    implementation/why implement a research-based curriculum or program, 132–134
    initiative overload and, 143
    next steps, 150
    pedagogy and, 129–130
    prioritizing, 144–145
    reproducibles for, 151–154
    research-based/backed by research, 131–132
    school resources and, 134–137
    SEL assessment and, 157, 169–171
    SEL for adults and, 38
    SEL ingredients, 8, 9
    SEL understanding and, 36
    supporting content beyond lessons and, 147–149
    team approach to, 145–146
    training and professional development and, 143–144
    what is SEL curriculum and instruction, 124–132
SEL for adults
    about, 33
    comprehensive SEL and, 10
    conclusion, 47–48
    environmental support and, 39–42
    importance of, 36–38
    next steps, 48
    reproducibles for, 49–52
    SEL assessment and, 157, 168
    SEL ingredients, 8, 9
    strategies to improve adult stress coping and well-being and, 42–47
    supporting SEL for adults in schools, 38–47
    what is SEL for adults, 34–36
SEL ingredients. *See also* assessments/SEL assessment; positive relationships; safe, predictable, and positive environments; SEL curriculum and instruction; SEL for adults
    five SEL ingredients, 8, 9
    how can schools assess SEL ingredients, 167–171
    role of social-emotional learning, 3
    what to assess, 157–158
SEL recipe
    about, 7
    conclusion, 28–29
    how can schools deliver/implementation of, 20–28
    next steps, 29
    reproducibles for, 30–32

what is comprehensive SEL, 8, 10–12
why is SEL important, 12–20
self-awareness, 34, 126, 167
self-care, 41–42
self-distancing, 43–44
self-efficacy, 25
self-management, 8, 126
self-reflection, 141
Shea, C., 22
Siegel, D., 43
sleep, 46
Social, Academic, and Emotional Behavior Risk Screener, 160
social awareness, 13, 35, 126
Social Emotional Assets and Resilience Scales, 160
social proofs, 24
social-emotional competence, 60–61
social-emotional learning (SEL). *See also* SEL curriculum and instruction; SEL ingredients; SEL recipe
    for adults. *See* SEL for adults
    assessments. *See* assessments/SEL assessment
    buy-in for, 23
    positive behavioral interventions and supports and, 68
    role of social-emotional learning, 2–4
    SEL understanding, 36
    use of term, 123, 125
social-emotional well-being, 14–15, 61–62. *See also* well-being
strategies to improve adult stress coping and well-being
    about, 42–43
    embracing social support, 46–47
    getting adequate sleep, 46
    practicing gratitude, 45
    reining in one's emotions, 43–44
    shifting one's stress mindset, 45
    tapping into one's sense of purpose, 44

stress
    children and, 15–16
    creating opportunities for connection and, 40
    identifying and mitigating sources of, 40–41
    impact of, 37
    safe, predictable, and positive environments and, 63–64
    SEL for adults and, 37–38
    shifting one's stress mindset, 45
    tend and befriend stress response, 46–47
student-centered conversations, 97
student-teacher relationships. *See also* relationships
    about, 93–94
    classroom management and, 69
    equity and, 113–114
    Establish, Maintain, Restore model and, 94–111
    getting out of relationship ruts and, 111–113
    impact of, 11
    positive relationships and, 85
    PROMPT method and, 75, 77
    SEL assessment and, 168–169
    SEL for adults and, 38
surveys
    disseminating surveys, 165–167
    gather, review, acknowledge strategy and, 98
    screening instruments, 159
    SEL assessment and, 156, 162–163, 168, 169

T

taking ownership for part of the negative interaction or problem, 108–109. *See also* restore strategies
teachers
    percentage distribution of teachers in U.S. public schools by race, 56

percentage of male versus female teachers in U.S. public schools, 55
teaching interaction approach, 76–77. *See also* PROMPT method
teams
    and implementing comprehensive SEL, 21–22
    SEL teams and conducting SEL assessments, 162
    team approach to implement SEL curriculum and instruction, 145–146
three D's (disrespect, disobedience, and defiance), 65
tiered fidelity inventory, 66
time
    and implementing comprehensive SEL, 26
    protecting time for delivery of SEL curriculum and instruction, 142–143
"to each their own" motivation systems, 72. *See also* motivation
toxic stress, 16, 17, 85. *See also* stress
training and coaching, 27–28. *See also* professional development
trauma-informed practices
    positive relationships and, 85
    social-emotional learning and, 15–18
    stress coping and, 64
trust and peer relationships, 92
twenty-first century skills, 19–20
two-by-ten, 100. *See also* establish strategies

U
unconscious bias, 167

V
validity, 166

W
Weiner, B., 22
well-being
    about, 1
    comprehensive approach to student well-being, 1–2
    educator well-being, 34–36
    social, emotional, and behavioral well-being, 14–15
    social-emotional well-being, 61–62
    strategies to improve adult stress coping and well-being, 42–47
whole-student approach, 60
wise feedback, 103. *See also* feedback; maintain strategies
workloads and supporting SEL for adults, 40
World Health Organization, 2

Empower Moves for Social-Emotional Learning
Lauren Porosoff and Jonathan Weinstein
EMPOWER students to discover the values they want to live by. You will learn twenty-eight activities, as well as extensions and variations for each, that will engage students and help them make school a source of meaning, vitality, and community in their lives.
BKG095

Embracing Relational Teaching
Anthony R. Reibel
When you shift to relational pedagogy, you establish connections that help students feel valued, respected, and heard, which leads to enhanced student engagement. This book explores the relational approach and offers strategies to embed student-teacher relationships into everyday interactions and learning.
BKF949

The Metacognitive Student
Richard K. Cohen, Deanne Kildare Opatosky, James Savage, Susan Olsen Stevens, and Edward P. Darrah
What if there was one strategy you could use to support students academically, socially, and emotionally? It exists—and it's simple, straightforward, and practical. Dive deep into structured SELf-questioning and learn how to empower students to develop into strong, healthy, and confident thinkers.
BKF954

Raising Equity Through SEL
Jorge Valenzuela
Activate social-emotional learning effectively in your classroom with this trusted source for sound pedagogy that addresses the academic and SEL needs of diverse learners. Each strategy, tool, and template shared is meant to facilitate your practice by making SEL easier to implement.
BKG041

Solution Tree | Press

Visit SolutionTree.com or call 800.733.6786 to order.

Wait! **Your professional development journey doesn't have to end with the last pages of this book.**

We realize improving student learning doesn't happen overnight. And your school or district shouldn't be left to puzzle out all the details of this process alone.

No matter where you are on the journey, we're committed to helping you get to the next stage.

Take advantage of everything from **custom workshops** to **keynote presentations** and **interactive web and video conferencing**. We can even help you develop an action plan tailored to fit your specific needs.

Let's get the conversation started.

Call 888.763.9045 today.

SolutionTree.com